Parent
Involvement
Begins
at Birth

Parent Involvement Begins at Birth

Collaboration between Parents and Teachers of Children in the Early Years

SALLY GOLDBERG

Nova Southeastern University

Allyn and Bacon
Boston   London   Toronto   Sydney   Tokyo   Singapore

Library of Congress Cataloging-in-Publication Data

Goldberg, Sally
    Parent involvement begins at birth : collaboration between parents and
teachers of children in the early years / Sally Goldberg.
        p.   cm.
    Includes bibliographical references (p.   ) and index.
    ISBN 0–205–17415–9
    1. Parenting—Studying and teaching—United States.   2. Child
development—Study and teaching—United States.   3. Infants—Care—
Study and teaching—United States.   4. Toddlers—Care—Study and
teaching—United States.   I. Title.
HQ755.7.G65   1997
649′.1′07—dc20   96–42956
                                                         CIP

The drawings on pages 29, 33, 34, 35, 37, 46, and 195 are based on material in *Teaching with Toys: Making Your Own Educational Toys* by Sally Goldberg, copyright © 1981 by The University of Michigan Press, Ann Arbor. Used with permission.

Photographs on pages 3, 32, 40, 87, 122, 142, 162, and 181 are by German Salazar.

Photographs on pages 19, 20, and 21 are by Paul Morris.

Printed in the United States of America
10 9 8 7 6 5 4 3 2 1   01 00 99 98 97

CONTENTS

PREFACE AND ACKNOWLEDGMENTS

Birth-to-five programming is slowly but surely finding its way into our educational system. The goal of this book is to take the focus away from the "slowly" and move it more on the course of the "surely." There are federally funded and state-funded programs aimed at helping our impoverished communities receive the necessary services related to prenatal care and early childhood health and development services; yet these programs reach only a small percentage of the people. There are hospital programs that provide childbirth preparation classes to parents-to-be and additional programs that provide follow-through child care classes for new parents; yet these, too, end up as support for the very few. There are many new books written specifically for the purpose of educating both the preparent and the new parent, but these too are specialized and not widely available. There are preschool, daycare, and Head Start programs, both federally funded and private, that care for children from infancy to age five, but these too are limited.

Yes, there is a system, but no, it is not working effectively. Guidance and support are not there for all parents. They are the ones who need the most up-to-date and complete parenting information.

Until the time when such programming becomes available to all parents, preschool, daycare, and Head Start professionals can provide the backbone for disseminating information to parents about ways to develop their children from birth to age five. They hold the key because, in today's world, they are a well-trained, knowledgeable group. They have the most up-to-date and complete information about early childhood education and its very important focus on developmentally appropriate practices. They can teach parents what they need to know to do their important part of the developmental and educational process effectively for their child.

In the 1980s an alarm was sounded nationwide and maybe worldwide. The great concern was over the impact long hours away from home, in a daycare setting, might have on a child's development. What would happen to children not reared full time by their mothers? People were frightened.

In the 1990s another alarm has sounded nationwide and maybe worldwide. This time the concern is over the impact long hours at home, not under a teacher's direction, might have on a child's development. Our preschool, daycare, and Head Start teachers know how to handle the children, but what is happening to them when they return to their homes, many in poverty, many with single parents struggling to meet life's demands, many in wealthy homes neglected by two overly busy parents? Once again, people are frightened.

To the first alarm educators responded with teacher training. They put together major programs preparing early childhood educators with techniques for handling children in an optimum fashion for growth and development. They ended up teaching teachers how to provide for children what would be closest to a high-quality home environment.

To the current alarm, educators are looking for a way first to focus parents back again on the importance of an effective home environment and then to teach them how to provide such an environment for their children. They are looking to professionals to take classroom knowledge and help parents apply it at home. We need teachers to teach parents how to provide a developmentally appropriate environment for their children. Parents need teachers to teach them how to use appropriate classroom techniques at home and how to maximize the home environment in terms of positive time spent with their children, effective discipline, and purposeful play activities.

Traditionally, parent involvement and parent training as part of a preschool or daycare setting have focused on connecting parents up with school programming as much as possible, letting parents know what is going on with their child in school. Now the focus must change. Parents need to know how to continue at home that which has been started at school. Positive time spent with children, effective discipline, and purposeful play activities for the child should fit together as one continuous process, with no split between school and home. Teachers already know classroom procedures; now is the time to advise parents on adapting many of these school procedures for home use.

What follows is a guide to providing the best possible in-home parent–child environment. Professionals can teach these skills to parents. This guide starts with the historical roots of parent involvement. It then presents the rationale and model for an effective, complete, and growing program that could be set up through a public system. It gives the basics of the kinds of interactions parents should have with their children from birth to age five. There is a lot of information on the toy, game, and play environment for the early childhood years. There is a method parents can use to set up exemplary language, writing, music, and exploratory environments for their young children.

Self-esteem development is a major concept. No parents should lack the basic information to develop children's self-esteem from birth to age five. This includes information on both child self-esteem and discipline. A practical parenting section outlines 15 pillars of parenting related to managing children's behavior. There is a method for helping parents solve child disputes. There is guidance for getting children to go to bed, and there is a current perspective on Attention Deficit Disorder, learning disabilities, gifted children, and the differently abled.

From the federal Goals 2000 program for the improvement of education, we know that getting children ready for school is important. This idea should not remain just a thought, a hope, or a wish. It should take shape as an official public program. Definite techniques exist for getting children ready to start school, and parents need to know what those techniques are. Parents have to be made ready to do the best possible job of parenting. They need to be given the information that development takes place in an interconnected fashion and that the goal is to have a well-developed, independent child who can work as part of a team with others and then take a positive place as a team player—an interdependent, functional member of society.

The play-and-learn system of play activities is the practical application of cognitive, motor, social, and language development. Self-esteem is developed through those four areas and then on its own through highly skilled parent–child interactions. Parents can be taught to use the play-and-learn system of play activities to interact in a positive, appropriate way with their children. The play activities, 185 in all, represent examples. Parents can use these, personalize them, and create their own related activities. Many activities that are designed for children at a young age can be expanded for children as they grow and can be enriched for continued value.

More than thirty years' research shows that early family involvement in children's learning is the critical link for a child's future academic success. Now the task is to make sure that no more years go by without our parents knowing how to apply that knowledge.

Basically, young children need consistency of care and attention. Times may have changed, and technology has changed; but no one has changed the children. The focus of early childhood education needs to be moved back to the parents. Infant-toddler programs and preschools are doing their best to emulate an exemplary home environment. Now it is time for teachers, skilled in child care, to teach the parents how to carry over these child care skills to the home. The result will be healthy, easy-to-care-for children who will grow up to be healthy, productive adults, who themselves will know how to bring up children.

ACKNOWLEDGMENTS

Appreciation goes to Dr. Jeri Serosky and Jon Page, Miami site administrators at Nova Southeastern University. They have given me the opportunity to teach early childhood education to master's students. Through a teaching environment I have been able to enrich and refine my ideas about the importance of education for children in the early years.

Special thanks go to Nancy Forsyth and Frances Helland, editors at Simon & Schuster Education Group at Allyn and Bacon, and to Judy Ashkenaz at Total Concept Associates. They worked long and hard to strengthen and protect my ideas about the critical formative years of children from birth to age five. Thanks also go to Wilma Robles Melendez of Nova Southeastern University and to Margaret King of Ohio University for their review of the manuscript.

Gratitude goes to Virginia Quan, computer expert. My computer was as sensitive as any person I know, and many times I did not know how to handle it. Luckily, Virginia did. I value all the time and effort she gave to me and my work.

Honor goes to my friends. I have three who can be reached at any time of night or day. Fran Schreiber is one who has been with me through thick and thin. The next is Diana Lee, and I call it an honor to be considered one of her friends. The third is my aunt, Betty Reiser, who knows just what to say at just the right time. I also have two friends, Miriam Salazar and Stella Matos. They give freely of their time for friendship.

Respect goes to German Salazar. He has always taken an interest in my work with parents, teachers, and children. As a talented photographer, he graciously accepted my request to take many of the photographs used in this book.

Recognition goes to the Florida Writers Assocation, chapter of the National Writers Association. They provide leadership and inspiration to Florida writers. Guidance from that group led me to finding just the right publisher. Being able to bring valuable information to people who can use that information is one of life's highest rewards.

Love goes to my family. They were always there with great support. I cannot thank them enough. My husband, Paul, made sure I had the equipment and the knowledge necessary to get my ideas into printed form. My children, Cynthia and Deborah, willingly gave up Mom-time to let me work on the book.

INTRODUCTION

Parent–child interaction is one of those things. I invite you to take a look . . .

Parent: I am wearing a big shirt. Bring me a little one.
Child: I have a big pencil. Bring me a little one.
Parent: I found your little sock. Bring me a big one.

This is Aileen and her daughter Jessica having fun with a play-and-learn activity from Chapter 11, "A Practical Approach to Cognitive Development." It is "Size It Up," Activity #36, based on Milestone #47, "Understands size." Aileen is starting the activity on a basic level because Jessica has a basic understanding of sizes. Soon Aileen will begin to refine the activity with terms like v*ery big*, *huge*, *giant* and *very little*, *small*, and *tiny*. Soon Jessica will be able to play this game with increased intricacy, speed, and even more fun. Both of them will enjoy the search for all kinds of household objects, and Jessica will grow and develop through a hands-on activity, dynamic with interaction.

Child: I did it. I tied a knot.
Parent: I did mine. Your turn.
Child: I did it. You go.

This parent, Rudy, and his child Preston are having fun with a play-and-learn activity from Chapter 12, "A Practical Approach to Motor Development." It is "All Tied Up in Knots," Activity #37, based on Milestone #42, "Ties a knot." Rudy is beginning the activity on a basic level because Preston has beginning fine motor skill related to tying knots. As Preston develops this skill, Rudy will increase the level of difficulty of the activity. He may do it by speed, by a thinner size string, or by teaching Preston how to tie more complicated knots. He will be sensitive to Preston and his skill level, and he will enjoy the activity with Preston at whatever level is appropriate. The two of them will continue to have fun as long as both of them want to continue to play the game.

Cost anything? No.

Fun? Yes.

These activities and 183 others at the end of this book are available to teach to parents. Teachers now have the opportunity not only to tell parents what to do but also to show them how to do it. Teachers can now give parents a developmentally appropriate way to play together, create together, and guide their children. Teachers can help them to be able to experience some of the most satisfactory experiences known to parents and children together.

Beginning with infancy and continuing through age five, teachers can teach parents about providing an optimal educational and emotional environment for their children. First through toys and play, and second through schedules and guidance, teachers can show them how to get their children ready to start school. They can show parents how to be ready to parent. Not doing enough, doing too much, and pushing are important parent concerns; and now teachers can address these issues with them. Teachers will be able to help parents learn about each area of child development, show them how to interact appropriately with their child in relation to the many milestones that are part of their child's early years. As teachers work with parents on an individual basis, they will be giving parents a system that allows them to optimize their child's development in all areas, an interconnected system that focuses on the whole child.

DEVELOPMENTAL REVIEW

At about age three, a developmental review should be carried out. This process is explained in Chapter 8. From an inventory filled out by a parent and from other available recorded and observed information, teachers can put together a report for the parent about the child's level of functioning. It should include recommendations pertinent to the child's particular situation, as well as a home program for the parent and child together. Usually, for children under three years of age, there is no need to carry out a full developmental review.

PARENT CONFERENCES

This new system lends itself to a new approach to parent conferences, a goal-directed approach that values parent concern and parent information. It is a system that involves the parent as a true partner in the education program in the classroom.

With this new system, the first two parent conferences take on new meaning. They become the developmental review. They are no longer simply designed to keep parents informed about what has been happening with their child in school. They are conferences that take place at the very beginning of school to set up goals and objectives for the child for the coming year.

With this new system, the other conferences that follow also take on new meaning. They are conferences to follow through on the goals and objectives that have been mutually set up for the child. They also provide an opportunity to update the goals and objectives. The child's "ready-for-school" program now has three parts. It is a program for how the teacher, the parent, and the child each carry out their individual parts, all focused on the child's development.

THE FIRST TWO CONFERENCES

The first two conferences, as part of the developmental review, are designed to exchange information about the child. A prepared teacher can provide the parent with an up-to-date picture of the child's development. The concerned parent can provide the teacher with relevant current information. Together at the second conference parent and teacher can draw up goals and objectives for the child. Together they can turn to the Play-and-Learn System explained in Part IV to put together an appropriate set of home activities for parent and child to work on together.

FOLLOW-UP CONFERENCES

First the parent can update the teacher on the program at home. Then the teacher can update the parent about the program at school. Then both can return to the Play-and-Learn System. Select goals (areas of development), objectives (milestones), and activities to update the program.

PARENT INVOLVEMENT HAS COME ALIVE

Parent involvement has now become part of the program. It will no longer be a struggle or a hard-to-accomplish goal. Teachers will find themselves sharing with parents. They will find themselves sharing with children. Children, too, will share with parents. These patterns of sharing will probably continue for a lifetime.

What is new here is a way to use parents as the wonderful resources that they are. They can give teachers valuable information about their children's level of functioning. They can provide that information in a natural way. Teachers can use that information to help parents and to help themselves provide educational and emotional guidance for children. They can use it to create a goal-directed program that will work well for children. This book is designed not only to help parents and teachers get children ready for school, but also to help parents be ready for their children.

PROLOGUE

The Importance of Early Childhood Education

by former Deputy Secretary of Education Madeleine M. Kunin*

While the country is engaged in a heated debate over what to do about welfare, it's time to revisit a common sense answer that begins at home—helping parents to enable children to start school ready to learn. The biggest difference between success and failure in school and in life is made in those early years.

The most important part of a child's education is not the first day of school, but the pre-school years, when intelligence, health, and confidence are shaped. That is when parents can enable their children to overcome the disadvantages of poverty and give them an equal chance to become productive, self-sufficient citizens.

The evidence that early childhood education makes a lasting difference is powerful. The High Scope Foundation's Perry Preschool Project found that preschool participation increased the percentages of persons at the age of 19 who were literate, enrolled in postsecondary education and were employed. It decreased the percentage labeled mentally retarded, school drop outs, and on welfare.

At age 27, the difference between the control group and children who participated in preschool were even more dramatic: higher incomes, higher percentage of home ownership, higher level of schooling completed, lower percentage receiving social services, and fewer arrests.

Not only do children do better when they get good health care, love and nurturing at an early age, but parents improve their own chances for success as well. A program called Even Start, which teaches both parenting and literacy skills to parents, produces win/win results. Children make significant gains in verbal IQ scores and parents get their GED's in great numbers. Most

---

*Reprinted with permission of Madeleine M. Kunin.

significantly, parents remain involved in their children's education, a key factor in academic success for all children, regardless of income.

We don't need new studies or further research to tell us that early childhood education is the best investment we can make. It is the first and most important goal of the national education goals: Every child will start school ready to learn.

Support of Head Start, and related programs like Even Start, the Parents as Teachers program in Missouri, and the HIPPY program (Home Instruction Program for Preschool Youngsters) have demonstrated their effectiveness. Now is the time to take this experience and apply it on a larger scale so that every child gets off to a good start—the best insurance this country could have against long-term adult dependency, called welfare.

PART I

The Optimum Educational Environment

"Parents are the best teachers when they allow their young children to be their guides; they have the best teacher-to-child ratio; the best overall knowledge of their child's needs; and they can allow continuous progress. Besides, it's great fun!"

—Barbara Clark, *Growing Up Gifted*

CHAPTER 1

A Historical Overview

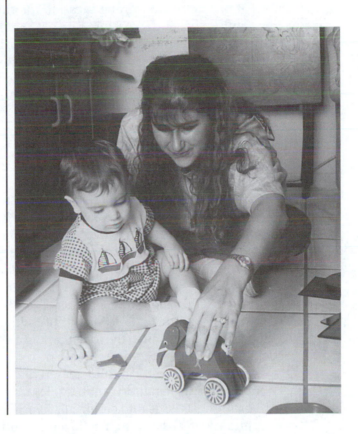

PREHISTORIC TIMES

While parent education and parent involvement stand out today as the most important methods for raising the academic achievement for children in our schools, they are not new. As a matter of fact, they date back to prehistoric times. Primitive societies did not have schools; but they did have families and communities. They had parents who taught their children by living with them and by being examples. Parents taught their children by telling and showing and by praising when appropriate. For thousands of years, every society's important customs, values, and laws were learned and internalized by children in this way. Parent involvement was integral to children's education from its inception, and it has been preserved in different ways throughout our history.

JOHANN HEINRICH PESTALOZZI (1747–1827)

The first preservation came in the late 1700s. To read about Pestalozzi, a great educational philosopher of the eighteenth century, is to read about today's most widely accepted ideas on schooling. Pestalozzi believed in the natural goodness of children. He based his teaching on the use of concrete objects, group instruction, cooperative learning, and what he called the self-activity of the child. As a follower of Rousseau (1712–1778), he was a proponent of free and natural education for children. Most of all, he believed in parents, a belief that earned him a reputation as the Father of Parent Education. "As the mother is the first to nourish her child's body, so should she, by God's order be the first to nourish his mind. For children, the teachings of their parents will always be the core, and as for the schoolmaster, we can give thanks to God if he is able to put a decent shell around the core" (Pestalozzi, 1951, p. 26).

THE TREND CONTINUES

Friedrich Willhelm Froebel (1782–1854), a great educational philosopher of the nineteenth century, well known as the Father of Kindergarten and also highly acclaimed for his curriculum innovation, advocated the mother as the first educator of the child. He wrote a book for mothers to use with their children at home. This book, *Mother Play and Nursery Songs with Finger Plays*, included verses, pictures, songs, and finger plays such as Pat-a-Cake and many more still used today. Froebel organized his birth-to-three curriculum to follow the natural unfolding of the child, with the mother facilitating development. He put forth the idea that the child and the mother should enjoy both language and activities together.

Throughout history, child-centered thinking got lost from time to time. Economic struggles and war struggles brought stresses on society that in turn brought stresses into children's lives. The ideas that children should be seen and not heard and that children should act in a subservient manner to all-knowing parents were resultant philosophies that left behind some unpleasant lifestyles for children.

After years of Calvinist doctrine in the 1800s, we can thank Margaretha Shurz for the return to the revered Father of Parent Education, Pestalozzi. She found herself in an era that advocated the idea of infant depravity, emphasized not spoiling the baby, and expected total and immediate obedience from children. "It was considered to be fatal to let the child win out" (Sunley, 1955, p. 160). In 1856 Mrs. Schurz revived the ideas of Pestalozzi and Froebel when she founded the first kindergarten in the United States in Watertown, Wisconsin. This school exemplified nurturing. Children were treated in a gentle and persuasive manner, with understanding and justice, consistency and firmness. This guidance was thought to enable children to reach their full potential.

On the coattails of Mrs. Schurz came Henry Barnard, then secretary of the Connecticut Board of Education and later United States Commissioner of Education, and Elizabeth Peabody, a sister-in-law of Horace Mann. Barnard discovered the ideas of Froebel and worked to spread them throughout the United States. Peabody crusaded to introduce kindergarten, with its inherent characteristic being an assumption of the intrinsic natural goodness of children.

With this shift in philosophy came a return to both parent education and parent involvement. Froebel's *Mother Play and Nursery Songs* was translated into English. This gave parents an opportunity to use Froebel's activities in their homes. Froebelian kindergarten became established in the United States, and with it came both Pestalozzi's and Froebel's beliefs that parents are integral components of their children's education.

THE TWENTIETH CENTURY APPROACHES

G. Stanley Hall played the next major role. Hall was a psychologist at Clark University who was elected president of Clark in 1889. His great contribution was the founding of the child study center. He was the first to study children scientifically to determine what was in their minds. After years of study, Hall counseled parents to be indulgent with children: "Treat them as young animals, who simply have to behave as they do. Childhood was an easygoing cavorting stage which youngsters must pass through peaceably if they were eventually to become mature, self-controlled adults" (Schlossman, 1976, p. 443). Hall's innovative work influenced the founding of the Parent–Teacher Association, or PTA, during the first decade of the twentieth century.

THE TURN OF THE CENTURY

In 1907 Maria Montessori introduced to the world another method of education, one that did not get its full recognition until the 1960s. In Italy she started a system of education by turning the educational environment into a Children's House. The role of the directress or teacher was to model herself after a mother. The teaching style was one of modeling to children and parents alike. The parents felt a sense of collaboration with the Children's House. They paid "rent" for their children to go there, which gave them a sense of ownership of the program. Parents were entitled to go there at any time to learn from the directress or to experience the life there on their own.

In 1916, twelve faculty wives at the University of Chicago established the first parent cooperative in the United States. These women wanted quality child care for their children, parent education, and time to work for the Red Cross during World War I. The parent cooperative had parent participation in a preschool setting under the direction of a professional teacher. Parents watched the teacher work, learned from the teacher, and then became proficient in early childhood education techniques.

THE 1920s: A BOOM IN PARENT EDUCATION

In 1922 Benjamin Gruenberg published *Outlines of Child Study: A Manual for Parents and Teachers.* This text on child rearing was used as a study guide for many parent groups. Each chapter included succinct discussions of issues of child development, such as speech development, early childhood, emotional development, heredity, obedience, testing, adolescence, and mental development.

Early childhood concerns and parent education were booming in the 1920s. As the decade drew to a close, however, the middle-class parents who were active in parent groups; optimistic about the future; and concerned about health, nutrition, and shaping their children's actions faced the crash of 1929 and a dramatic change in lifestyle.

THE 1930s: PARENT EDUCATION CONTINUES UNDAUNTED BY HARD TIMES

At this time the U.S. government developed *Infant Care,* a publication that it distributed to more than eight million families. This publication continued important child-rearing information for parents. Updated each year by the United States government, it is still available for parents today.

During this period the following statement from the Pennsylvania Department of Public Instruction supported parent education:

> The job of the school is only half done when it has educated the children of the nation. Since it has been demonstrated beyond doubt that the home environment and the role played by understanding parents are paramount in determination of what the child is to become, it follows that helping the parent to feel more adequate for this task is as important from the view of public education and the welfare of society as is the education of the children themselves. Moreover, an educated parenthood facilitates the task of the schools and insures the success of its educational program with the child." (Pennsylvania Department of Public Instruction, 1935, p. 12)

The public library system entered the parent education arena around this time. In 1935 Clarence Sumner, director of the Youngstown, Ohio, Public Library and author of the *Birthright of Babyhood,* started the Mothers' Room program. The Mothers' Room was designed to encourage literature-sharing activities between mothers and preschoolers, not with the purpose of teaching young children to read but with the aim of exposing them to the pleasures of literature. The Mothers' Room contained books and magazines on child care as well as picture books for children. Later the Youngstown library employed a lecturer on a regular basis to talk to mothers about children's reading, child care, and family relations.

Influenced by the Youngstown prototype, several public libraries around the country established special rooms or alcoves in their libraries as a way of spreading the Mothers' Room concept. Effective as it was, however, it never became the national movement expected. The reasons are unclear, but women's involvement in World War II probably played a role (Greene, 1991, p. 1).

THE 1940s: DR. SPOCK

Educators, psychoanalysts, and pediatricians all had made clear the need for greater understanding of children and for flexibility in their care. Dr. Benjamin Spock took the information and brought it to the public in 1946 in his well-received book *Baby and Child Care.* The book, which has been revised since that time, gave Dr. Spock the primary position as the authority on raising children. At the time he had virtually no competition from other books or other professionals. Although the book is mostly about children's medical well-being, it also contains high-quality information about other aspects of child care.

Because Dr. Spock is a pediatrician, his book became a mother's first step in getting a doctor's help. If you had a question about your child, you could first look it up in your volume of Dr. Spock. If you could not find an answer there, it was time to call your doctor. Because of his relatively flexible and supposedly permissive approach to child rearing, Dr. Spock came to be seen as the person responsible for the youth rebellion of the 1960s. Today his book shares an eminent position with a select group of other books, especially *Your Baby and Child: From Birth to Age Five* by pediatrician Penelope Leach (1978).

THE 1950s: WHEN PARENTS WERE STILL INVOLVED

By 1950 the PTA had more than nine million members and thousands of study groups among its 30,000 local chapters. The attitude of the times was, "Send your child to school, we will do the teaching; your responsibility as a parent is to be supportive of the teachers and the schools" (Berger, 1991, p. 67).

On a limited scale, books and magazines were available about child care, discipline, and child development. This was an era when the economy was thriving, and many women had the luxury of staying home to bring up children. Modern conveniences, "instant" products, and efficient household technology were not yet well established. Most women were not college educated, and most did not prepare for careers. Bringing up children was well understood to be a full-time job. This combination of diverse factors boded well for parent education and parent involvement.

The thriving economy, however, also had a down side for children. Parents were beginning to focus more on what they could give their children materially and less on what they could give them in terms of spiritual and moral values. Making life easier became a major national goal, and children experienced less of a major purpose to their existence.

Another turn of events took place in 1957 with the launching of Sputnik by the Soviet Union. That event prompted great concern in the United States over children's academic prowess. A major quest was begun to raise the academic functioning level of our student population, a quest that has continued into the 1990s. At that time the goal was to improve our students' achievement, particularly in math and science, in order to win the Cold War and, in particular, the space race against the Soviet Union. This impetus led to a multitude of theories and programs designed to help children learn more. The idea of "more" led to a trend toward teaching academics to children at an earlier age.

Later, this competition with the USSR spread to a competition with other countries. In the 1980s we learned that our students were behind those in Japan, especially in science. For years the Japanese had used a hands-on science approach. The whole world watched them succeed in the marketplace with electronics and automobiles. We discovered that in reading our students were far behind those of New Zealand, who scored at the top of international tests of literacy. The world began to seek out New Zealand's texts and teachers. Looking toward the Netherlands, we found that their students excelled worldwide in math. Dutch children liked math and, like the Japanese, scored high on standardized tests. The Netherlands, a small country, developed an extensive foreign language program that enabled almost all of its students to master English. The Dutch also taught French and other languages with a high rate of success.

The quest to raise the academic functioning level of our students, begun in 1957, continues today. The most recent manifestation was developed as America 2000 in 1991 under the Bush administration and expanded as Goals 2000 in 1993 under the Clinton administration.

THE 1960s: BRINGING PARENT INVOLVEMENT TO THE NEEDY

No one can think of the 1960s without thinking of change. While gradual change is always a part of life, major change characterized life in the 1960s. All institutions were criticized and questioned. In the late 1960s, major change hit parents and children alike. The mission of President Lyndon Johnson's Great Society was to bring the advantages of the high-functioning upper middle class to minorities, the handicapped, and the economically disadvantaged. The War on Poverty was begun, with the children of the poor as the target. Research showed that the early childhood environment was the place to start. If children could be given equal environmental opportunities, then the cycle of poverty could be broken.

On the basis of years of compelling research indicating that parent involvement and family background were positively correlated with academic success, Head Start was founded in 1965. First the program was started for three- to five-year-olds. Later it reached the two-year-old population. At first, "parent involvement" meant training parents for positions within the Head Start system. Later it expanded to include parent education and other kinds of parent participation intrinsic to the program. Parent involvement continued as an integral part of the Head Start program.

The Perry Preschool Study grew out of the Head Start concept. In Ypsilanti, Michigan, data were gathered to see the effect on children's lives of a nurturing preschool environment supported by a parent program. This was the first longitudinal study of its kind. Year after year, the High/Scope Foundation, as it is now called, has studied that same group of inner-city children. Year after year, that group shows up as a more advantaged group—less likely to be involved in crime, more likely to be in stable marriages, and more likely to be experiencing productive lives than a representative group of their counterparts who were not in the program. After the first positive findings came in from that study, the High/Scope Foundation began developing its High/Scope preschool into a widely used, effective system, with parent involvement as a strong component.

The changes of the 1960s mounted. Few of our institutions seemed to be working for the population as it existed, and schools were no exception. College students stirred up their campuses in search of more relevant education, and all schools suffered nationwide. Concern for the poor and needy in the United States became a major focus, and it looked as though parents were about to get help.

THE 1970s: A TURNING POINT

But the help never quite arrived. The economy began to change, and the problems got worse. More women went to work. Values began to change, and more families broke up. In addition, our country found itself with a high number of female college graduates seeking careers in the work force. Moreover, since the 1960s had set the stage for opening work opportunities to both women and minorities, life for families had become complicated. Child care was not available for the numbers of children who needed it, nor was there consistent high quality. Conditions for children grew worse. As parents worked through many struggles, they questioned the schools at the same time. The closely knit parent–school partnership that had been developed so well before all these struggles was broken apart.

Eventually, the turmoil of the 1960s settled down. The late 1970s saw the rise of an enormous number of programs and advocacy groups for the poor, the disabled, and eventually the general population. In 1978 Barbara Rollock, the coordinator of children's services at the New York Public Library, started a one-year pilot project for parents that was so successful that it never closed. Designed for adults, it has three parts: a resource collection, an ongoing program of workshops and seminars on early childhood topics, and a family room designed to encourage interaction between children and their parents or caregivers. Later, other centers similar to this New York program opened around the country. In 1979 the Orlando Florida Public Library initiated the "Catch 'em in the Cradle" program, offering information to parents in hospital maternity wards. Parent workshops were started, and parent education programs began to spread throughout the country. Many children's library centers were developed where parents and teachers could work with preschool children to promote intellectual and social growth. They were designed for adults and children to interact with each other and to have a parent resource corner with information for parents (Greene, 1991, pp. 3–9).

THE 1980s: DIVISIVE FACTORS CONTINUE TO PLAGUE FAMILIES

Years of research showed the positive effects of parent involvement on child academic achievement. But even with the increased availability of resources and programming, parents still found themselves unable to respond as they would have liked. Rather than being able to focus on their children's development, they found themselves drowning in practical problems. They were putting in forty- to sixty-hour work weeks just to meet their basic responsibilities. Crime, drug use, teenage pregnancy, and unwed motherhood were on the rise. Very young mothers were not prepared physically, educationally, or intellectually to rear children; and there was an increase in the number of mothers who were single because of divorce, death of a spouse, or preference. In more than half of the two-parent families in the United States, both parents worked (O'Connell & Bloom, 1987). Although this gave parents economic flexibility, it also posed great difficulties in rearing their children. The result of all these demands was the development of a large number of child care facilities. Unfortunately, many of these centers had very low standards and were run by caregivers with inferior training.

Much was done to combat these problems. The Council for Early Childhood Recognition established the Child Development Associate (CDA) degree, awarded on completion of a two-year program offered at many community colleges, which became a requirement for employment in many early childhood centers. In addition, training for teachers became available at conferences throughout the country. By the end of 1989, our country was proud of 31,000 credentialed caregivers who had either achieved the CDA or earned certificates in other educational programs.

The National Association for the Education of Young Children (NAEYC), a strong and growing national organization, also responded. It became a major advocate for sound early childhood policy. In 1986 the NAEYC published a landmark book entitled *Developmentally Appropriate Practices in Early Childhood Programs Serving Children from Birth through Age 8.* This book, which contrasted appropriate with inappropriate early childhood practices, caught on well and played a major role in guiding early childhood educational practices nationwide. It became a part of many teacher education programs, as well as a staple in the hands of early childhood professionals. In 1989 the NAEYC published a handbook, *Accreditation Criteria and Procedures of the National Academy of Early Childhood Programs.* This book explained how a center can receive NAEYC accreditation. It presented the highest standards for an early childhood program, and it took its place as a major influence on the shape of early childhood education.

Programming for parents as their children's first teachers also came to stay at this time. One program for the economically at risk that continued to grow was known as HIPPY (Home Instructional Program for Preschool Youngsters). It was developed in Israel to help the large immigrant population adjust to Israeli culture. It was brought to the United States in the 1980s by Avima Lombard and was adapted to U.S. culture. Hippy was originally designed for mothers of four- and five-year-olds. Its two-year curriculum included materials to help mothers teach specific skills to their children to increase readiness for kindergarten. The program, which included home visits and group meetings, was later extended for mothers with three-year-olds (Riley, 1994, p. 24).

Another parent training program for the economically at-risk population was the federally funded Even Start program. Public schools were used to teach parents of babies early parenting skills. This program also helped struggling parents obtain basic resources and further their education.

A third parent training program was the Missouri New Parents as Teachers (NPAT) program, which became available to parents throughout the state. As soon as babies were born, parent trainers helped parents learn valuable skills designed to prepare children to do well in school. NPAT used a group meeting and home visit format.

These programs and others that were generated from the same concepts made up a strong parent development system, but only for the very few. Most parents still found themselves arriving at the day of new parenthood almost totally unprepared.

During these troubled years, schools did not regain parent support. The basic parent agency of the times, the Parent–Teacher Association or PTA, became weaker and weaker. New kinds of programming for parents were planned—parent information nights, guest speakers, spaghetti dinners, bake sales, volunteer activities, and more. Yet year after year, the same parents turned out—mostly the ones who did not need the support. In general, parent program attendance was notoriously low. Parents left teaching to the schools and were unable to add a fully committed school spot to their already overcomplicated lives.

THE 1990s: FAMILIES AT RISK

By the 1990s information was disseminated more widely, teachers were better trained, and child care centers were reaching higher standards. There were programs for those in poverty, those stricken with AIDS, those affected by drug and alcohol abuse, families overburdened with stress, undereducated youth, and the homeless. However, the actual situation for a massive number of children in our country did not improve. Many parents found themselves worse off. Crime had risen sevenfold since 1960; the teenage pregnancy rate had doubled since 1972. Since 1960, the teenage suicide rate had tripled, and the divorce rate and the proportion of families with single parents had more than doubled. Average television viewing per household had increased from five to seven hours a day, and SAT scores had dropped 75 points (verbal and math combined). The 1994 census reported that only 50.8 percent of the children living in the United States lived in a traditional nuclear family.

By the mid-1990s, accounts of children in terrible situations had increased. Poverty and substandard living conditions of some parents led to enormous stress and sometimes to children's abuse or even death. Cases were reported of children being shaken to death, shot, and even dropped from high buildings. In a congressional report released in 1995, it was reported that 2,000 children were killed annually by violence and upwards of 140,000 children were injured. Abuse and neglect became a leading cause of death for young children, and the majority of abused and neglected children were under four years old.

In some advantaged areas, by contrast, schools of the past were beginning to turn into schools of the future. Paper, pencils, and desks were being replaced with personal computers for students and staff. Tight curriculum materials and rigid standards were crumbling, and strongly child-centered study—augmented by Internet access, telecommunications, appropriate field trips, and the concept of the teacher as a facilitator—was on the rise. These "schools of the future" were being looked at carefully, and funding was becoming available for them (Des Dixon, 1994).

Amid all of these new developments, the quest for parent education and parent involvement still captured the hope of our leading educators. New technologies and new schools were not sufficient to create students who were competitive worldwide. The most important research result still prevailed: High-quality parent involvement is positively correlated with child achievement. Such involvement was no longer considered a luxury, but a necessity for educational success.

A school opened in Miami, Florida, that understood this concept well. Claude Pepper Elementary School, under the direction of principal Billie Gimenez, was designed as a parent involvement school. It activates the resources of its parents for the benefit of the children. Other proposals were submitted for the design of this school. It could have been set up with another theme, another type of special expertise, or another focus. But the decision makers believed that parent involvement had shown itself to be the direction for true success in raising child achievement.

Society has changed, but children have not. Society has become technologically advanced, faster paced, move competitive, and more materialistic; but children still need coddling, nurturing, and care. Society brought many children into the homes of two busy parents, working hard to make a living. It brought many children into homes where schedules were a thing of the past and expectations changed from time to time and from caregiver to caregiver. It brought still others into homes where there was only one busy parent, working hard to do the jobs of two. Many children who still needed vast amounts of attention from parents found themselves with a multitude of caregivers giving shallow, unstructured, and diverse care.

FOR THE TWENTY-FIRST CENTURY

Technology should and will be the driving force behind education in the twenty-first century. It is likely to impact schools and children in a revolutionary manner. In the 1990s, technology has begun changing so fast that even incredible advances are quickly going out of date. CD-ROM and on-line technologies have opened up the availability of virtually a limitless supply of information. It is truly unknown what will be the state of the art in the year 2000 and beyond.

RETURNING TO OUR HISTORY

There has been a tradition in public school education from kindergarten through grade 12 of schools assuming an authority–client relationship with parents. This tradition started at the turn of the twentieth century, when the population of the United States more than doubled with non-English-speaking immigrants. To "Americanize" the foreigners, kindergarten teachers especially were asked to make home visits and start mothers' groups. The intent of the parent involvement at that time was to activate the resources of the parents in developing "good citizens" (Gartrell, 1994, p. 22).

PUTTING THE PACKAGE TOGETHER TO WORK FOR TODAY

It is time to pick up on the authority–client tradition. We are in great need of "Americanizing" our population and in great need of turning out "good citizens." Once again we must turn to the parent population for their support. Pestalozzi is our "Father," and he taught us well. He taught us about teaching parents, starting when they are new parents. New parents, now more than ever, lack parenting skills. Many are far from the support of their own parents or any kind of extended family. They find themselves with busy lives unable to give sufficient time and energy to what was meant to be a full-time job. They use the techniques they know but that may not necessarily be the best. In addition, many parents are, as they were in the early twentieth century, in need of major socialization concepts to be able to succeed in a new land.

A NEW IDEA

If the schools need parents, why not think about teaching the parents when they are new parents? Schools can bring the parents into the school structure in an appropriate way as soon as their baby is born. They can make a parent–school partnership with a strong foundation, one that will grow as the years go by. This will not be just another way of raising children's academic achievement: It will be the most effective way.

This approach will give parents the opportunity to learn about child development and techniques for facilitating it. It will give them the opportunity to be part of their child's education from the beginning and with a depth that will grow in strength and meaning in later years. It will give them the opportunity to be part of the school. Loss of parent support will disappear as an issue if parent support is started in the school system from the ground up, during the years from a child's birth to age five.

PARENTING CLASSES THROUGH THE PUBLIC SCHOOLS

Taking the authority–client position, the schools should require that all parents register their child with the public schools as soon as their baby is born. They can register in a program that ideally will provide a full range of services. Churches, temples, hospitals, and other private or public settings could also provide these services. Community schools and full-service schools are new concepts that could provide appropriate alternatives for including ongoing parenting classes.

PERSONALIZED PARENTING

Personalized Parenting classes should be set up for parents of children from birth to five years throughout the school day and into the evenings so that there are viable choices of times for all parents. These should be set up as seminars meeting once a month, with no more than 15 sets of parents in each. Sometimes only one parent would be able to attend, but attendance by both parents would be optimum. For parents of children in the birth-to-three age range, these classes should focus on early childhood development—what it is all about, how to interact with children in a way that develops the child in all areas and culminates in high self-esteem. For parents of three- to five-year-olds, these classes should be a follow-through program emphasizing readiness for school.

As part of this program, "Mommy and Daddy and Me" developmental classes should also be set up for parents of children in the birth-to-three age range throughout the school day and into the evenings. These should include no more than 15 parent–child combinations in each group. The purpose of these classes should be to expose the parents to activities that they can use to facilitate development in all areas (see Part IV). Songs, motor activities, concepts, socialization, language, and creativity should all be part of the program, along with the opportunity for the infants and toddlers to experience a stimulating environment under the direction of a trained teacher. Classes should be set up to meet once a month. In addition, this program should include a set of audio tapes containing the songs and activities from the classes that could help parents continue with their programming at home.

Teachers for the program should come out of the educational setting. New certification is being put in place for early childhood teachers that includes parent involvement training. Until a sufficient cadre of teachers can be trained, however, an interin system should be set up. One suggested model is to allow any interested teacher with elementary school certification and at least six credits earned in early childhood education and three credits earned in parent involvement to be considered as a candidate for the position. Sufficient orientation and inservice training should be part of the program at all personalized parenting sites.

Also as part of the program, developmental review should be set up for children when they turn three years old. Developmental review is a procedure for reviewing each child's developmental progress with parents and responding to their questions and concerns in a way that enables them to parent better. It is an enabling process for both parents and children because it offers affirmation of a child's developmental level, information about child care and child development, and the opportunity for parents to raise questions and express concerns about their child. Developmental review assumes a positive orientation that goes beyond "screening for defects." A child's progress is reviewed with the parent in a way that is beneficial for parents and normally functioning children as well as for developmentally delayed children.

Developmental review is carried out in two parts. The first is a consultation focused on parental concerns as well as child strengths and potential. Parents will have the opportunity to give a professional background information about the child, both informally, through conversation, and then more formally, through filling out a questionnaire about their child. The second consultation is for giving the parent a report with recommendations based on the assessment made from the verbal and written information obtained at the first consultation. It should include a home program based on the report. For children with possible developmental problems, the review is oriented toward the parents' questions or concerns. For children functioning in the normal range or above, discussion is oriented toward enrichment planning. Referral for follow-up evaluation or special services is made when needed.

For children who had any deficit areas at age three and who went through any kind of intervention programming based on the deficit areas, developmental review should be repeated at age five. This review will be meaningful for placement in a kindergarten program.

Personalized Parenting seminar classes should be continued after the child enters a full-time program in the school. In this way parent involvement and parent education will play a role in the schools that is integral to the system and is not left to chance or diminished by other priorities.

For parents of older children, the emphasis should be on self-esteem, discipline, and the practical implications of both. Self-esteem is the area of development that encompasses all others (see Chapter 4). Role playing for parenting skills should be part of the program along with the opportunity to trouble-shoot current individual problems. If parents need any special services, these classes would provide the opportunity to find out about those services. Classes should meet once a month. The program should include a set of audio tapes and a workbook to help parents truly understand the concepts they need to know and the practices they need to use.

These classes hold the key to enabling children to achieve their full potential. They represent the type of parent programming that current educators are seeking. Book after book has been written to communicate excellent techniques of parenting to parents, but the information in those books still finds itself in the hands of only a few. It also can be hard to put written information into practice. Stating, "Here's what you should do" is rarely as practical as, "Here's how you should do it."

Role playing is a teaching technique that is tailor-made for ongoing parent seminars. It provides two strong teaching benefits to the parent. First, while role playing the parent part, it becomes an opportunity to practice effective parent–child interactions. Second, while role playing the child part, it becomes an opportunity to experience how a child might feel when handled in different ways by a parent. No book, class, or lecture can come close to role play in which the parent not only is exposed to optimum methods of parenting but also is given the opportunity to practice those methods.

The information offered in parenting classes also finds itself in the hands of only a few. Parents need more than a six- or eight-week session. They need a lifetime membership in such a course. Parenting skills are people skills. They must be practiced. As children grow and change, the practicing has to grow and change as well.

PERSONALIZED PREPARENTING

Personalized Preparenting should be the next priority. These classes should be set up for parents expecting a baby and those in the process of adopting. The time before a baby is born has a powerful effect on the life of the baby-to-be, and it is important that all preparents understand this. Research has shown that a mother's use of drugs, alcohol, or tobacco during pregnancy is responsible for many birth defects. Another cause is inadequate prenatal care. The 1989 White House Task Force on Infant Mortality found that 400,000 children were born with disabilities every year and that more than one-fourth of these impairments, including impaired vision, learning disabilities, hearing problems, developmental delay, autism, and cerebral palsy, could have been avoided in the prenatal stage (United States Department of Education, "What Other Countries Are Doing," 1992, p. 6). Another half million potential lives are destroyed by miscarriages and stillbirths every year, largely because of faulty fetal development. Disabilities have become our nation's most serious health problem. They account for 30 percent of the hospitalizations of children, cost billions of dollars in medical care, and cause great human suffering and anguish to children and parents alike (March of Dimes, 1994).

Preparenting classes are important for teaching prenatal care. The following advice comes from a 1994 guide from the March of Dimes titled *Be Good to Your Baby Before It Is Born: Your Guide to a Healthy Pregnancy:*

> Eat right while you're pregnant so your baby will grow the way it should. Drink at least 6 to 8 glasses of water, fruit juice or milk every day.
>
> Don't take any drugs without the advice of a health care provider who knows you are pregnant. Even store-bought medications like aspirin or cough syrup can hurt your baby.

Preparenting classes are just as vital for fathers-to-be. Throughout pregnancy, an expectant father can take steps to help his partner have a healthy baby. The father's lifestyle and emotional support of his partner can affect her behavior and even her level of psychological stress (March of Dimes, *Men Have Babies Too: A Guide for Fathers-to-Be,* 1994). Research has shown that maternal stress and attitude can influence the baby's future (Clark, 1988).

These classes are necessary not only to teach the importance of prenatal care but are also to teach preparents about the wants and needs of the children soon to be born. They need the information about being prepared to set up an optimum environment for child development and the information on being prepared to guide and support their child. Preparents need to be ready.

PERSONALIZED FUTURE PARENTING

Personalized Future Parenting is the next logical step. These classes should be set up in both high schools and colleges. Just as teaching parenting skills to new parents and to parents-to-be is now seen as essential, teaching parenting skills to future parents should be seen as essential, too. Ideally, we should teach parenting skills to our high school students and also to our college students. Personalized Future Parenting classes are the true necessary classes for our young people. Our students in high school and in college need to know not only the information taught in Personalized Parenting and Personalized Preparenting, but also how to begin preparing themselves and their bodies for the possibility of becoming parents in the future.

The physical condition of both the father and the mother influences the unborn baby long before conception. Scientists used to think that infertility, miscarriage, or genetic damage to the fetus was caused only by what the mother did *during* pregnancy. Now they know that such problems can occur because of what she did even before pregnancy. They also know that such problems can occur because of things the father did before conception. Teenagers and young adults must learn that smoking cigarettes, drinking alcohol, taking nonprescription drugs, or being exposed to toxic chemicals in the environment can affect reproduction and fetal development. Young men should know that even damaged sperm may still fertilize an egg and that some toxins may alter the sperm's chromosomes, which carry genetic information. If this happens, the results may range from infertility and miscarriage to stillbirth, birth defects, learning disabilities, and even childhood leukemia and kidney cancer (March of Dimes, *Men Have Babies Too*, 1994).

Our knowledge of how children develop and learn has increased tremendously in the twentieth century, especially since the 1960s. Research has become more accurate. We know now beyond a shadow of a doubt that all children need an excellent start. We also know beyond a shadow of a doubt that an excellent start is not available to all children. Our practices in early childhood education lag far behind our knowledge. Parent education and programming are absolute necessities if we have any hope of improving the quality of life in the twenty-first century (Greene, 1991, p. 11). We owe it to our children, those who should be given the opportunity to grow into a responsible adult population.

CHAPTER 2

Parent Involvement at Its Best

HIGH PARENT INVOLVEMENT, HIGH STUDENT SUCCESS

There is a reason for involving parents in the classroom. As involved parents become more interested in their child's success at school, their child will actually become more successful.

More parents will try to find the time for visiting their child's classroom if they feel needed and wanted. "Needed and wanted" is the key. Lilian Katz, the 1994 president of the National Association for the Education of Young Children (NAEYC), suggested that the school "focus on making sure that the day-to-day interactions of children with their teachers and with each other are engaging, interesting, rich, satisfying, and meaningful. This strategy can attract the interest, involvement, loyalty, and support of parents better than all the usual incantations about parent involvement and support (Katz, 1994, p.2).

The "new" ideas about parent support, therefore, are the old ideas. We cannot successfully create a need for parent involvement from without and try to draw parents into what is virtually a closed system. We must build the system from within and make it so enticing that the problem will become keeping parent involvement from overwhelming it.

A WORKING MODEL

Many schools today are making a major effort to get parents involved. Why? Because parent involvement is correlated with a child's school success. While different programs have been implemented in different ways, most principals report poor attendance at programs planned for parents. The turnout rises when food is part of the program, but the crowd is biggest when parents come to programs with their children, come to see their children, or at least come to see their children's work. While few schools have been successful, most are still trying. They try because they know such in-

volvement correlates with student success. When parents tell their children that school is important, they encourage school success. By simply walking on the school grounds, they influence it even more. By talking to the child's teacher(s), meeting with a classmate's parent(s), or even participating in a school program, they have a major impact on children's achievement.

One successful format for parent involvement includes morning meetings. Morning meetings are often held first thing in the morning with groups of classes that are organized into communities. Parents not only are invited to attend these meetings, but play a role in them. They have responsibilities and also power by having a voice in the affairs of the community. Teachers are also a part of these communities. They are able to communicate to parents the important responsibilities they have in preparing their children to be successful in school. They tell them things as basic as the importance of bringing their children to school on time and giving them breakfast and as creative as modeling techniques for helping children to follow directions. This gives children the opportunity to experience a connection between home and school. Morning meetings give parents and children alike the feeling of belonging to a caring community.

Besides meetings there are frequent parent conferences. Parents might have a scheduled appointment with their child's teacher once a month. The first conference takes place during the first month of school and is primarily for individualized goal setting. After that the conferences are to monitor the goals and set new ones if applicable. Children are made aware of the goals, and the teacher–parent–child trio work hard all year long to accomplish goals and continually set new ones. The focus of the conferences is on success. First the children are made aware through the school program of their own successes.

At the conferences these successes are communicated to the parents. Once the parents see their child's successes and the rise in self-esteem that follows, they tend to get more involved in the school and with their child's schooling.

When parents are an integral part of both meetings and conferences, they also will find themselves spending time at school. This already makes their parent involvement different than for most. Generally children set off for school five days a week to a place largely unknown to their parents. Although schools often think they are keeping parents well informed, parents usually get only a glimpse of school life from what their children say, from their homework, and from notices and newsletters. It is only when frequent contact is built into the system that parents have the opportunity to see and experience some of the exciting activities in which their children are participating. This contact activates the classroom as its own force of parent involvement. When the innovative Southpointe Elementary School program was originated in Miami, Florida, it had an exemplary parent involvement program that included a successful version of morning meetings, parent conferences, and parent involvement in the classrooms.

Although this model is the most effective one we have, it is not widely used. It is also limited by its connection to schools as they currently exist, starting children at age five. We now know that the years from birth to five are not only not too early to start parent involvement but the right time for beginning to initiate the resources of parents in the process of developing children to their highest potential. We also now have all the information necessary for starting parent involvement under school direction as soon as a child is born and even before.

NEEDED FROM THE BEGINNING

Burton L. White, a psychologist and researcher from Harvard University in Cambridge, Massachusetts, culminated thirty-three years of research on infants and toddlers by publishing in 1975 a landmark book titled *The First Three Years of Life.* In it he explained the important learning that takes place from birth to three. He also carefully described the kinds of child-rearing practices that enhance learning in those first three years. White's book was different from other books because he discovered that children who are reared well in the early years have adequate preparation to succeed in school, whereas children who are not reared well at this time are likely not to be successful in school. He uncovered that successful children had parents who knew how to lead them onto the path of success, all during the first three years of their lives. He was clear and simple about the importance of educating parents of children in the birth-to-three age range in order to prepare them to prepare their children. But White's concepts have been largely overlooked. Instead of birth-to-three programming in our schools, all educational efforts have gone into the development of preschool programs serving children ages three to five.

White's research included the Brookline Early Education Project (BEEP) in Brookline, Massachusetts. This project was set up to find out whether it should be recommended to the public schools that they run programs for parents and their children from birth to age three. Although no conclusive answer was ever reached, the information gathered about the effectiveness of positive child-rearing techniques on the lives of infants and toddlers turned out to be extremely valuable. It was publicity about that information that led to the development of Missouri's innovative and successful program for parents and their children ages birth to three.

NEW PARENTS AS TEACHERS IN MISSOURI

After twelve years of building support in the political, medical, business, and community spheres, Mrs. Mildred Winter, director of elementary education in Missouri, succeeded. With the help of Mrs. Jane Pane from the Danforth Foundation, the project was born and came to fruition as the New Parents as Teachers (NPAT). It too succeeded. It too demonstrated what knowledgeable parents could accomplish with infants and toddlers. Through this program, new parents were taught what babies learn as they develop, what effective child-rearing techniques are, and how not to interfere with optimum development. Just as was explained in White's book, the babies who were reared from birth to three under the direction of professionals according to the most up-to-date information were the ones who were successful starting school at age six.

What went wrong? A lot. The program was so successful that Missouri started to expand it without paying proper attention to quality control. White witnessed his high-quality design turn into a watered-down version. He fought for many basic services that did not get funded. "Since 1985 the state has been making a mess of the program and, worse than that, exporting the mess to twenty-six other states!" (White, 1993, p. 350). Eventually White severed his ties to the program.

THE CARNEGIE COMMISSION REPORT

The third set of conclusive information about the importance of early experiences for children from birth to three was released in April 1994. The Carnegie Commission, in a report known as *Starting Points,* warned the nation about the devastating conditions in which many infants and toddlers were living. From a three-year multimillion-dollar study, they concluded that such conditions will have an irreversible effect on the lives of those children. They showed that unless we do something about our current conditions, more and more children ages birth to three will have this detrimental exposure that is likely to result in their growth into dysfunctional adults in our society.

The first three years of life, the report said, lay the foundation for all that follows. Ideally, this learning time should be spent with adults who offer nurturing love, protection, guidance, stimulation, and support. Instead, infants and toddlers are society's most neglected age group. One in four lives in poverty and in a single-parent family. One in three abused children is a baby less than a year old. The information was clearer than ever before. Once again we learned that an adverse environment can compromise a young child's brain function and overall development and can place a child at risk of cognitive, behavioral, and physical difficulties.

TIME FOR ACTION

When a report tells us that millions of American children are at risk of a bleak future and many face a lifetime of dysfunction, the time has come to respond. When a report warns us about the harm we are doing to our children and hence to the future of our nation, it is time to listen.

> "One of the big problems in Washington," declares Congressman Nick Hanfli, "is that we have too many fact-finding committees and too much reluctance to face the facts once they've been found!" (Burton Hillis in BETTER HOMES AND GARDENS, February 1994)

We have to face the facts. Child-rearing information is for rich and poor alike. Public school programming for parents and their children from birth to five should no longer be just an idea, or just a pilot program. It should be made available for the benefit of all children and, most important, for the benefit of our entire nation.

ARE WE REALLY TOO LATE AFTER THREE?

When asked if programming after age three comes too late, White often hesitates. On the one hand, it is never too late to help people. But White truly believes that missing opportunities from birth to three means missing major opportunities. There is a lack of ability to make fundamental personality changes after the early years. In his research he found that "children doing remarkably well at three years of age are much more likely to exhibit the major elements of competence that distinguish the outstanding six-year-old." What he found between the ages of three and six was "a process of refinement of abilities already in place rather than the emergence of new abilities" (White, 1993, p. 325).

EARLY LEARNING

There are some basic interactions and principles of parenting that should be learned and implemented by all parents in the first five years of their child's life. These principles should be available to everyone. All of them will be usable throughout their entire lifetime as parents. Some will be usable in the exact form and only adapted to the child during growth; others will be usable in a modified form because of the nature of children's growth. All of them should be taught during the first five years for the maximum effect on child development. Some of them must be taught continually throughout the years as both parents and their children grow together.

WHAT PARENTS NEED TO KNOW FROM BIRTH TO EIGHT MONTHS

Luckily, they do not need to know too much. Nature provides an "orientation period" to allow the family to get used to the baby in a natural way. According to White, parents need to provide love, attention, and physical care, and then let nature take care of the rest. During this period there is no such thing as spoiling a child.

There are four basic types of interactions that parents should do at this time to keep their child on the track toward optimum development. These are adapted from White's original work.

1. *Respond.* Parents should be as available as possible to respond to a child's needs.
2. *Touch.* They should follow their natural instincts for handling, caressing, and loving the baby. Touching in itself provides security necessary at this time.
3. *Play.* Parents should also begin play at this time. Much of play is demonstration with babies at early age. However, there is also a part of play that flows naturally from parent–baby interaction. Whoever smiles first will get a smile back. Whoever touches first will get touched back. Whoever makes a sound—a coo or anything else—will get an appropriate vocal response. Play should also be affectionate and should include a lot of talk about what the baby is doing.
4. *Act natural.* They should be warm and loving. Overall, they should be themselves.

These four concepts are little more than what comes naturally.

FOUR STYLES OF CHILD REARING FROM EIGHT MONTHS ON

From eight months on it is important to adopt principles of parenting that will work throughout the early years. Once parents know these they can adapt them to all situations as their baby grows. The following four principles of child rearing, adapted from White's work, will be worth their weight in gold to any parent in terms of providing the opportunity for optimum development for a child.

1. *Provide an enriched learning environment.* All learning takes place through the five senses. Whether we are infants, toddlers, preschoolers, school-age children, adolescents, or adults, that is the only way we can learn. Therefore, it is good for parents to ask, "Does the child have something to see, hear, touch, taste, or smell?" If the answer is no, they can do something about it. The more senses an activity encompasses, the more powerful it is as a facilitator of development.
2. *Be responsive to the child's needs and interests.* Just being a child means needing help in one way or another almost all the time. It is important for a parent to be there to provide assistance and encourage-

ment. When the child's needs subside, it is still just as important for a parent to be there to provide support and development of the child's interests.

3. *Be firm but positive in the areas of behavior management and limit setting.* Maintaining authority is the key. A parent should feel free to love, caress, play with, and in any way possible enjoy the child. However, the parent should not forget about being a parent, fully in charge of the growth and development of a little one. Parents have access to much information, and their strength is a source of great support to a child. They give a child both roots and wings.

4. *Provide a language-rich environment.* Once parents know that talking to a child is of the utmost importance for development, they can build it into their lifestyle. Reading to a child, talking, and singing can become frequent activities. Research tells us that adult speech has a more important positive influence on later child development than any other activity or procedure a caregiver can do. (Goldberg, 1990, p. 1) After about eight months, when the baby starts to make many sounds, there is a direct progression of language—sounds, words, phrases, sentences, and then conversation.

STAGES OF DEVELOPMENT

An understanding of the interactions helpful to a baby and an understanding of the principles of child rearing are the basics. They can be even better applied if parents have information about each broad stage of development. Since each stage should be looked upon as an exciting opportunity for growth, it is important for a parent not only to know the stage the child is in but also to be interacting with the child in a way that is preparation for the next stage.

Year 1: Time for absorbing and developing foundation skills—cognitive, motor, social, language, and self-esteem
Year 2: Time for testing limits and risk taking—"the terrible twos"
Year 3: Time for building social skills
Year 4: Time for moving from "me" to others
Year 5: Time for developing independence

These stages are additive. Development takes place in different ways at different times, but it is also a lifelong process.

Somehow we always have the secret hope that we can get ourselves together, work out all our issues, discover all our talents, accept our life's work, and then relax and get on with it. What a shock it is when we finally recognize that character building is a continuing lifelong process.—Anonymous

LEARNING RATE

Strong input, support, and commitment on the part of parents helps children learn faster and better. Parent support that is truly responsive and personally interactive speeds up development. Children who succeed on the highest levels generally come from homes in which they have learned a willingness to do great amounts of work, a determination to do their best at all times, and the ability to learn rapidly. Innate ability is a factor, but favorable learning conditions provided in the early years have the greatest influence on learning (Clark, 1988, p. 120).

TOYS

When we think of the years from birth to three, we think of toys. A good toy challenges a child to do, think, and feel. Therefore, the toys that are the most formed have the least value, and the toys that are the least formed have the most value. Some of the best toys are balls, blocks, building sets, putty or clay, pegs and a pegboard, dolls (male and female), sand, water, and objects for pretend play. These toys all provide open-ended experiences for children.

Toys have play value if there is something intrinsic to them that invites play. Certain attributes of a toy invite play:

1. Something appealing to see
2. Something interesting to touch
3. Something to manipulate
4. Something to generate a surprise

This section describes a core set of ten exemplary toys. They have all or most of these characteristics, and they also facilitate development maximally in all areas: cognitive, motor, social, language, and self-esteem. According to *Developmentally Appropriate Practices in Early Childhood Programs Serving Children from Birth through Age 8*, a respected reference on early childhood toys and play, there are principles and guidelines about interactive play and creativity that are important for facilitating early childhood development. These toys all reflect these principles and guidelines. .

Because learning is interactive, it is necessary to prepare a child's environment for active exploration and interaction with adults, other children, and materials. Finished products or correct solutions that conform to adult standards are limiting. Much of young children's learning takes place when they direct their own play activities. Activities should be designed to concentrate on emerging skills through creative play and involvement (Bredekamp, 1986, pp. 3–4).

These toys have beginning qualities for infants and toddlers, and they also have more advanced qualities for the preschool years. The play activities possible with all of these grow with the child. The child will not outgrow the toys. Both parent and child can continue to use all the toys in new and different ways. The end result from exposure to and play with these special toys will be a child who knows from play, love, and experience how to think, problem-solve, and create. The child will understand major concepts and will have absorbed the core of academics that educators call the building blocks of learning—colors, letters, numbers, shapes, and reading.

With these toys, concepts will not be taught in a traditional manner but will be learned through interaction in a meaningful and lasting way. These toys, designed for open-ended play, maximize the use of the five senses and enhance all areas of development. They never have to be used in the same way twice. In addition, they serve as stimulation both for the development of many related toys and for the creation of an infinite number of parent–child play activities.

1. Color Boxes

Simple plastic containers, covered with colored lids and filled with toys of the same color, are highly unformed. Intrinsic to them are a myriad of experiences with the containers and all of their varied contents. They invite play. On the outside, the colored lids are attractive. Inside are a variety of interesting items to touch. Babies like to shake containers; toddlers like to empty and fill them. Preschoolers like to collect and sort their own items. When children get to open these containers and find out what is inside, that is a surprise. This kind of toy can include something to see, hear, touch, taste, and smell. It is personalized, too. Whatever is in the containers is put there by the parent, by the parent and child together, or by the child. If there could be such a thing as the perfect toy, this would be it (Goldberg, 1981, p.146).

These boxes can be embellished easily with index card labels with the color words in black on one side and the color words in the identifying color on the other. They can also be enriched by color books, bracketed colored folders filled with matching colored paper and then filled with items that color, either cutouts or the actual items. Descriptive words or sentences can be added as much or as little as is desired (see Figure 2.1).

2. Unbreakable Mirror

A mirror has its own way of being unformed. An unbreakable mirror is an excellent toy. What the baby, toddler, or preschooler sees—his own image—is the most interesting thing that could be seen. A first look causes a reaction. That reaction causes the image to change. That change causes a reaction which again causes the image to change. This process goes on and on. It fits in with the stimulus–response theory, which underlies the major dynamics of play. The toy is the stimulus, the child responds, and the play process goes on and on. Very few people can pass an available mirror by without taking advantage of the opportunity to see themselves, react, see themselves again, and so on. The mirror is something appealing to see, interesting to touch, and full of intrinsic surprise qualities (see Figure 2.2 on page 30).

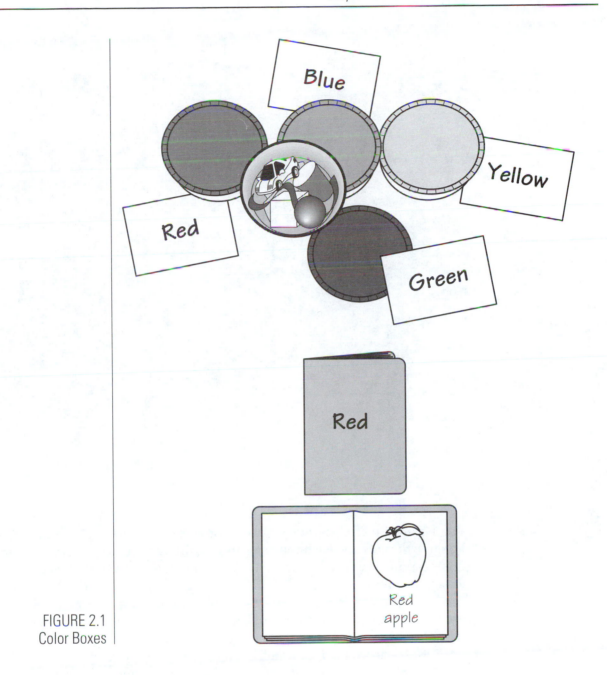

FIGURE 2.1
Color Boxes

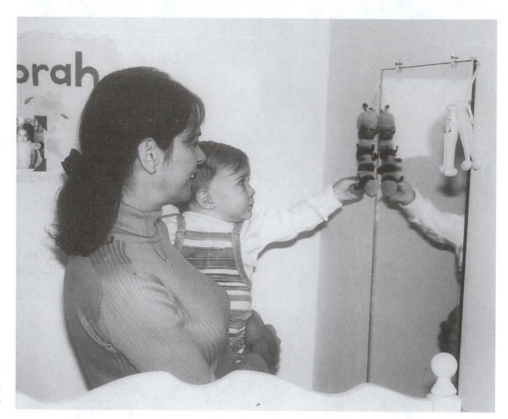

FIGURE 2.2
Unbreakable
Mirror

3. Simple Ball

A ball is unformed in its own way. It too is an excellent toy. A ball never does the same thing twice. Each roll or bounce is different. It too fits with the stimulus–response theory of play. What someone does with the ball is the stimulus. The child responds by catching and then doing another roll or bounce stimulus. Then the other person responds by catching and then doing another roll or bounce. The simple ball has a capability all its own that can give a child many happy hours of play (see Figure 2.3).

Our fascination with the ball begins early and lasts a long time. We like it first to roll, then to bounce, and then to throw and hit in all kinds of ways. Later we use it in sports and never see it do the same thing twice. Children and adults as well play softball, football, volleyball, basketball, soccer, and more. Our interest continues and even grows as we become spectators of sports that we may or may not play ourselves. Why go to another football or basketball game? We go because no two games are ever alike. We have no way of knowing beforehand how well that ball will be played by either team or what the outcome of the game will be. The fascination is never-ending. The ball is something appealing to see and interesting to touch, and it has the qualities for intrinsic surprise.

FIGURE 2.3
Simple Ball

4. Van-like Pull Toy

An original toy designed by Creative Playthings is an example of a specific toy with a minimum amount of form that provides a maximum amount of play. A child will easily be able to do many things with it, think both analytically and creatively, and feel a wide variety of feelings.

Ten different children will call the toy ten different names: van, bus, car, wagon, truck, and so on. Ten different children also will play with it in ten different ways: deliver milk bottles or juice, count the pegs, take it on a family vacation, practice addition and subtraction with the pegs, and so on. The block of wood on wheels is appealing to see, interesting to touch, easy to empty and fill, and full of surprises (see Figure 2.4 on page 32).

FIGURE 2.4
Van-like Pull Toy

5. Name Toy

The Color Boxes mentioned before are personalized toys because what goes into them is selected by the parent or child or both. Another way to personalize toys is by using household photographs.

A parent can make a simple name toy by attaching a child's picture to an index card and clearly writing the child's name on another index card and ataching it to the back with double-stick tape (see Figure 2.5). To the child and to anyone playing with it with the child, whatever is on either side means the same thing. This can be made to stand up for a crawling baby by taping the two cards together from the inside so that they can stand up when spread apart at the bottom. You can see in Figure 2.5 the two versions of this toy. The introduction of the baby's name in large, clear letters is an excellent first exposure to the reading process (Goldberg, 1981, p. 36). These cards can be protected with clear adhesive paper or laminated for increased durability.

A parent can make a new name toy for the child every few months as the baby grows and changes. The toddler can then have the experience of carrying them around from place to place. The preschooler can enjoy looking at them all, putting them in order, and seeing how growth took place from a baby to a young child.

Front   Back

FIGURE 2.5
Name Toy

6. Family Book

A parent can expand the picture concept to a photo album family book
(Figure 2.6 on page 34). In this toy the child will see more pictures and
more corresponding words. While Name Toy was a way to learn to read
a child's name, Family Book is a way to learn to read the names of all family members. This book also teaches the concept of family by showing that
only those in the family can be in this book. The concept of the family can
be whatever the parent wants it to be. It can be a traditional nuclear family plus any number of grandparents, aunts, uncles, and cousins, or even
a dog or other pet (Goldberg, 1981, p. 38), or it can be a nontraditional
family.

Another way to teach reading is through action words. Start with five
simple words that look different from each other. A parent can take turns
with the child picking a card, reading the word on the card, and then following the direction. Good starting words are: *hop, jump, clap, stand,* and
walk. Other word cards can be added after the child learns the first five. Then
two-word, three-word, and even longer sentences can be made: *Get up. Tie
your shoe. Open the door. Give me a pencil.*

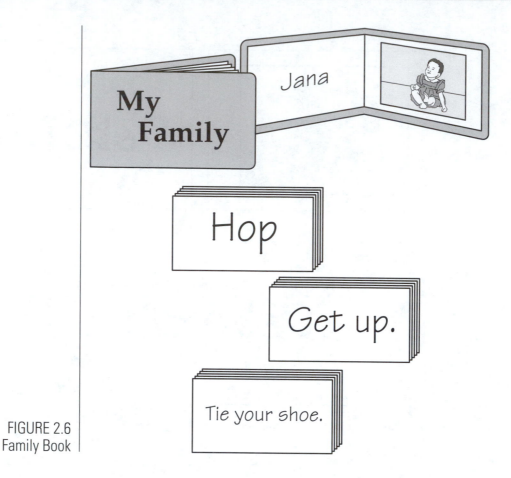

FIGURE 2.6
Family Book

7. Letter Cards

People learn only 10 percent of what they hear, 50 percent of what they see, and 90 percent of what they experience. Infants, toddlers, and preschoolers are no exception. Letter Cards can be made out of 5" × 8" index cards, folded in half so that the lines will not show (Figure 2.7). They provide an excellent way to teach letters by experiencing them. They should have clear letters on them and have a small yarn loop on each one. The letters can be made from yarn, with markers, or using adhesive-back letters available in most office supply stores. Covering the cards with clear adhesive paper or laminating them will protect them and give them a longer play life. The loop is good for playing with the letters. A baby or toddler can hang them from a high chair or on a set of hooks. A preschooler can carry them around. While the child enjoys them simply as play items, the parent can identify them by letter by saying something like, "You have the B," or, "Please pass the D." These Letter Cards have play value. Everyone will enjoy playing with them in creative ways. They are appealing to see and highly interesting to touch. Young children like cards and paper. The cards can be hung on various types of hooks, and they will generate surprise as there is a different letter on each side (Goldberg, 1981, p. 54).

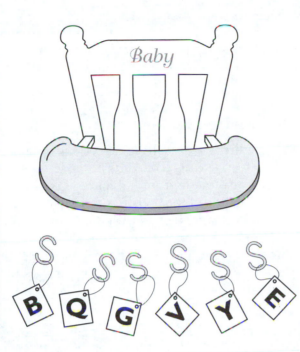

FIGURE 2.7
Letter Cards

8. Number Books

Everybody likes books, and infants, toddlers, and preschoolers are no exception. That is why teaching numbers through books will be a successful experience. Like Letter Cards, Number Books can be used as manipulatives. Each number is presented in one book only, and each number is represented by a numeral and the corresponding number of pieces of yarn to go with that number (Figure 2.8). The pieces of yarn provide practice in one-to-one correspondence, counting, and truly experiencing the number. Basic Number Books can be made from file folders and yarn. Whereas most number books you can buy start with 1 and go on up to 10 or more, with these Number Books each book is about one number only. In the others, by the time you get to 10, you no longer have a good concept of 3, 5, or 7. Young

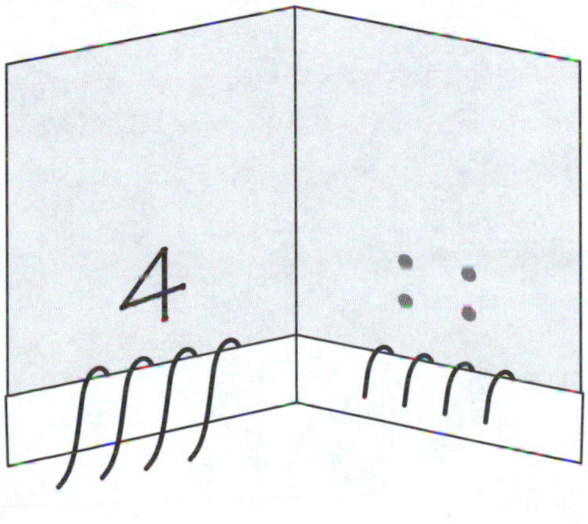

FIGURE 2.8
Number Books

children like folders and soft yarn. They can experience these books, have something appealing to see, something interesting to touch, something to empty and fill, and a vast number of creative activities that can generate surprise (Goldberg, 1981, p. 62).

9. Shape Books and Shape Boxes

Shape Books (Figure 2.9) are a little like books because they open from left to right, and they are a little like cards because they have no enclosures or words. They are also made from file folders. Each shape is represented in one book only. The title of the book has the word for the shape in it, and the book itself is in the shape. Just as with the Number Books, young children like folders. They can experience these books, have something appealing to see, something interesting to touch, have some matching and sorting activities, and design some surprises by covering shapes up, either fully or partially, inside the folder (Goldberg, 1981, p. 72).

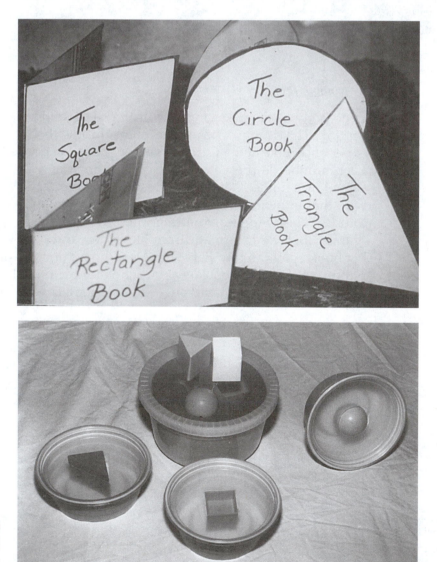

FIGURE 2.9
Shape Books and
Shape Boxes

These books can be enriched with Shape Boxes made from simple plastic containers with lids. A shape can be cut in the lid, and a matching shape can be used as the puzzle piece. A larger lid can have more than one shape cut in it. This medium used as a manipulative is complementary to the aforementioned books.

10. Reading with Surprise

From one sheet of paper, a parent can make a personalized child's book (Figure 2.10). As children get older, they will be able to make these books themselves. The book format is good because young children like books. The paper is good because young children like paper. In addition, this book is manipulative and based around the principle of surprise. This book will have something appealing to see as well as something appealing to touch.

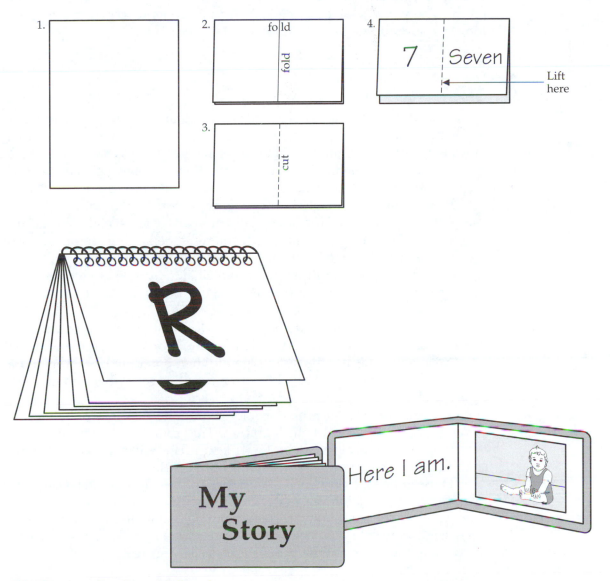

FIGURE 2.10   Reading with Surprise

To make the book, a parent has to fold a sheet of construction paper in half, and then in half again. Then the parent cuts open the second fold only one thickness. This allows a word to be on the top of the page and some kind of surprise to be under the page. The book can be about any subject: people in the family, colors, letters, numbers, shapes, categories like flowers, food, jobs, or any others of interest. This is truly the easiest type of book to make and the most fun to use. It cannot help being an effective medium for exposing infants, toddlers, and preschoolers to the pleasures of recognizing words.

Index card notebooks make a nice addition to these manipulative books. Such pages are more durable and also many more in number. In these books, a parent can collect for children favorite words, letters, or numbers. The parent can point out for the child the word, letter, or number at which the child is looking. Small photo albums similar to the one used for the Family Book are also practical for these books. Such albums can be used with all kinds of family pictures and descriptive words on the opposite pages. The words could be one-, two-, or three-word sentences, or even longer if appropriate to the reading level of the child.

ROTATING TOYS

Just as having toys that are too formed is not valuable, having too many toys is also not valuable. When toys are stored in some kind of toy chest, in a set of shelves, or in some other kind of order where all toys can be seen, they are often left untouched. When they are stored in such a way that only a few are available at any one time, they are played with much more.

Plastic crates, available in office supply stores or in bath and linen shops, are recommended for storage. Parents can try to get eight in four different colors, two of each color. Red, yellow, blue, and green are recommended, if available. However, any four colors, especially if they match a room decor, are fine. These crates store well side by side anywhere, even under a standard crib. They also store well one on top of the other. Parents can store as many toys in these crates as possible.

They also can use the crates in a system for rotating toys. They can take out one color (two crates) for one day, a few days, or a week, depending on what works. Parents are the best judge of when boredom has set in and a new set of toys is needed. Then they can return that set of toys and take out a new color.

The color of the crate is not for color coding the toys. It is for being able to remember and order the toy rotation. This rotation system will make many toys seem like new over and over again. This will help parents avoid spending money on new toys when it is not necessary.

These crates are very good at clean-up time. Children can be asked to put everything back into the crates before they are returned to the child's room or other selected spot. If crates are out belonging to two different siblings, a separate color for each sibling can be used to make it easier to sort toys and return them to their proper places (see Figure 2.11).

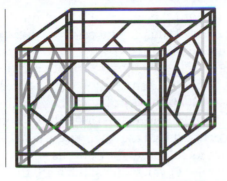

FIGURE 2.11
Crate for
Rotating Toys

GAMES

When we think of the years from three to five, we think of games. A good game should possess the following attributes:

1. No special knowledge needed
2. Flexible number of players
3. Flexible amount of time to play the game
4. Interaction between players
5. Tasks geared to a specific age group

All games, by their nature, are educational activities. A simple game like "Simon Says" teaches following directions, auditory discrimination, and creativity; and it enhances gross motor development. A more complicated game like Monopoly teaches following directions, reading, mathematics, strategy, planning, visual discrimination; and it enhances fine motor and language development. There are traditional games that have been passed on from generation to generation, and there are new games that are being created all the time. They all teach social skills—competition, getting along together, and more. The key to parent teaching is that it must be done through a game format. If a child has a weakness or a special interest in an area, the parent can initiate a game that focuses on that area.

PLAY

"Play is a child's work." This is not a new idea today. Most parents of young children have heard it often. However, most of them do not understand what it means. That sentence implies that play is like prelearning, getting ready for a time when formal or important learning will take place. It also carries with it the idea that infants, toddlers, and preschoolers should not be allowed to learn academic information like reading and writing.

But play is not prelearning. Rather, it is a vehicle for layer upon layer of important learning. Academic information, reading and mathematics in particular, will—and should—emerge through play exposure and experience in the early years.

The problem is not with the sentence but with the reality of scheduling for today's young child. True play takes a long time and should not be limited by artificial time constraints. Once a child starts playing, one idea leads to another, and the activity takes on true depth. Play calls for active and total engagement. It can be done only when there is a true wish to do the activity (intrinsic motivation). In play, attention is placed on what is being done rather than on the end result or goal. It can be compared more to a dance than to a race. In a dance the full process is to be enjoyed, whereas in a race the focus is on the outcome. Play entails symbolic and representational behavior (make-believe). It has rules that arise from the play situation itself, with no external rules imposed. Play in the early years has the potential to facilitate development in every area—cognitive, motor, social, language, and the all-encompassing and all-powerful self-esteem.

"Play is a child's work, and children learn from it."

Why? Because it is natural.
When? Any time.
With what? Almost anything.
How? Through the five senses.

Piles and piles of bottle caps provide an excellent way for children to experience play. They can provide endless activities—from matching, to sorting, to making up all kinds of games. Caps can become game pieces for games as thought-provoking as checkers, chess, or backgammon; and they can become creative building blocks as interesting and as exciting as their colorful plastic counterparts. One form of play leads to another. True play is the beginning, and true learning takes place.

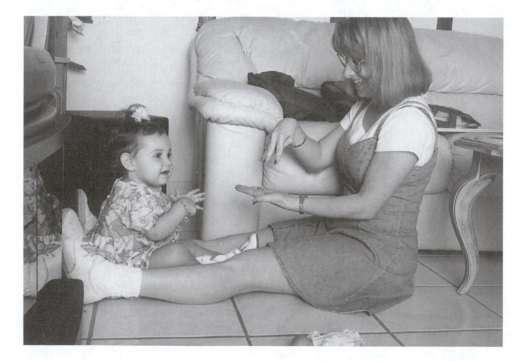

Parents play a major role in child's play as well. They are natural teachers. No one else knows their child as well as they do. They can be a part of their child's spirit of adventure, responding appropriately and with sincere interest. They can allow a child's natural curiosity to emerge and can watch their child experience the joy of learning. Research shows that the amount of time parents spend playing with their preschoolers is directly related to an increase in verbal intelligence test scores (Clark, 1988, p. 121).

CHAPTER 3

Emergent Literacy and Early Learning

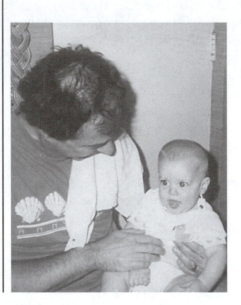

LANGUAGE DEVELOPMENT

Emergent literacy is defined as the natural, gradual development of a young person's listening, speaking, reading, and writing abilities. It includes an awareness of print and writing and other uses of language. It is multidimensional and involves development in all areas. It is child-directed and grows from the child's continuous active participation in listening, speaking, reading, and writing. Children set their own pace as they explore and play with language. Growth in literacy varies from child to child. Children who have fewer opportunities to interact and explore print or language may take longer to become proficient in literacy skills (Morrow, pp. 3–5).

Current research has changed thinking about early literacy. Very young children are now viewed as children with literacy skills. Whereas oral language development was once considered a preschooler's preparation for reading, it is now considered part of a literacy process that starts before birth. Language learning starts as soon as hearing develops and clearly depends on hearing. We now know that hearing starts even before birth, somewhere around the fifth month of fetal development. The language(s) to which babies are exposed will be the language(s) they learn to speak. If a child is to learn more than one language correctly, at least one person will have to speak only that language with the child. If one person speaks both with the child, there is more of a chance for the child to mix the two languages together and not learn either one correctly. The period from 18 months to 4 years old is a critical time for excellence in language learning. While a language-rich environment is important from birth on, recommended especially from eight months on, it is absolutely necessary for this period. Never again will the child have the ability to learn language-related activities with such ease.

The new ideas about literacy development have impacted our thinking about young children and the corresponding activities that go along with that thinking. These new ideas have led to a whole new set of parent–child literacy-oriented interactions:

1. Because literacy learning begins in infancy, parents should be taught to read to babies as soon as they are born and to provide a continuing, stimulating language environment.
2. Because parents need to provide a rich literacy environment to help children, they should be taught to fill a home with much talk, many books, and eventually writing materials.
3. Because school personnel are now aware that many children come to school with poor knowledge of oral and written language, parents should be taught to be free to help their children develop reading and writing skills.
4. Because each child is exposed to different information, parents should be taught how to present early reading and writing experiences that build upon a child's existing knowledge.
5. Because learning requires a supportive environment that builds a child's positive feelings, parents need to be taught how to create that kind of environment.
6. Because children learn from what they see their parents doing, parents should be taught to model high-quality literacy behavior by exhibiting involvement and enjoyment with books and print.
7. Because children's learning is an active process, parents should be taught to set up early literacy experiences for children that are meaningful, are concrete, and actively involve the child.
8. Because literacy development is a holistic process, parents should be taught to facilitate child speech, listening, reading, and writing. (Adapted from Morrow, 1994, pp. 2–3)

READING

Reading is a visual language experience that may aid in language development from the time of emergent speech. Research shows that children exposed to reading from age two to four become early readers with ease and never lose their edge. New research suggests that reading is as natural as walking; if we let it emerge, it will.

Imagine if we prevented children from walking until age three or four. We would have to teach balance, left–right sequencing, how to place one foot in front of the other, shifting weight, and other incremental skills. In reality, at age six, we employ a complex set of procedures to teach reading, a skill that can be learned naturally at an earlier age. Children who enter school reading have a distinct advantage that continues to accelerate during the school years. Early reading has been linked to higher intellectual development in children. Reading seems to be easily accomplished by younger children. It also enriches play and results in happier, more well rounded children (Clark, 1988, pp. 101–104). Emergent literacy and whole language are today's response to this information, but our system still does not have access to the children until they are past the critical years.

Learning to read naturally does not mean that a child will suddenly pick up a book and start reading it with no instruction. It does mean, however, that the homes where children learn to read naturally have certain characteristics. These homes are rich in supportive and interactive behaviors conducive to a child's learning to read. Specific studies of home storybook readings indicate that parents share reading experiences with children from an early age.

According to Jim Trelease, author of *The New Read Aloud Handbook,* children learn to read by having books read to them. This process teaches a child to want to read, the real precursor to being able to read (Trelease, 1989, p. xxi). The single most important activity for success in reading is reading aloud to children (Trelease, 1989, p. 2). Reading aloud exposes a child to the delights and pleasures of reading. It ensures that reading is not painful or boring. It is important to read aloud enough in the critical years from birth to age five, especially from birth to age three. If this is done, the school experiences of sound-by-sound, syllable-by-syllable, and word-by-word exercises; skill sheets; workbooks; flashcards; and test scores will not be what reading is all about to the young reader. Instead, the school experience will be a return to the enjoyment of reading that someone had provided by exposure to the magic of stories.

Because learning to read is as natural as learning to speak, opportunities to experience reading should be as prevalent in the life of a baby as opportunities to experience speech. From birth to eight months, the time to be natural with the baby, parents should introduce books in a natural way, by reading simple stories. At this time, they should point to pictures of interest and any words that are in large print. They should let the baby participate in turning the pages as much as possible. When a baby is holding a book, it is important to make sure it is right side up. There are many books available that a parent and baby can enjoy together at this time. Many have stiff board pages, appropriate simple pictures, and large, clear words; some even have textures for the baby to feel.

From nine months to two years, parents can continue to read to their children. The stories can become a little more complex, and more attention should be paid to showing the child the connection between what is being read and its visual representation, both in words and through pictures. Scrapbooks are appropriate to make, and personalized storybooks based on photographs of the child and the family are effective. Enthusiasm is the key. A parent who loves reading and shows that love to the toddler plays a major role in fostering the child's eventual love of reading. From age two to five, reading should be off to a good start. Parents should continue to read

to their children, with increasing amounts of child participation. Children should be encouraged to read the last word in a sentence, the last two, and then more. As reading skills progress, the parent can read the left-hand pages while the child reads those on the right. This is an exciting time to witness and enjoy emergent child reading.

As soon as children begin to say their first words, there is a way for parents to introduce to them the visual representation of their words. This is how it was explained in *Teaching with Toys:*

When you hear your child saying a word with a big smile and enjoying it, show him the word in his book. He will like seeing the written form of what he is saying. When the book has only one page with a word printed on it, have him read it that way. As you add individual words to other pages, he will be reading a longer book. The reason we present the words on pages in a book labeled "Book" and not on cards is to give the child the idea that words are written in books (Figure 3.1) (Goldberg, 1981, p. 79).

In general, children who are successful in school are avid readers. In general, children who are avid readers have parents who started reading to them as soon as they were born. Usually they were not told to do this, but

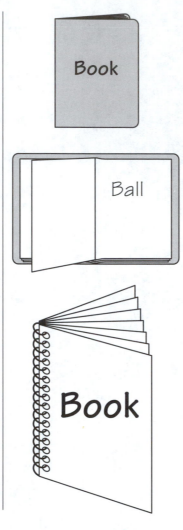

FIGURE 3.1
Books of Words for
Beginning Readers

they loved reading so much themselves that they desired to share their joy with their child.

Avid reading means an avid love of learning, thinking, and intellectual growth. Through reading, we learn the meaning of life, living, and success. What we learn from reading can be as basic as obtaining specific information or as complex as a way to design solutions for personal problems.

In earlier times books were read aloud as family entertainment. However, stories always do more than entertain. They teach the lessons of life. To the Greeks and Romans, the Iliad, the Odyssey, and the Aeneid provided moral education. Stories have an emotional impact that lectures or sermons can never match. A story can create a desire for goodness. Since life is a story, the stories we read or hear help us carve out our own life stories. "Beauty and the Beast" teaches love and commitment by hooking the imagination. It teaches an important lesson without even revealing an attempt to teach, mold, or develop character.

Books lay the foundation for exploring experiences, feelings, and ideas. One mother reads *Are You My Mother* to teach about the special bond that forms between a mother and her child. One father reads *The Berenstein Bears Go Out for the Team* to teach his son how to be ready for Little League try-outs. Reading to children whets the appetite for the time when children will read on their own.

WRITING

Writing is a tactile language experience. Our newest research shows that writing is as natural as reading. Our awkward old way of teaching writing was by introducing a lot of rules after a child could read. Now, on the basis of the research of Donald Graves, known as the Father of the Writing Process, we are starting to teach emergent writing in our schools. We start in kindergarten by allowing children to express themselves by combining letters whether or not the words are spelled correctly. Whatever is correct we build on, and whatever needs improvement we work on with the child. This is a child-centered approach, one that is driven by the child. It also is part of the emergent literacy and whole language approach. It too can be taught to parents of younger children through the Personalized Parenting classes.

Parents provide models and encouragement as babies learn to walk and talk. They act as facilitators as babies express a strong desire to accomplish the developmental milestones. Babies learn simply by trying and failing and succeeding. Adults do the helping by cheering them on in their successes and by ignoring or making light of their failures.

Young children will often show the true beginning of learning to write in a similar way. They will start to pretend and imitate adults. One way this will show up is through scribbling. Parents should be taught to take that opportunity to point out to their children whatever in the design looks like letters or other representations. Another way this might show up is by seeing a child put letters together. Graves tells this story:

> One day a four-and-a-half-year-old named Emily called to her parents, "Look. I made a word! I spelled SIR with my blocks." Her parents looked down and saw S-G-H-Y-R. They had an important decision to make in a matter of seconds. Emily had shown that she understood the importance of the written word. She knew that words have meaning, letters make words, and at least some of those letters correspond with the sounds of words. She wanted to write and had taken the risk of trying on her own. Her parents had two choices. They could point out all that she knew: how to place letters from left to right and how to sound out the first and last letters. Or they could say, "That's not how you spell *sir*." In short, they could encourage her to keep trying or convince her, and themselves, that she wasn't ready to write.
>
> Comparing the event to her first tooth, first step and first word, Emily's parents chose to congratulate her. (Graves, 1985, pp. 1–2)

Researchers have defined the developmental stages of writing in early childhood. Because these stages, like those of the reading process, are not rigorously distinct or necessarily sequential, parents should be taught to expose children to writing early, often, and with genuine love and enthusiasm. There are considered to be two basic stages of children's prewriting development. From birth to age three, children explore writing by scribbling. From three to six the scribbling gradually develops into objects children can name. Then the scribbling gradually acquires the characteristics of print, including linearity, horizontal orientation, and the arrangement of letter-like forms (Morrow, 1991, p. 240).

Parents should be taught to use various strategies for encouraging and responding to children's self-initiated writing efforts. From birth on, parents should consider even the youngest child's marks on paper as early attempts at writing, rather than as random marks. Parents need to know that speaking, reading, and writing are dynamically linked in child development. Reading to children contributes to speaking and writing, and writing contributes to speaking and reading.

Parents should be made aware of what their children see as print on signs, television, and around the house. Then they can point out to their child many letters, words, and sentences in familiar view. Aware of how often their child has seen the familiar *M* on the well-known McDonald's sign, they can then show a child how a particular scribble might look like an *M*.

Parents should also be taught how to assist a child in first attempts to mark on paper. When children are in their first stage of writing development, parents should be able to show their child how to hold markers or crayons. They should guide small hands without making marks for the child and should help the child understand that the paper is the place for writing. To encourage children's writing, they should express genuine pleasure in their child's markings, whether or not those markings resemble writing.

Beyond responding supportively to children, parents should model writing for children by writing in their presence. Parents should be taught to invite their children to sit with them while they write and to participate as much as each child is able.

There are specific items parents should be taught to use that can help their child with writing skills. Pieces of junk mail provide a natural medium for many activities. Coming in all different sizes, styles, colors, and shapes, they can be used for scribbling, tracing, or writing in blank spaces. Certain toys have particular value in preparing children for writing dexterity. These are hand and finger puppets, puzzles, any type of children's clay or dough, crayons and markers, finger painting, chalkboards, and painting, especially on easels. Moreover, just reading to children directly stimulates them to want to write, design, and create their own books.

There are also specific ways parents should be taught to set up a comfortable writing environment for their child. Recommended are comfortable spots with rugs and child-size tables and chairs. There should be safe storage for writing materials, which could include markers, pencils, crayons, and chalk. There should be varied sizes of large, unlined paper and a chalkboard. Materials should be stored consistently in the place provided for writing so that the child can learn how to select materials and put them away independently (Morrow, 1991, pp. 246–249).

MUSIC

Learning songs gives children exposure that promotes language development. Receptive vocabulary grows first and then has a positive effect on expressive language. Both the language exposure and the beat are foundation experiences for memory development.

Exposure to music in the early years is exposure to magic. Research has shown that babies who were exposed to certain melodies while still in utero can recognize and be calmed by the same music. Centuries of experience have proved the power of lullabies for putting babies to sleep.

Music has other benefits. It is a pleasant activity that promotes bonding between a parent and a child. When rocking to the music, a baby receives important brain stimulation necessary for proper growth and development. Music also provides a natural way for a parent and an infant or toddler to communicate.

Classical music is difficult for older children and adults to learn, but easy for young children who have been lucky enough to have been given this kind of exposure. In addition, there is new research that ties exposure to classical music in the early years to improved mathematical ability.

Because children learn so well by two principles, familiarity and repetition, it is beneficial to expose children to several selections of classical music in the infant/toddler years. It is best to use repetition to have the child become familiar with a symphony or concerto by Beethoven or Brahms and then, after familiarity is achieved, to introduce another composer like Mozart or Chopin, again by repetition.

PARENT ACTIVITIES

There are certain activities that all parents should know. They are activities to do with all children, those who excel as well as those who need help. They are activities that help a child to develop into an independent, autonomous learner, with inner locus of control, intellectual achievement, and a sense of responsibility.

1. Organize the child's environment so that it allows for choice, variety, and novelty. Rotate toys to achieve this type of organization. Also include the opportunity for a child to follow through on an activity to its completion.

2. Expose the child to situations in which the child can discover basic concepts in math or science. Count fingers and toes with a baby, and later count the sugars in a restaurant. Lead the child through discovery situations to build problem-solving skills. Participate in and create as many of these natural interactions as possible.

3. Allow the child's language to emerge to its highest levels in all of its aspects—listening, speaking, reading, and writing. Remember to cheer on successes and ignore failures.
4. Provide a variety of child-safe materials. Some suggestions are colored paper, beans, yarn, crayons, markers, clay, play dough or therapy putty, magazines, wrapping paper, material scraps, and more.
5. Invite other children to spend time with the child for enjoying group games, cooperation, and shared experiences. Children need the opportunity to develop social skills with peers.
6. Take the child on outings in the community. Experiences beyond the home stimulate higher levels of learning.
7. Try to bring into the life of the child a major relationship with at least one other adult. This introduces the child to other interests, language patterns, and vocabulary. (Adapted from Clark, 1988, p. 119)

The development of lifelong learning skills and success habits are a direct result of well-trained parents who are fortunate enough to have acquired effective parenting skills. There is a major need for parent direction, especially during the earliest years of a child's life. This need transcends income, race, and socioeconomic level. Every parent has the right to know what to do to raise successful children, and parents should be given this information. Not only will the child and the family benefit, but society will benefit as well.

SUMMARY

All children are different. They are born with different genetic potentials, and they will all be exposed to different environments. Children all develop at different rates and in different ways. They will all enter school with different backgrounds and different skills. However, they should all be given the privilege of entering school with the best possible early experiences behind them.

Certain skills can be developed for children through the home environment from birth to age five. They expose children in a playful way to colors, shapes, and sizes. They give children the opportunity to experience position, direction, time, and order. They present reading and writing readiness opportunities through reading, talking, listening, drawing, and writing. They introduce children to numbers and counting. They even provide optimum conditions for physical development. Most of all, they let children experience positive social interactions. Such directed attention to a child's feelings promotes the development of self-worth. Self-worth and self-accomplishments, together, are the building blocks of self-esteem.

It is easy to look at a young child and overlook the vital importance of childhood experiences. High-quality childhood experiences lay the foundation for later school success, poor-quality ones are equally detrimental. As a matter of fact, early experiences are so important that Maria Montessori cautions us by saying there is no such thing as an eraser.

From the personal observation of a young mother, we learn it in another way. This mother tells us that she had made a card for her baby. She had put black sandpaper on one side and black smooth paper on the other side. While the color was constant on each side, the texture was different. For play, she took each one of her baby's hands and rubbed each one on both sides, saying, "rough" when she rubbed the rough side and saying "smooth" when she rubbed the smooth side. She did the same for each of the baby's feet. She and her baby played with the card often when the baby was under one year old. Then they lost the card. One day when the baby was over two years old, she went into her closet, found the card, and came running to her mother saying, "Mommy, Mommy, rough, smooth!"

SELECTED READINGS

Bredekamp, S. (Ed.). (1986). *Developmentally appropriate practices in early childhood programs serving children from birth through age 8.* Washington, DC: National Association for the Education of Young Children.

This landmark book is a complete guide to developmentally appropriate practices for teachers, parents, and other primary caregivers taking care of children from birth through age eight. It can be used as a handbook for evaluating current practices or for developing new ones.

Clark, B. (1988). *Growing up gifted.* Columbus, OH: Merrill.

This book covers all aspects of information about gifted children. It covers all ages, but it has excellent information about optimal conditions for the early years.

Elkind, D. (1987). *Miseducation: Preschoolers at risk,* New York: Knopf.

This book was written as a caution against trying to teach children too early by inappropriate methods. Play is a child's work. It is instructional and explains appropriate methods for teaching young children.

National Association of Elementary School Principals and Worldbook Educational Products. (1992). *Little beginnings: Starting your child on a lifetime of learning.* Chicago: Worldbook, Inc.

This little pamphlet has excellent practical play and learn ideas for babies. The pamphlet is easy to use and is a helpful guide for new parents.

PART II

The Guidance Approach to Self-Esteem, Independence, and a Productive Life

Parents night at Judy's school was billed as "Meeting Our Children's Needs," which Christine and I suspected was an indirect appeal for more funding. On the way to the meeting, we talked about how we made do with less when we were kids, and that better facilities and more equipment won't solve every education problem. But principal Gael Humphrey had another priority in mind. "Take time each day to talk with your children," she urged. "Read to them, ask them about their day's events. Show an interest in their activities."

A child whose efforts are recognized and appreciated, she said, will become an even better student. To Chris and me, that made great sense. In today's busy world, it is sometimes so easy to concentrate on giving the children what we didn't have when growing up that we forget to provide them with what we did have.

—Burton Hillis, in *BETTER HOMES AND GARDENS*,
February 1994

CHAPTER 4

Guiding and Supporting Children

NEW PARENTING SKILLS CAN BRING GREAT REWARDS

Sometimes a small change in what you do can make a big difference. Did you ever comb your hair in a slightly different way and then notice a great improvement in how you look?

> Did you ever learn to do a task in an easier way and find that the end result was better? You learned to expend less energy to do the work and achieve a better result because of it.
>
> Another way of looking at this challenge comes from the perturbation theory. A simple example of a perturbation is a cyclist riding along a road without difficulty. Suddenly the bike hits a small pebble and skids off course. The rider falls, and her whole life is changed either by injury or by the long-term consequences of meeting a passerby: either way the rider's life is changed in big and fundamental ways. (*Young Children*, p. 2)

The most important information about parenting must be made available to parents. Much of this information is new. It is information that if used properly by parents can change the lives of both parents and children. For parents, less effort will bring more success. For children, less time will be spent on resistance and more on positive growth and development. With this information, parents can find themselves interacting more appropriately with their children, not working as hard at it, and not working as much at it. They will then have more time to themselves and also more time to enjoy their children.

SELF-ESTEEM DEVELOPMENT

> "O.K. means adequate, worthwhile, important."—Thomas A. Harris (Freed, p. 44, 1983)

From birth to age 5 children develop concurrently in five areas—cognitive, motor, social, language, and self-esteem. Of these areas, self-esteem is the least understood and the hardest for facilitators of development to handle. The reason for this difficulty is that self-esteem develops by a complicated two-part process. The major part develops through experiencing success in all the other areas of development. When children know that they can do something, their self-esteem grows. What they can do cognitively, through motor skills, socially, and through language skills will largely determine their self-esteem. The other part of self-esteem develops when others communicate to children that they are loved and worthy in their own right. Parents who show respect for their child's uniqueness help their child to feel self-assured. That is a direct yet more subtle process.

Children's destiny is to grow and develop. They will do so the way we all grow and develop in any area—by making mistakes. Mistakes in the cognitive and language areas are usually handled well by parents, who expect them and tend to deal with them in a facilitative and appropriate manner. But parents often mishandle mistakes in the social domain. Mishandling these mistakes can be damaging to children's self-esteem. Mistakes are considered the most powerful learning tool available, yet parents often do not know how to handle in an optimum way these social mistakes of their child's learning. They need to learn how to channel the mistakes in such a way that effective learning will take place. They need to learn to do it in such a way that children will not only not lose self-esteem but will also gain it. However they do handle it will be the way their children will eventually handle it for themselves and for their own children. Self-esteem development is the true path to children's success.

> Researchers have noted a steady decline in self-esteem of children as they progress through the grades. 80% of children enter first grade with high self-esteem. By 5th grade only 20% have high self-esteem. By the time they finish high school, the number has dropped to 5%. School experiences such as failure, embarrassment, and other facets of conditional acceptance have a deleterious effect. (Gartrell, 1994, p. 248)

From Transactional Analysis, developed by a medical doctor, Thomas A. Harris, we learn that children who have grown up with parents who do not have the necessary training in self-esteem development do not feel O.K.

about themselves by age two. In his landmark book *I'm OK—You're OK,* we learn that the low self-esteem, when developed early, lasts forever. By the third year of life, most of our population, successful as well as unsuccessful people, have adopted a negative life position that contaminates their adult potential, leaving them vulnerable to inappropriate, emotional behavior (Harris, 1973).

From Parent Effectiveness Training (P.E.T.) we learn that children with parents who have the necessary training in self-esteem development do feel O.K. about themselves by age two. These children will not have temper tantrums at age two and will not become rebellious teenagers (Gordon, 1975).

While parents tend to be tolerant of children's mistakes in some areas, like academic learning or even the mastering of certain games, they do not have the same tolerance for children's mistakes in social behavior. In reality, children do make mistakes in social behavior, and they should be helped to learn from these mistakes as well. This learning will be positively related to self-esteem.

DISCIPLINE

The word *discipline* has the same root as *disciple.* A *disciple* isn't somebody you beat over the head. It is somebody who apprentices to a master and learns a craft by working at the same vocation. This is the new concept of discipline as well. The parent should be a model of good behavior and character, someone who displays exemplary values. The children will then have good behavior and character and become people with exemplary values. Built into the system is a guidance approach. If we do not moralize or tell children what to think, our sheer direction will help them gradually develop moral judgment. If we allow children to think and experience, they will internalize learning. This approach will not create the resistance and rebellion that children so often develop in reaction to an authoritarian approach. Yelling at children will create children who yell, and hitting children will be the precursor to violence.

The goal is for children to have an internalized morality. No society, not even the most totalitarian, operates solely by external control or coercion. Because sanctions are too limited to cover all, or even most, situations; and because every society seeks to develop citizens who can conduct themselves in a productive manner without seeking rewards or avoiding punishment, there is a worldwide need for children to have a moral code.

For a democratic society such as ours, it is of the utmost importance to help children develop sound moral structures. Parents are the ones who face this challenge. Parents have a lifetime responsibility to interact with their children in such a way that their children will develop a commitment to maintaining the common good and then develop the skills for putting that commitment into practice.

Psychology, child development, and other behavioral sciences have amassed new knowledge about children, parents, interpersonal relationships, how to help another person grow, and how to create a psychologically healthy climate for people. Much is known about effective person-to-person communication, the effects of power in human relationships, and constructive conflict resolution. This knowledge is now available for use on a practical level by parents.

From Transactional Analysis we know about a contracting system, how each member of the family can have a clear idea of the expectations each of the other members has for him or her. From P.E.T. we know that punishment can be discarded forever in disciplining children; that parents can be taught to raise children who are responsible, self-disciplined, and cooperative without relying on instilling fear; and that parents can learn how to influence children to behave out of genuine consideration for the needs of parents rather than out of the fear of punishment or of the withdrawal of privileges.

Research shows that children of authoritarian parents who control their children with absolute standards are not as successful in school as are the children of parents who use a style that includes setting clear standards, recognizing children's rights, expecting mature behavior, and including healthy verbal exchange. The correlation between parenting style and success in school goes across ethnic boundaries. Too much emphasis for punishing or rewarding children for grades results in lower child performance and poorer grades (Clark, 1988, p. 122).

The newest method of discipline is through effective management of conflict based on a contract system. This is the heart and soul of effective parenting. P.E.T. calls it the master key to parent effectiveness. Parents who are given the opportunity to learn it will be richly rewarded beyond their hopes and expectations.

The newest method turns the parent from a technician into a professional. Whereas a technician is concerned only with whether or not a rule has been violated, a professional recognizes that each situation is different and attempts to understand it at a deeper level. A technician is inflexible, able to determine only that X happened and that Y is the punishment. A professional uses a problem-solving approach to solve the immediate conflict and also to teach an alternative behavior pattern. The first goal is to teach the child to solve the problem. The second goal is for the professional to learn from the experience to improve the quality of the relationship with the child for the future.

The newest method acknowledges mistakes in behavior and classifies them into levels. Behavioral mistakes at the lowest level come from interacting with the environment, curiosity, or experimentation. A child's desire to explore and touch may lead him to break something delicate and valuable or to lose something small. This level of mistakes is bound to happen. The second level is socially influenced. A child can be exposed to another child's or even an adult's inappropriate behavior and copy it. This level is frequent as well. The third level is the most serious and the hardest to handle. It occurs with a child who has very low self-esteem, who is experiencing a troubled and painful home environment, and who is acting out against it. Fortunately, this level is least common.

There are two major causes of mistakes in behavior. One is a mismatch between the child and the situation going on for the child. Either the activity or the place or both are inappropriate. The parent did not set up the circumstances for success. The other is a mismatch of communication between the parent and the child because the parent did not make expectations clear before putting the child in the situation.

The newest method acknowledges that the end goal of discipline is that children will be able to discipline themselves and therefore interact on appropriate and functional levels with one another. This goal is so important for children's functioning both now and as future adults that "relationships" will probably become a component of preschool curriculum for the 1990s. The personal/social skills essential to democracy need to be part of basic education (Gartrell, 1994, p. 249).

VALUES

Parents have little understanding of the way they instill values in children. Most aspects of parenting are direct, but instilling values is indirect. Children surmise their parents' values on the basis of observation of their parents' activities. The process is probably best summed up in the expression, "Children will do as you do and not as you say."

If a parent spends a major portion of time in the workplace, a child will surmise that the parent values work. If a parent spends a major portion of time caring for children, a child will surmise that the parent values family commitment. If a parent spends a major portion of time reading, studying, or working on a skill, a child will surmise that the parent values self-improvement. If a parent merely talks about work, family commitment, or self-improvement and follows through with no personal actions in any of these areas, a child will not surmise that the parent values work, family commitment, or self-improvement.

Whittled down to its most basic terms, our society values self-respect and service to others. Healthy high-functioning adults learn to first respect themselves and then to use their resources to serve their fellow humans in effective ways. As they develop respect for themselves, they become capable of doing more for others and ultimately of modeling values. Value development in children can be talked about and explained, but it is essentially taught by example.

Without traditional direct instruction, values are taught to children. The father of one kindergarten child was a great sculptor. This man came to the kindergarten once a week for a whole semester. He did not teach about clay. Instead, he *loved* clay in front of the children. Little by little, the children began to love clay, too, and little by little they learned to work with it and make things with it (Rogers, 1994, p. 33). These children learned a value by exposure to a man who did something out of love. Subsequently they showed by what they did that they held the same value.

While parental resources related to the teaching of values are circumstantially limited, parents should take comfort in the world of books. Most stories written for children have powerful value-packed messages. An excellent example is the well-known book *The Little Engine That Could.* The language and the suspense have not only entertained several generations of children but also taught them the important value of not giving up. Such a value is intrinsically connected with the larger value of self-respect. "I think I can, I think I can" is free for the asking, and no parents should let their child be without it.

PHILOSOPHY

A parent's understanding of the importance of self-esteem development, discipline as a modeling process, and the instilling of values makes up a philosophy for handling their children. A philosophy provides a personal foundation from which to operate. Once parents absorb the foundation, they will be able to create practical solutions to everyday problems and situations.

The next chapter has information on practical techniques for implementing the ideas presented about self-esteem development, discipline, and values. This chapter will have full coverage of the many important methods for interacting appropriately with children. It will be helpful to parents.

Even more helpful, however, will be the day when these ideas can be presented to parents nationwide through ongoing parenting classes. The most effective parent training uses a seminar approach. It gives parents the opportunity to ask their own personal parenting questions of their own instructor. It gives them the opportunity to role-play situations using their newly learned information, to practice the information, make mistakes with it, and learn well from those mistakes. Nobody knows what the new day will bring, and parents need the opportunity to keep sharpening their skills to be ready. Reading about parenting skills or being told by an instructor what to do represents one level of knowledge, but being shown how to interact effectively with children and being able to practice such interactions represent a much higher level. This interactive approach is ideal for breaking some ineffective parenting patterns and for building new, more effective ones. It is also helpful for knowing when to use the new techniques. Personalized Parenting classes on a long-term basis through the public schools should provide the forum for establishing such an interactive approach.

CHAPTER 5

Practical Parenting

There are fifteen pillars of magical parenting. Parents who master these techniques will find themselves in control of easy-to-handle children who will experience high self-esteem and the ability to achieve a high degree of satisfaction in their lives.

The fifteen pillars should be the core of the Personalized Parenting Classes. They are fifteen parenting skills that should not be regarded as frills but should be seen as necessities. Children spend 91 percent of their lives from birth through age 18 in places other than schools. Parents, who are responsible for much of that time, cannot afford to face that responsibility unprepared.

These pillars should be presented to parents as soon as they have their baby, if not before. They should begin using many of the skills at around the time their infants begin to crawl or walk, about eight months on average. It is at that time that do's and don't's become important and that parents need to take steps that will last them a lifetime with their child. New parents must develop understanding of the importance of self-esteem and the true meaning of discipline. They should try to develop a broad understanding of what parenting is and to start good habits early. The job that remains will then be modification of the skills to fit their children as they grow and change.

These pillars are based on a positive philosophy about children's capabilities and on a modeling and guidance approach to discipline. They teach parents how to show respect and display understanding to their children. They focus on teaching children to develop their own standards for exemplary behavior. Ultimately, the pillars help children develop their self-esteem, the true key to the development of high-functioning members of society.

When Greg Norman hits a golf ball, he makes it look easy. By extending a little effort, he sends the ball sailing a great distance. When Jennifer Capriati hits a tennis ball, she makes it look easy. By extending a little effort, she sends the ball over the net with high speed and impeccable accuracy. Norman and Capriati are pros. Professionals in any arena extend less effort than amateurs to accomplish the same goal, and they achieve that goal with a much higher degree of expertise.

If parents are taught to use the fifteen pillars of parenting, they can become parenting pros. They will have tools of parenting that will relieve stress and make their day-to-day activities with their children run smoothly. They will have information that will help them meet their responsibilities, expend less effort, and reap the rewards of the job of parenting.

These pillars are trustworthy. They include the finest parenting and leadership techniques available. From a review of many resources, these fifteen themes emerged. The themes were then narrowed down and refined to this easy, clear, and effective form for presentation to parents. The fifteen pillars are further broken down into three parts. The first three pillars are preparation states, the next five are attitudes, and the last seven are techniques.

PILLARS OF PARENTING

I. Preparations

1. Set up conditions for success.

Parents should try to set up appropriate conditions for their child that will minimize the occurrence of unacceptable behavior. They should try to avoid inappropriate conditions that will most likely lead to unacceptable behavior. Table 5.1 contrasts inappropriate and appropriate conditions. When a child acts up in a store, theater, or religious service, it may be because the child is surrounded by conditions inappropriate for children.

Parents also should try to avoid setting up "yes-or-no" situations that can easily turn into "no" situations. For example, instead of asking if a child wants to go shopping, a parent should ask in which store the child would like to shop. Choices are helpful for initiating a child's cooperation.

Sometimes breaking up the situation into smaller segments increases the child's chances for success. If a child is going to be asked to shop in a

Table 5.1   Conditions for Successful Child Behavior

Inappropriate Conditions	*Appropriate Conditions*
Requiring the child to sit and listen for a long period of time	Giving the child ample time for moving around
Requiring activities be done to exacting standards	Setting up open-ended activities with child-choice and creativity, and not emphasizing a right answer
Using critical evaluation of what the child has done	Being supportive of what the child has done
Rejecting the child because of unacceptable behavior	Accepting the child and facilitating problem solving
Communicating unclear child expectations	Communicating clear child expectations
Keeping inappropriate schedules	Having flexible routines

Source: Adapted from D. Gartrell, *A Guidance Approach to Discipline* (Albany, NY: Delmar, 1994), p. 160.

particular store for a long time, a suggestion is to break up the time into smaller sequences and then to pay some kind of appropriate attention to the child after each sequence and before beginning a new segment of store time. In that way, even if there are problems during the second segment, the child will feel the success from the first one.

If the child has difficulty sitting for the reading of a complete book, a solution is to read only one or two pages. After completing those pages, the parent should ask the child if one or two more pages are desired. In that way, even if the child does not want to continue, the child will feel the pride of accomplishment and not the distress of failure.

Example

Parent: Here is some play dough to use while I am on the telephone.
Child: (Busy and involved)
Parent: That bowl looks like a real bowl. Here is another color to make some fruit.
Child: (Busy and involved)

2. Make expectations clear.

An excellent way to encourage acceptable child behavior is for parents to make clear to their child before going into a situation how they want their child to act. Simply said, an ounce of prevention is worth a pound of cure.

An excellent way to set up expectations for difficult situations is through holding regular family meetings. They give the child the opportunity to have a say in the situation and possibly even help to determine it. Being part of the rule-setting process makes a child more likely to abide by the rules. These meetings are excellent for allowing all members of the family to present their concerns. As children grow, their wants and needs continually change, and the family will be better able to respond when they address these changes regularly.

One way to settle particularly troublesome issues is by using a technique called "Upfront Contracting." The parent starts out by saying that a decision has to be made about something like putting toys away at night. Then the parent will say to the child that he or she will ask each other questions about the issue to determine all possible considerations about it. Then the question-and-answer session starts. On the basis of the discussion, the parent will come to a decision. Since the decision will be made with much child input, it is likely that the child will follow it.

When setting up expectations, it is crucial to present the consequences that will occur if the expectations are not met. Then it is important to follow through with those consequences if necessary.

Example

Parent: We are going to the library. How many books do you want to take out?
Child: I want six books. Can you read me one in the library?
Parent: You may take out six books. I will read you one in the library. If you take any more than six, you will have to put all of them back and go home with none.
Child: I understand.

3. Use praise and encouragement appropriately.

Parents should learn to use praise appropriately, not indiscriminately. It should be reserved for major achievements. "Good," "Excellent," "Well done," and the like are appropriate for a child who has expended much effort and has reached a goal as a result.

In many situations, parents should use encouragement rather than praise. Encouragement is recognition of effort and is not dependent on achievement. Encouragement should be specific, descriptive, and nonjudgmental. Personal recognition is better than an impersonal reward like a sticker. Encouragement may be just what a child needs to be able to finish a whole activity.

Praise is appropriate after a true accomplishment or after a major outlay of effort. It is best done privately, not in front of a sibling or another child who, hearing it, may feel less adequate and thereby suffer a decrease in self-esteem. Private praise is well appreciated by the child. General platitudes of praise should be avoided. Children have all kinds of thoughts about themselves, both positive and negative. If parents praise a child at a time when the child is thinking negatively, the parents will lose credibility in their child's eyes.

If no apparent opportunity arises for a while for encouragement or praise, then recognition of a past event or praise for a past success is appropriate. Encouragement by acknowledging child endeavors should be a part of a child's daily experiences. Such recognition should be shown regularly and naturally.

Example

Parent: You put in two of the hardest pieces. Now I see part of the house.
Child: I think I see the flowers on the side of the house too.

The first two pillars of preparation are important for setting ground rules. There are no surprises for anyone, parents or children, as behavior occurs and is guided. Setting up for success and making expectations clear provide the best chance that a child will not misbehave. These pillars start off the system and are used again and again throughout the whole practical parenting process. As children grow and learn, they will always be making mistakes in behavior. After each mistake, parents can learn from the situation and then be ready to make better preparations for the next time. The third pillar continually helps a child to develop self-worth. The feeling of capability is always being reinforced. When parents use praise and encouragement appropriately, the child will grow in self-esteem, the true quality needed for appropriate functional behavior.

II. Attitudes

4. Separate the behavior from the child.

Parents should always think of the behavior, not the child, as the problem. A child may have feet inappropriately up on a table or be drinking purple grape juice near a white linen tablecloth. It is helpful to start off with the phrase, "There is . . ." or "There are . . ." to focus on the actual situation. Being able to solve a problem is the goal. Criticizing the child or designing a punishment is not.

When parents isolate the behavior and try to work with it, they are likely to get positive change. It is proper to treat a child like a friend, with respect. Instead of ordering, directing, commanding, or giving the solution, parents should show a sincere concern about the particular behavior. If the concern does not automatically produce a change in behavior, they should make a polite request. An effective type of request is often made in reverse or in a negative form. While direct instructions are often met with resistance, a negative statement, as demonstrated in the example, is often followed by a positive response. Children respond well when they are respected and made to feel trusted and equal. They respond poorly when they are not respected and made to feel immature or irresponsible.

Example

Parent: I always get nervous when purple juice is near a white tablecloth. That kind of juice causes a permanent stain. I don't suppose you could put your glass on the counter?
Child: That's fine. I can do that.

5. Look for the cause of the misbehavior.

Parents should always look for an underlying cause when their child is misbehaving. Children may act out because they are uncomfortable, in need, or frustrated. When parents accept the behavior as a result of an underlying circumstance, try to understand that circumstance, and then work on removing or ameliorating the circumstance, they are likely to effect positive change.

Active listening—listening and then responding appropriately—is a way to understand a problem. Active listening helps children become aware of their own feelings and better able to find their own solutions. It is open-minded. It directs children away from limited thinking and leads them toward taking more control of situations.

Example

Parent: What's bothering you?
Child: I'm hungry.
Parent: Yelling at your brother won't bring the food any faster. I know you
    are hungry and that makes you irritable. We are on our way home.
Child: How soon will we be home?

There is a way to implement this kind of understanding with infants and toddlers as well. Infants have needs just as older children do. They also have their fair share of problems getting those needs met. They get hungry, hot, cold, tired, thirsty, frustrated, sick, bored, and so on. Just as parents can actively listen to the verbal communication of older children, so they can decode the nonverbal behavior of infants before making a determination of the problem. Just as with older children, this kind of interaction will give infants and toddlers more autonomy. Active listening helps a parent determine the cause of a problem and provide a proper solution. It also helps a baby feel respected and understood.

Example

Parent: That kind of cry tells me you want attention. I see you want to get
    picked up. I'm coming right over to hug you.
Child: I love you (or some beginning version of these words).

6. Be positive, warm, and supportive, and believe in the child.

Parents should try to form a warm, supportive relationship with their child. Children are inclined to emulate adults with whom they have a positive relationship. Being the recipient of warmth and support is basic to developing empathy and moral affect. Parents should focus on what children *can* have as opposed to what they cannot. It is better to tell a child to play with a toy after a friend is finished than simply to tell the child not to play with the toy. Parents also should try to acknowledge good behavior when they see it. They should try to remember to comment about toys put away or excellent sharing. If a parent believes in a child, the child will end up believing in himself. If a parent believes that a child has a special ability, the child will usually end up having that ability. Parents should support children by providing opportunities for becoming outstanding and should instill in their child the confidence necessary for success in a given area. With this open-ended warmth, parents are expressing unconditional love.

One thing a parent cannot give a child too much of is love. The child is a special kind of container for contributions of love. It is a container that cannot ever run out of room. It has the capacity to take as much as it gets and always to have room for more. Therefore, the job of the parent is to give as much love as possible to the child, in all possible ways at all possible times, and to keep on giving it. Filling the child with love is providing ongoing fuel for success.

Example

Parent: I see you really like that doll. You can play with it after Allison is finished with it.
Child: I will color now.

7. Be a person, not a god.

Parents should not pretend to have unlimited patience or to have all the answers. It is better for them to acknowledge that they have real feelings and that there is much that they do not know. It is better for a child to see a parent as a real person. Parents should share with their child real thoughts and ideas. They should also be free to make mistakes and to apologize for those mistakes. They should show respect and admiration for their child. Children's opinions should be sought and children's feelings acknowledged.

In addition, parents should show respect and admiration for the many people and things in the world around them. In this age of information and advanced technology, parents should convey to their child that they do not know everything. They should make it clear that there are many experts and professionals who can be called on to provide help. There are even computers to provide us with great support. A quick look at a current CD-ROM encyclopedia program can show any child the vast amount of information that is fingertips away from any person at the time an answer is sought.

Sometimes parents should sit back, relax, and enjoy a child's initiative. They should join in when appropriate. They should remember to encourage children's endeavors. If a child is just relaxing, that is fine too. It is an opportunity for a child to develop positive thinking skills and a strong sense of self-direction. The parent–child relationship, the first and most important relationship, should be as honest as possible. It will be the model for all other future relationships.

Example

Parent: I get tired by 8:30 P.M. Sometimes I rush through your bath so I can relax. I am sorry I was impatient with you.
Child: That's O.K., but you didn't have to take my boat away.
Parent: I agree with that. I didn't have to take your boat away.

8. Make the child feel needed.

Parents should seek children's help whenever possible. If a parent is trying to prepare dinner for a certain time, it is appropriate to ask the child to fold napkins, pack up some toys, or beat an egg to get the job done on time. Another way to show that the child is needed is by calling on the child to help with a task the parent does not know how to do—for example, putting a set of blocks back in a container as it was originally packed, or trying to accomplish a task on a computer. It is O.K. to call on the help of the child even if the parent really can do it alone.

Example

Parent: I need your help carrying this.
Child: I can help.

The attitude pillars are also important for decreasing children's misbehavior. They are supportive and respectful of children. Separating the behavior from the child and looking for the cause of misbehavior help a parent learn about preventing a situation from developing again. These attitudes also help to preserve a child's self-esteem after misbehaving. Being positive, not acting all-powerful, and making a child feel needed guide a child toward productive and functional behavior.

III. Techniques

9. Use behavior-messages, not child-messages.

Behavior-messages describe the behavior and then the parent's feelings about that behavior. This kind of information helps children to be more aware of their actions and of the impact of these actions on others. Child-messages express direct anger at the child. This kind of disapproval is damaging to a child's self-esteem. If a parent first identifies for the child what the bad behavior is and then tells the child about the effect of the behavior on a person or a situation, that gives the child important information about what has been done. If a parent criticizes a child for an action, that tells the child that he or she is "bad." A parent should try to identify bad behavior and not a bad child. Children can try to correct bad behavior more easily than they can correct what seems like a bad self. Once they are told more about their behavior, they usually want to be more considerate. This is a way to turn thoughtlessness into thoughtfulness.

Example

Parent: The spilled milk gets all over the table and on the floor. I don't like to clean up these messes.

Child: I am sorry you have all the extra work. I will try to be more careful next time.

Behavior-messages are just as important to infants and toddlers. On this level, behavior-messages still teach consideration, and child-messages still damage self-esteem. The messages can be verbal because even infants can understand language at a much higher level than they can speak it. There are also nonverbal versions of behavior-messages.

Example (Verbal)

Parent: Pulling all the boxes off the shelf makes a lot of work for me. I don't like having to pick them all up.

Child: (Stops pulling all the boxes)

Example (Nonverbal)

Parent: (Puts hand flat on the baby's tummy at changing time)

Child: (Stops moving)

10. Listen and communicate.

Parents should be able to listen to and communicate with children. It is an effective way to find out the cause of misbehavior if the cause is not already clear. It is also a way to find out what is on a child's mind. That helps a child understand himself as much as it helps a parent understand a child. Hearing is accomplished by a 70/30 ratio of communication. This means that parents should listen to the child about 70 percent of the time and talk about 30 percent of the time. Talk should be made up mostly of either nurturing the chlid's talk or asking questions that will stimulate more talk on the part of the child. Nurturing can be done with responses like these: "I understand." "Oh." "And." "That's a good point." "That sounds important to you." "Tell me more about that." Questions can be asked: "Why did you say that?" "How did that happen?" "What do you mean by that?" Through this process, the child will feel the true focus of parent attention. Knowing that a parent understands can put a child's mind at rest and ultimately open up for the child the ability to cooperate.

Parents should also plan time to have conversations with their child. This is a time to exchange ideas about activities or events. It is a time to communicate together. It is a time to show that a parent will take active steps on behalf of the child. It is a time for the parent to come alive to a child first with understanding and then as a real person with likes, dislikes, and interests. Included in these conversations should be the protection of child ideas and feelings. It is a time to encourage developing thoughts and actively facilitate their growth.

The best way to communicate with children is by being in rapport with them. A parent should use a similar pace and tonality to the child's. This will take away the "talking at" style and replace it with a sincere "talking to" style. In conjunction with this type of rapport, it is helpful to be at the same level physically with the child and even, if possible, in the same position.

Example

Child: My whole lunch fell on the floor. It was a big mess.
Parent: I understand.
Child: So then I ate the ice cream.
Parent: Oh.
Child: It was so good!
Parent: And . . .
Child: It got all over my face.
Parent: That must have been funny!
Child: It was great! I licked it all up. I ate some with my fingers. I thought you'd be mad at me. I'll be more careful next time.

11. Change the environment.

Parents should change the environment to bring about a change in behavior. This method is widely accepted with infants and toddlers, but it is effective with children of all ages. There are a wide range of possibilities: enrich the environment or improve it, substitute part of it, or move to another place.

Example

Parent: Come over here with me. I have a brand new set of markers.
Child: I love the neon colors.

12. Use a sandwich method for supervision.

Precede and follow a suggestion, recommendation, or request with a statement of encouragement. It is important to keep this "sandwich method" tightly connected. First, focus on a part of the activity that the child is doing well. Then request an expansion of that activity. Then go back and focus either on the noticeable improvement or on another part of the activity that the child is doing well.

Example

Parent: You hold the fork with a strong grip when you eat.
Child: I don't like the spinach.
Parent: I don't suppose you could keep a little on your fork.
Child: I can do that.
Parent: You balance food directly in the middle of your fork.

13. Use humor when appropriate.

A parent who accepts the humor in a situation is building a positive relationship with the child, creating a friendly atmosphere. While parents should not laugh *at* a child, they should be encouraged to laugh *with* a child. When parents look openly at why a child has acted in a particular way, they may find a perfectly consistent and understandable reason. Often that reason is humorous.

Example

Parent: I've been looking all over for you. Where have you been? I told you to wait outside.
Child: I *was* waiting outside. I was on the playground.
Parent: You're right! I was waiting outside the classroom, and you were on the playground. Next time I mean outside the classroom, I'll say "outside the classroom."

14. Touch.

Parents should feel free to touch their child. Physical closeness accomplishes what no words can in forming a healthy attachment with a child. Patting, holding, rocking, and hugging perform true magic. They are all positively related to bonding. Research has connected touching with physical health. One touch can successfully accomplish what 1,000 words might miss.

> "Parents should hug their children every chance they get," the Rev. George Hall declared last Sunday. "After all, there will probably soon come a time when they won't let you."
>
> —Burton Hillis in BETTER HOMES AND GARDENS, February 1994

15. Be a part of the solution.

It is helpful for parents to make themselves part of the situation as much as possible. If the task is for the child to set the table, a good idea for the parent is to put out the silverware. If the task if folding the clothes, a positive approach is to offer to fold all the towels or items of a particular size, or even those of a particular color.

Example

Parent: Let's make a salad. I will cut the tomatoes. You tear the lettuce.
Child: I love making the salad.
Parent: I will cut the carrots. You mix everything together.
Child: I will put it in the salad bowls.

The techniques fit well with the attitudes. If a parent can separate the behavior from the child, the parent will be able to use a behavior-message instead of a child-message. Often it is easy to figure out the cause of child misbehavior. In other cases, however, the technique of listening to and communicating with the child will be helpful. A major cause is often the environment, and changing it is a valuable technique. The sandwich method for supervision, humor, touch, and being part of the solution all go with the positive attitudes presented.

THE PARENT PARTNERSHIP

All the pillars of parenting together are important for a smooth running, effective, and efficient parent–child relationship. Not one of the fifteen takes precedence over another, and not one should be eliminated. However, there is one important parenting situation that exists over and above all the pillars that has the most important impact on child development. That situation is the quality of the parents' relationship with each other or, in the case of a single parent, the quality of that parent's relationship with the self. If the parent relationship runs smoothly and is highly effective, the roles of the children will most likely fall into place. However, if major difficulties in the parent relationship exist, these can be the primary cause of child unrest and disruptiveness.

USING THE PILLARS

Parents often ask professionals questions like these: "My child often bites other children. What do I do?" "My child will not go to bed at night willingly. What do I do?" "My child continually throws tantrums. What do I do?" Professionals often answer these questions with specific advice like, "Give the child a time out until he stops biting, goes to bed, or calms down from the tantrum. Then talk to the child about the bad behavior, and suggest alternative methods of good behavior." The advice, though reasonable, may or may not work for the particular parent in a particular situation. It also does not help the child to evaluate the situation and learn from it.

The pillars offer the parent a whole new approach that is efficient, personalized, and highly effective. They give the parent all the information that is needed to design an individual solution. Once familiar with all of the pillars, the parent can run through all of them and choose the ones that should be applied in the particular situation at the particular time. It works something like this:

A parent has a child who keeps reaching for something that shouldn't be touched by a child. The parent wants to stop the child from doing it. The parent then quickly thinks through the pillars:

Preparations

1. Set up conditions for success.
2. Make expectations clear.
3. Use praise and encouragement appropriately.

Attitudes

4. Separate the behavior from the child.
5. Look for the cause of the misbehavior.
6. Be positive, warm, and supportive, and believe in the child.
7. Be a person, not a god.
8. Make the child feel needed.

Techniques

9. Use behavior-messages, not child-messages.
10. Listen and communicate.
11. Change the environment.
12. Use a sandwich method for supervision.
13. Use humor when appropriate.
14. Touch.
15. Be a part of the solution.

Using these pillars as a guide, parents can find the intervention that is appropriate to the situation, easy to implement, and effective for the child. First the parents should consider the preparations, then the attitudes, and then select some appropriate techniques. The goal is to have preparations that will make misbehavior unlikely, attitudes that will show respect and understanding for a child, and techniques that will not only stop misbehavior but also encourage appropriate behavior in the future.

HANDLING DISPUTES

The fifteen pillars can be helpful when disputes arise. The more we place children in differing age groups, the less friction there will be. The more we place them in groups of children the same age, the more friction there will be, because the wants and needs of all the children will be similar.

The first level of dispute solving is as a mediator. The mediator follows a three-step process:

1. Identifies the problem.
2. Generates possible solutions.
3. Gets the participants to agree on a solution to try.

The second level is as a guidance expert. The guidance expert empowers the children to handle their difficulties more effectively in the future. This takes place after the problem has been solved. It is a private discussion with each individual involved that should take place when the problem is still fresh in each child's mind. The expert first accepts each child's perceptions and feelings and then helps each one understand the consequences of behavior. The child is then led to figure out more productive possibilities for reconciliation. This technique is a supportive,

Table 5.2   Handling Disputes

Situation	*Intervention*
Reasonable chance children can work out difficulties	Monitor, but do not intervene. If needed, coach children on mediation skills.
Disruptive argument	Redirect the activity. Play the role of *mediator*. Then follow up as *guidance* expert.
One or both have lost control. Children are yelling or fighting.	Separate the children for a cool-down time. Use the *mediation* and *guidance* process after tempers have cooled down.

Source: Adapted from D. Gartrell, *A Guidance Approach to Discipline* (Albany, NY: Delmar, 1994), p. 232.

conversational process. The guidance expert follows a second three-step process:

1. Provides encouragement in the form of recognition for specific efforts to work out the difficulty.
2. Makes a suggestion, recommendation, or request between two statements of encouragement—the sandwich model.
3. Accepts the child by using active listening, acknowledging the reason for the behavior, and then directing the child to come up with an alternative solution.

The larger the part a child plays in the solution of a problem, the less resistance that child will have. The more the child joins in, the less threatening the situation will become to the child. There will be less talking at and more talking with the child, thus creating an atmosphere of cooperation.

Table 5.2 shows a way to troubleshoot arguments of different degrees. There is also a way to keep a little problem from becoming a big one, by using humor. Humor can be a direct verbal statement, or it can be subtle. It can come from eye contact, physical proximity, body carriage, gestures, or facial expressions. A humorous solution is friendly and full of smiles.

BEDTIME

Bedtime is notorious as the hardest of parenting tasks. Many infants, toddlers, preschoolers, and school-age children do the same thing at bedtime: They cause problems. Depending on their age and experience, they do every trick in the book: They cry, ask for water, insist on another story, and so on. They do everything but ask for the very thing they want—their parents.

The best solution for all age groups is to utilize bedtime for intimate discussions. If children can count on this kind of undivided attention session from the parent or parents, they will actually look forward to going to bed. Older children will even become more efficient at getting themselves ready for bed in order to have the grandest reward of all, their parents' full attention. If parents are truly able to listen, the child will be able to share fears, hopes, and wishes. This kind of intimate attention will relieve the child of anxiety and prepare him or her for a pleasant sleep (Ginott, 1973).

Stories at bedtime are traditional and serve many purposes. First, they require an adult, preferably a parent, to be there to read them. Second, they can be part of a routine. Third, from the child's point of view, they can be packed with all kinds of assets: One story may be new, one may be familiar, and so on. The familiar will probably be the most soothing.

There is also an individualized kind of story that is probably the most effective of all—"The Story of the Day." It gives the child the opportunity to improve memory, learn some information, and develop listening and thinking skills. Because the most interesting story children can hear is one about themselves, and because information for this kind of story is readily available, a story about children's own experiences during the day is fun and easy to tell. It is especially good because it can include information about what will happen the next day and therefore create expectations for exciting coming events. It develops the child's sense of time by establishing the past, present, and future (Goldberg, 1986, p. 54). Since this is a story that is told each night, it is a golden opportunity to teach some of the information children learn by rote. For example, a parent can begin the story each night by saying something like, "This is the story of the day of [Child's Name]." In this story, the parent can also repeat the child's address, telephone number, birthday, and any other facts that he or she would like the child to learn. Then the parent can go on to tell the events of the day. The child can participate in the story at whatever level of language is possible. It is also an opportunity to discuss any events of the day that might have been either particularly troublesome or exceptionally happy (Goldberg, 1986, p. 55). See Chapter 14, Activity 36, for a write-up about this activity.

CHAPTER 6

What about Special Needs?

Guiding a child to develop self-esteem, to become independent, and to lead a productive life is not easy. At the very least it requires much knowledge and a true commitment on the part of the parent. Guiding a child with special needs poses all the same difficulties as guiding a child without such needs, plus the added consideration of dealing with special circumstances. Parents of children with special needs require all the information available about general child development, plus all the information available about their child's particular situation. It is the job of the professional to educate these parents that the child is first and foremost a child, and only secondarily a child with special needs. The professional must first communicate to parents that the child has attention-deficit disorder (ADD) or a learning disability (LD), that the child is gifted, or that the child is differently abled—and then communicate that there is no such thing as an ADD child, an LD child, a gifted child, or a differently abled child. These are all characteristics that affect certain aspects of the child's functioning but not all areas. These are children who must be guided as children to grow up to be adults to live in the same world as everyone else. That is the job of the professional.

ATTENTION DEFICIT DISORDER (ADD) AND ATTENTION DEFICIT HYPERACTIVITY DISORDER (ADHD)

These are syndromes characterized by impulsiveness, hyperactivity, and a short attention span. They often lead to learning disabilities and behavioral problems. ADD, which is milder and easier to treat, is greatly influenced by environmental conditions. Strict scheduling and highly consistent child care have been found to be an effective intervention for this disorder. ADHD is more serious and harder to treat. Both disorders are probably caused by some kind of chemical input to the body, either during pregnancy or prior to pregnancy in one or both parents. The parents of today's babies have taken a wide variety of prescription and over-the-counter drugs for years. Many parents also have used drugs for pleasure at some point in their lives. In addition, many pregnant women or women who have had difficulty conceiving have received various drugs.

Other chemical factors are also probably involved. Over the years it has been harder and harder to keep chemicals out of our foods. Many of today's parents drink large amounts of soft drinks, which contain chemical flavorings and sweeteners. In addition, the general food supply both in supermarkets and in restaurants contains large amounts of chemicals in the form of artificial color, artificial flavor, and preservatives. Not enough information is known about the exact effect of this chemical intake on these problems.

Correcting ADHD, which has a major dysfunctional effect on the child, is difficult. As with ADD, strict scheduling and highly consistent child care is necessary for the treatment. However, it is not enough. The hyperactivity component can only be controlled with medicine, and Ritalin is the most commonly used. There are other medicines as well.

Current theories hold that today's high-tech lifestyle plays a part in creating the poor environmental conditions that cause ADD. Our fast-paced lifestyle deprives infants and toddlers from every socioeconomic class of the opportunity to follow a child-centered schedule and to have consistent child care. Many of today's parents are on the run, and their hurried children are forced to be on the run with them. Because the first three years of life are the foundation years, we find that many children who experienced this inconsistent foundation develop an erratic way of operating and end up with a diagnosis of ADD. In apparent support of this theory, the condition is on the rise. When children with ADD are put into a highly structured situation, they usually settle down greatly. This change seems to help those with ADD, but it does not seem to be enough to solve the more serious problems of ADHD.

To return to a historical perspective, the 1960s were years that tore many of our institutions apart. During those years, our society made monumental changes that affected the lives of children as well. Child-rearing guidelines like these began to disappear:

- When your baby wakes up, set up a nice healthy breakfast.
- Leave enough time for your baby to be adequately fed, participating in the feeding process as much as possible.
- Take the time to hold your baby as you nurse or give a bottle.
- Do not worry about messes at this time. It is all part of the process.
- After breakfast, give your baby a bath. Let the baby enjoy the warmth of the water and some appropriate play.
- Dress your baby to go for a walk. A younger baby should go in a baby carriage, and an older baby should go in a stroller.

- After you walk the baby, put the baby down for a nap.
- After the baby wakes up, give the baby a comfortable place to enjoy free and interesting play.
- Make some time to sing, recite nursery rhymes, and share other appropriate happy activities.

In child-rearing books of today, the advice has begun to center around making the most of the limited time parents have with their baby. Many a child is whisked off early in the morning to some kind of child care center or in-home child care. Many a child is awakened from a deep sleep to do this, and then cries when dropped off for the day. When greeted on arrival, all caregivers say the same thing to the parents, "Your child will be fine after you leave." They are right. Their child usually is fine. However, the question remains, "How good is it for the child to be awakened from deep sleep and cry each day?"

The important focus is the lesson for parents. For all children, including those with ADD or ADHD, parents should try to provide a structured environment with as much consistency of caregiving as is possible. This kind of environment will prevent the problem from occurring or ameliorate the symptoms of the problem if it has already occurred. Ideally it should be provided from birth on, and especially from birth to age three.

LEARNING DISABILITY (LD)

According to the latest edition of *The American Heritage Dictionary of the English Language*, learning disability means, "difficulty in understanding or using spoken or written language, affecting a person of normal intelligence and not arising from emotional disturbance or impairment of sight or hearing." For this condition, there seem to be three possible causes. One is the direct result of ADD or ADHD. Another comes from the same unpredictable environmental conditions that cause ADD or ADHD. The third comes from the same parental exposure to drugs and chemicals both before and during pregnancy. Like ADD and ADHD, learning disability is on the rise.

Children with learning disabilities will always have their disabilities, but they can learn to raise their level of functioning in the problem area(s). Sometimes auditory, visual, or memory training can be so effective that a learning disability will eventually have minimal or no impairing effect. Sometimes the child can learn to compensate for the problem area by using other areas.

Unfortunately, because children with learning disabilities are often treated by parents and teachers as if they are lazy, irresponsible, and unmotivated, they suffer from strong feelings of low self-esteem. It is important for parents to understand that they do not have "an LD child." There is no such thing. What they may have is a child with one or more learning disabilities who also has many strengths.

If parents suspect their child has one or more learning disabilities, they should follow the proper procedure to verify their suspicion. This is difficult to verify because many characteristics of learning disabilities are present in all children. When a professional makes the diagnosis, the degree of the characteristic displayed by the child is what makes the difference. The following are possible characteristics:

1. *Hyperactivity:* Moves continually/restless.
2. *Hypoactivity:* Reacts slowly.
3. *Attention problems:* Is easily distracted by others, by noise, or by any activity.
4. *Impulsiveness:* Acts without thinking and is unconcerned with the consequences.
5. *Understanding:* Does not interpret correctly what others say.
6. *Interpersonal skills:* Misunderstands social cues and nonverbal communication, might stand too close or too far away, might convey inappropriate information.
7. *Memory:* Has poor memory and exhibits problems.
8. *Decision making:* Has poor reasoning.
9. *Fine motor skills:* Has poor handwriting and poor object manipulation.
10. *Social skills:* Has problems with relationships.
11. *Directions:* May confuse left/right, up/down, east/west.
12. *Punctuality:* Has difficulty being on time.
13. *Procrastination:* Delays taking care of responsibilities.
14. *Learning:* Learns more slowly or differently than expected.

The procedure begins with developmental review at age three as explained in Chapter 8. At that time, if a child is low in any developmental area, intervention can be initiated to remediate that area. A report will reveal a child's strengths and weaknesses, and a professional will be able to provide the parent with a home program of activities both for intervention and for enriching the child's strengths. If services for a child with one or more learning disabilities are still needed by the time the child is five, the kindergarten program should be able to provide the support. A school program should be able to provide subject matter taught in an appropriate manner for the child and exercises in the area of the disability that will help to minimize its effects. Such exercises could include visual discrimination, visual perception, auditory discrimination, auditory perception, memory, various kinds of language patterns, gross and fine motor activities, and other personalized learning experiences. If a program is of high quality, the above mentioned LD characteristics should become less acute, and the school learning problems associated with them lessened.

GIFTED

About 2 percent of the population is gifted. One way a child who is gifted is identified is by scores on an intelligence test. In early childhood giftedness is best identified by:

1. Observation of the child in the process of learning
2. Observation of the child's performance or product from a learning or problem-solving experience
3. Reporting from the child and from his or her parents, teachers, or peers

Testing young children under the age of six should be avoided because tests do not have high reliability or high validity for this age group. Children in this age group are not consistent about what they do and are easily distracted. In addition, because child development is rapid, it is hard to rely on a test score that could undergo major changes in a few days, a week, a month, or a year. It is equally difficult because child development is uneven across areas.

Testing becomes more reliable and valid beginning at around age six. That is the recommended time to have a child tested for placement in a gifted program. The 2 percent of the population who are gifted are different from the rare genius, sometimes called the highly gifted. The gifted are as different from the rare genius as they are from the average learner. As with children with learning disabilities—and as with all children—the gifted also differ in ability in all human traits. Everyone is unique.

Intelligence, though a single word, has a composite meaning. It "includes the capacity for insights into complex relationships, all of the processes involved in abstract thinking, adaptability in problem solving, and capacity to acquire new capacity" (Clark, 1988, p. 8). The last phrase holds the fascination and the window to giftedness that parents can experience with their children in the early years. It tells us that children have the capacity to grow and change, that they can be influenced by their environment. What they become is the result of the interaction between inherited and acquired characteristics. No two people have either the same heredity or the same physical, mental, or emotional environment.

Parents of young children have the principal control over a child's environment. They are the ones who can either hold back a child or aid the child in developing to unknown heights. To aid the child, the parents should do the following:

1. Allow the child to learn at his or her own rate.
2. Allow the child to pursue ideas and activities to whatever depth possible.
3. Encourage the child to be curious.
4. Be responsive to the child's curiosity.
5. Treat the child as an individual and not as a generalization.
6. Build on all evidences of the child's strengths.
7. Facilitate rather than restrict the child's growth and development.

By age 4 children have developed 50 percent of the intelligence they will develop by age 18. By age 8 they will have developed 80 percent of it. All parents should have this information. It is the critical data that emphasizes the importance of the first years of life. It makes the "preschool years" the optimum time to develop the child's intellectual capacity necessary for success in school. Intellectual capacity is what is necessary for the child to experience school on the highest level possible. Intellectual capacity development is what parents of children who are gifted should be doing.

Since identifying giftedness is difficult under the age of 6, it is a good idea for all parents to work from birth on toward developing a child who will be gifted. Research shows that among the eminent people studied, all had grown up in a stimulating environment. All the prodigies studied were educated from the first months of their lives. All of them experienced a stimulating early environment (Clark, 1988, p. 75). The years from birth to 3 are the most critical for human development.

Learning opportunities will facilitate or inhibit the development of inherited intellectual capacity. Learning opportunities are more than exposure. They require interaction with the environment—acting on things, interacting with people, and having the people in the environment be responsive. Long-lasting benefits occur as a result of these interactions, while lack of stimulation has irreversible detrimental effects. Environmentally produced individual differences begin at birth and even before.

Information on the importance of an optimum environment for children from birth to three pales in comparison to the information available about the optimum prenatal environment. By the fourth month the fetus can frown, squint, and grimace. By the fifth month the fetus is sensitive to light and touch and reacts to sounds and melodies. By the sixth month the fetus can hear clearly. By the seventh or eighth month the fetus is capable of supporting consciousness. Self-esteem, the highest level of development, has its first important roots in the sixth and seventh months of pregnancy because the mother's attitude is communicated to the baby. Even if the mother pretends to be pleased with the pregnancy and is not, the baby picks up the true feelings and reacts to them. Intense stress or prolonged discomfort in the life of the mother is deeply felt by the infant she is carrying.

A discussion of the optimum conditions for a child to succeed in life would still be incomplete without mention of the important influence on the child of the mother's condition even prior to pregnancy. A mother's healthy body bodes well for a healthy baby. The mother's use of drugs, alcohol, and cigarettes prior to conception affects her ability to conceive a healthy fetus. A proper diet and other sound health habits are also essential for a high-functioning child. A poor diet and unsound health habits, along with anxiety and poor mental health, are all reflected negatively in the child after conception (Clark, 1988, pp. 79–81).

THE DIFFERENTLY ABLED

It is difficult at best to guide and support young children and get them off to a good start in life. Ideal conditions no longer exist, and parents have to try to compensate for the effects of a fast-paced lifestyle on children. This is even more difficult when parents have to deal with a child who has a disability or handicapping condition. According to the March of Dimes Birth Defects Foundation, a birth defect is defined as "an abnormality of structure, function or body chemistry, whether genetically determined or the result of environmental interference before birth. It may present at or before birth or appear later in life." Although few parents expect such a problem, high percentages of birth defects continue to plague our growing population. According to the 1994 statistics from the March of Dimes, "Birth defects strike one out of every 14 infants" (March of Dimes, 1994).

It is important for parents who face this situation to know that the child is a child first and only secondarily a child with a disability. The child is abled with individual strengths and with all the other needs and wants of any child. There is every reason to treat the child as a parent would treat any child and then try to help the child overcome and cope with the disabling characteristic(s).

There are both general and specific guidelines that apply to bringing up a child who is differently abled. Generally, all the information about bringing up any child is important. Then there are specific guidelines that can be applied from our knowledge and experience with children who have other identified special needs. From children with ADD and ADHD, we learn the importance of being child-centered and providing schedules and consistency. From children with LD, we learn the importance of being tolerant of weak areas while enhancing areas of strength. From children who are gifted, we learn that an optimally supportive environment is important in order for a child to reach full potential. Parents of children with disabilities have the hardest job of all. They have to try to implement all the general guidelines, plus all that has been learned from special situations, and also try to lead their child through the area(s) of disability with the highest skill possible. That is not an easy task.

Early intervention programs have recently become available for parents and their children born with disabilities. Such programs are not just beneficial; they are essential. Infants, toddlers, and preschoolers born with major problems need help, and so do their parents. They need programs that will teach the parents how best to facilitate maximum development. In some cases it will be best to have the child go to a special program where learning will take place under the direction of trained early childhood special education teachers and therapists. In other cases it will be best for the parent to go to a special program with the child and get help and guidance for working directly with the child. The entire range of programming proposed through Personalized Parenting should also be helpful. This kind of programming as described in Chapter 1 would provide important information and guidance that would help to keep these families and their children in the mainstream. The seminar classes about the pillars of parenting; the "Mommy and Daddy and Me" classes with songs, activities, and exercises; and developmental review for personalized home programming are effective vehicles for promoting parent effectiveness.

SUMMARY

Some children have special needs, but all children need their parents to treat them in an optimal fashion. Bringing up a child is difficult. Taking a baby from a helpless and totally dependent state to adulthood as a self-controlled and independent human being is the task. All this must be done while the parent looks for and builds a unique place in a world full of ever-growing complication. There are principles and techniques to learn and few of these can be learned easily or quickly. To help with the task, however, parents can and should be taught.

A few themes ring out about how parents should treat children. One theme is the significance of self-esteem. Children need to be believed in so that they will believe in themselves. Second is respect. Children need to be trusted in such a way that they will gain confidence to be able to solve their own problems. The last theme is choices. Limits and restrictions will be placed on children, but they will all be useless unless children are taught that there are options for moving forward.

Underlying it all, professionals must help parents find satisfaction in their own existence. Through that satisfaction, children will find in their parents the modeling of excellence that they need to see. In addition, professionals must help parents learn to be the leaders of their children. Parents need to be taught how to guide children firmly and positively in what to do, and how not to discipline children with the old what-not-to-do parent–child directions.

All this can be summed up in what is known in education circles as "The First Grade Teacher " story.

Two first-grade classes were going on a field trip. One first grade teacher handled the situation in one way; the other handled it in another way.

The first teacher said to her class: "We are going on a field trip. There is a bus outside waiting. We are going to walk in a single line out of the building, down the path, to the bus. On the path near the bus is a puddle. Do not jump in the puddle. Then get on the bus." Each child walked in a single line, out of the building, down the path, jumped in the puddle, and got on the bus.

The other first grade teacher said to her class: "We are going on a field trip. There is a bus outside waiting. We are going to walk in a single line out of the building, down the path, to the bus. On the path near the bus is a puddle. When you get to the puddle, jump over it. Then get on the bus." Each child walked in a single line, out of the building, down the path, jumped over the puddle, and got on the bus.

SELECTED READINGS

Gartrell, D. (1994). *A guidance approach to discipline.* Albany: Delmar.

This book describes the classroom perspective of guidance discipline. All the techniques presented are designed to raise the self-esteem of young children, so vital to their future development.

Gordon, T. (1975). *Parent Effectiveness Training.* New York: Penguin Books U.S.A.

This book presents the basics of tried and tested effective parenting techniques. These techniques have served as a basis for many parenting classes nationwide.

Harris, T. (1973). *I'm O.K.—You're O.K.* New York: Harper & Row.

This book is a classic in the development of self-esteem. It includes foundation concepts on which many programs have been built.

White, B. L. (1993). *The first three years of life.* New York: Fireside.

This landmark book was the first to make clear the importance of learning during the years from birth to three. This information is highly valuable to all educators, especially those who work with children in the early childhood years.

PART III

Education from Birth to Five

"General intelligence appears to develop as much from conception to age 4 as it does during the 14 years from age 4 to age 18."

—Benjamin Bloom, *Stability and Change in Human Characteristics*

CHAPTER 7

Children Ready to Learn

Not Just Important, Imperative

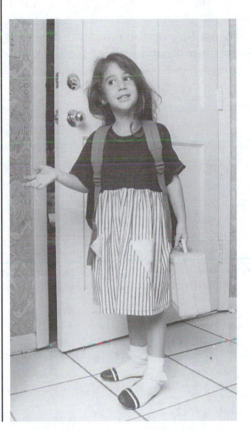

GETTING CHILDREN READY MEANS MAKING THEM PREPARED

Do you take a test before you have studied for it? Do you run in a marathon before you train for it? Do the New York Yankees play baseball games before spring training? The answer to all of the above is, of course, no. What does the good student say before taking an exam? The good student says, "I am ready to take the test."

When Bryant Gumbel was interviewed in September 1994 about how he maintains such a high level of on-TV grace and self-confidence, he said it all has to do with being prepared. He gathers all his information and then has his staff put together a massive briefing book.

Would you put a child in the water to swim without first making sure the child has basic swimming skills? No. Nobody would. By the same token, why do we put children in school without first making sure they have the basic developmental readiness skills to succeed in school? We should not do so anymore. Being ready for school is not just a good idea; it is an absolute necessity. Children who come to school ready are guaranteed of success the first day, the first month, and the first year. Those who succeed the first year are guaranteed success for the rest of their schooling, barring any unforeseen circumstances.

Children who come to school not ready are almost guaranteed to lag behind for their entire school career. They are likely to become frustrated, and they will be our major candidates for school dropouts. A good start bodes well for a good finish, and a bad start becomes tougher and tougher to overcome.

GOALS 2000

Richard Riley, Secretary of Education under President Bill Clinton, brought us the Goals 2000: Educate America Act. It provides resources to communities to develop and implement comprehensive education reforms aimed at helping students reach challenging academic and occupational skill standards. President Clinton signed the bill for this act into law in March 1994. It was designed to build on the previous administration's America 2000. America 2000 programming was established to raise the educational functioning level of our school system nationwide, and Goals 2000 programming, guided by the following goals, is well underway:

1. All children in America will start school ready to learn.
2. The high school graduation rate will increase to at least 90 percent.
3. All students in the United States will be competent in the core academic subjects.
4. U.S. students will be first in the world in science and mathematics achievement.
5. Every adult American will be literate and will possess the knowledge and skills necessary to compete in the economy of the twenty-first century.
6. Every school in the United States will be safe, well disciplined and drug-free.
7. Every school will promote parental involvement in children's education.
8. All teachers will have the opportunity to acquire the knowledge and skills needed to prepare U.S. students for the next century.

STRATEGIES

In addition, Goals 2000 programming gave us four strategies to meet these goals. These strategies focus on: (1) making our more than 110,000 schools better for today's students; (2) inventing new schools for tomorrow's students; (3) keeping studies alive for those out of school; and (4) involving our communities in doing this. School systems around the country are busy implementing these strategies and, much to our good fortune, the strategies are working. Little by little schools are changing, students are functioning better, and the educational level of many Americans is on the rise.

Change in education, however, occurs slowly. Only a small number of our students are doing better, and for every student who is benefiting from a rise in educational level, thousands exist who are left unaided by current reform.

GOAL NUMBER ONE

Building a sound educational system follows the same rules as building anything else. Success lies in the foundation. When looking at the eight goals that now lead our country in its pursuit of educational reform, one of the eight stands out above the rest. It is goal number one, the goal of foundation: By the year 2000, all children will start school ready to learn. It is imperative that we focus our time, money, effort, and untiring spirit in the pursuit of reaching this goal. Through investment in building a foundation, we have the opportunity not only to accomplish goal number one but also to see the seven other goals fall into place.

THE FOUNDATION YEARS FROM BIRTH TO FIVE

For a child to be ready to start school and achieve maximum potential, it is important for the child to be exposed to the finest experiences for development during the first five years of life. To achieve this goal, this kind of exposure optimally begins in the birth-to-three age range. By three years of age, advanced skills in cognitive, motor, socialization, language, and self-esteem development are predictive of success in school by age six.

A three-part program is needed to get children ready to start school and achieve maximum potential. First, schools must be taught how to reach parents as soon as their babies are born so that they can enlist them as facilitators of their children's development. The Personalized Parenting program, which includes seminars and "Mommy and Daddy and Me" classes explained in Chapter 1, is an exemplary way to carry this out. Second, children must be worked with directly using a diagnostic-prescriptive framework to develop a program based on their individual strengths and weaknesses. Developmental review, also explained in Chapter 1, was designed to facilitate this service. Third, parents must be taught an enjoyable way to interact with their children that will help them enrich all areas of their children's development. The Child-Centered Activity-Based Program described in Part IV explains a play-and-learn system that parents can use with their children from birth through age five.

Preschool programs are being started in our public school system for all four-year-olds, but such programming is still years away from becoming a reality, and even that programming comes too late. Extending our preschool programs down to the three-year-old population is under consideration, further away in years, and also comes too late. Teaching parents and their children in the birth-to-three age range is still a mere thought, manifested in a handful of programs for parents and their children who come from our lowest socioeconomic level. Parent–infant/toddler programming is currently overlooked by almost everyone—but that is the type of programming that is necessary.

The solution is twofold. First, society must learn to understand that parents are children's first and most important teachers, that parents have important roles to play in the educational success of their children, that those roles must be taught to parents early, and that those roles must be taught in such a way that parents will enjoy them and will become proficient in them in the early years of their child's development, from birth to age five. Second, society must recognize the value of parent involvement throughout all schooling for the educational success of children. Many areas of development for children come together in an integrated way to form the whole child—the whole educated child, educated in the areas of cognitive skills, motor skills, social skills, language, and self-esteem. All of these areas work together, and all are developed in a major way by parent input. What a responsibility, and what a reward for parents who do them successfully.

A child's foundation is built by parents, who enter the child's world from infancy. A child's foundation is built by parents who know how to be responsive—to imitate gestures and facial expressions; to talk to their babies; to play, sing, hold, comfort, and delight in new life. Responsive parents will spend time with their child, support their child's interests, and respond by offering appropriate instruction. Parents who know how to be responsive in the early years are likely to continue to be responsive, delight in discovering a new little person, and then continue to guide and watch who their child becomes. Responsive parents are those who help children grow in all areas of development, who create the whole child. In the process, those parents will learn the true meaning of "the more you put into it, the more you get out of it."

Of the eight excellent national goals of education, there is one that is foundational. It is the goal that must grab the attention of legislators, educators, and parents. It is the goal that says that all children must start school ready to learn. Parent programming must start through the public school system when children are in the birth-to-three age range. High-functioning children at three years of age are predictive of being successful in school at age six. Knowing this fact, we are remiss if we wait until age five, or age four, or even age three to begin. Knowing this fact, we must begin at the beginning, build foundations, teach teachers to work with parents and teach parents to work with children. We must develop the talents of our children, who are the future of our country. Society will reap the rewards of "an ounce of prevention is worth a pound of cure." This is a chance of a lifetime, and we cannot afford to miss it.

PARENT INVOLVEMENT

The research is done; the information is clear (see Figure 7.1).

The next step is to take this model and turn it into a usable and practical form. Parents and teachers are true partners, and this partnership should begin as early as possible.

Traditional parent involvement has been directed toward informing parents about the child's program and how the child is doing in the program. But the newest ideas about parent involvement go further. Today's well-trained preschool educators know that programs cannot adequately meet the needs of children unless they also recognize the importance of the child's family. These educators develop strategies to work effectively with families. They communiate with families based on the concept that parents are and should be the principal influence in their children's lives.

It is of the utmost importance that staff and parents communicate about child rearing practices in the home and in the program in order to minimize potential conflicts and confusion for children. Because many of today's early childhood caregivers have received a high degree of training, these caregivers are able to communicate to parents about extending some of the school's child-rearing practices into the home. A well-trained staff is able to give parents specific ideas for promoting children's healthy development and learning at home. To promote consistent child behavior, there must be consistent caregiving.

Parents have important information that teachers need to know in order to work effectively with children. On the other hand, the expertise of early childhood professionals is a rich source of information for parents. Such a respectful give-and-take relationship between caregivers at a center and parents at home provides an excellent opportunity for parents to receive knowledge and guidance and for teachers to receive support (White, 1991, pp. 26–27).

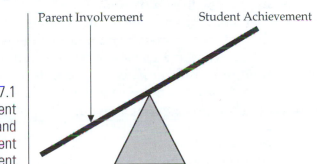

FIGURE 7.1
Parent Involvement and Student Achievement

CHAPTER 8

Parents Ready to Parent

Not Just a Good Idea, a Necessity

GETTING CHILDREN READY MEANS PREPARING THE PARENTS TO GET THEM READY

It is clear that children must have basic developmental readiness skills to succeed in school. It follows that parents in charge of getting children ready for school should have the information available to them for how to do it. Being ready to parent is not just a good idea but an absolute necessity. Parents who know how to set up an optimum environment for their children and who know how to guide and support their children are guaranteed to have children who will achieve to their full potential and ultimately succeed in school.

READINESS DEVELOPS UNDER OPTIMAL CONDITIONS

Parents must be taught how to set up optimal conditions for their children in the home. Optimal conditions include having parents committed to child accomplishment and education in a caring and loving environment. The analogy to a flower growing in a garden is an excellent one. An uncommitted, uncaring, and unloving gardener will turn out a neglected flower in a garden full of weeds. A committed, caring, and loving gardener will turn out a beautiful flower in a garden glowing with beauty.

The child's garden is, of course, the family. Within the family setting, readiness develops. The more positive the interactions are during the first five years, the more likely the child is to be ready. The more parents learn about and practice setting up an enriched early learning environment for their child, and the more parents learn about and practice child guidance and support techniques for their child, the better they will be able to do their job.

Children need room to explore, and parents need to be there, ready to assist them. Children need to blaze their own trails and, when competent, create effective methods of their own; and parents need to be there to encourage such efforts. Children need to follow their dreams wherever they lead, and parents need to relinquish controls unless they are needed for safety. Parents are like gardeners, tending children as gardeners would a plant (Collins, 1995, p. 22).

While readiness develops from birth to age five, the critical period for readiness is from birth to age three. Between four to five readiness becomes a process of extension and expansion.

GOAL NUMBER 7

The Goals 2000 program started with six goals in 1993. In 1995 Richard Riley created two more goals. The first was related to teacher training, to prepare new teachers to understand and be able to carry out the original six goals. The second was related to parent involvement. It was based on the recognition that parents play a vital role in providing their children's first quality education.

This goal, declaring that by the year 2000 every school will promote parental involvement in their children's education, became goal number 7. In the summer of 1995, President Clinton signed a bill establishing a new discretionary grant program to create parent information and resource centers in order to help provide parents with the knowledge and skills needed to participate effectively in their children's education. While goal number 7 was originally focused on parent involvement with school-age children, new funding has become available to set up programs to help parents prepare their children in the early years for school.

GETTING READY FROM BIRTH TO THREE

Time spent with infants and toddlers shapes and defines their world. Simple daily habits provide a secure and stable environment for children. The true best time turns out to be an ordinary schedule. Here is an example:

> Up at seven, breakfast, play and household activities, a stroller ride or walk, lunch, nap, play and household activities, supper, bath, teeth brushed, storytime, kiss and a hug, and lights out by eight.

Familiar, regular routines are the ideal. Through these routines, children learn values, self-discipline, work and play habits, and other personal characteristics. While all this can be done by an alternative caregiver—nanny, au pair, baby-sitter, or other designated person—it is done best by the parent or, as a close second, a grandparent. The critical link, according to Urie Bronfenbrenner, child psychologist and founding member of Head Start, is that the child needs the enduring, irrational involvement of one or more adults. When asked to restate what he meant by "irrational involvement," he said, "Somebody has to be crazy about the kid" (United States Department of Education, "What Other Countries Are Doing," National Goal #1, 1992, p. 2).

While that sample schedule sounds simple, it is packed with opportunity. On the most general level it provides the time for parents to instill values and expectations in their children. Parents are a modeling team. Children grow in the image of their parents. Much of what they learn to do will come from trying to do things as their parents do. Much of what they think will come from the influence of their parents. Even much of how they eat and take care of themselves and their belongings will be based on how their parents handled those responsibilities. In situations of family dysfunction, children can learn not to model their parents but to program their lives in a different manner and in a different direction. However, such a task is difficult, fraught with problems, and sometimes impossible to do well.

The schedule described here provides the opportunity to read aloud to the child. Being able to read is the single most important skill for success in school, and reading to a child is the single most important activity contributing to a child's learning to read. Reading is the most important skill for success in almost every other area of learning. It is recommended that parents begin reading to children from the day they are born. Infants love being talked to and sung to, and they love hearing the rhythm of Mother Goose rhymes and other poems and stories. Reading, just like talking and singing, is part of the bonding process.

This schedule provides time that is not spent in front of the television set. The average two to three year old watches nearly 28 hours of television a week, approximately 4 hours a day. Although there are some worthwhile television programs for young children, none are as beneficial for a child as attention from a parent or other caring adult.

Such a schedule provides a wealth of teachable moments. Folding the clothes, for example, provides the opportunity for much cognitive development—sorting by color, size, item, similarity, and more. Unpacking groceries is another activity for facilitating cognitive development. Again, sorting can be done—this time by category, size, color, temperature, and so on. Coupons can be used for matching, and words on the grocery list can be part of the fun. Counting and reading are both activities that can emerge naturally from a variety of home activities. Almost any household task, chore, or activity is packed with possibilities for interactive, pleasant learning experiences.

From a quick look at a baby, it is easy to miss the importance of daily caregiver–child interactions. Because the baby cannot verbally express thoughts and feelings, it is easy to think that thoughts and feelings are not there, and that even if they are there they are not very important. However, when you start to communicate with a baby, you will receive powerful communication back from facial expressions, vocalizations, and body language. You will soon see that what you say and do has a major effect on that child.

Brain development, stimulated by a rich environment, is rapid as soon as a baby is born. With continued stimulation, it gradually slows down until the brain almost finishes growing by the age of eight. Learning still takes place during one's entire lifetime, but never as rapidly or as easily as during the first eight years of life. It is said that 80 percent of a person's intelligence is established by age eight, a time when the brain almost reaches its adult size.

All learning takes place through the five senses. In the early years, cells that are not stimulated by such sensory experiences die. Of the billions of brain cells with which babies are born, nature acts as a sculptor, chipping away at them by the stimulation pattern of the early environment. It is evident that the more the stimulation, the higher will be the brain functioning for the particular child (Otterbourg, 1994, p. 8).

Spending time with children and doing things together are the twin pillars of school readiness (United States Department of Education, *America 2000, An Education Strategy,* 1991, p. 6). Cognitive skills, as already mentioned, will flourish. Motor skills of every kind will unfold as infants and toddlers find themselves in a mobile yet protected environment. Social skills will develop naturally from their first and most important close successful relationships. Language will grow and expand with great clarity and effectiveness by exposure to adult interactive models. Self-esteem, the heart of all development, will be nurtured to its best formation.

PARENTING SKILLS

Because what happens to a child from birth to three is so important, it should not be left to chance. No one should take that primary caregiver position who does not have all the information necessary to do it well. In September 1994 Education Secretary Richard Riley, in a coalition headed by the Reverend Jesse Jackson, spread the message that parents are the most important influences in a child's education. Part of the message was that this influence will not be positive if parents are not properly prepared. The new message was to redirect a futile general call for "parent involvement" to a specific call for purposeful programs of parent readiness beginning in the prenatal period. While birth-to-three parent programming remains a logical beginning, and while preparental programming should be next in line, it is time to plant the seed for future parent programming to be set up in our colleges and even in our high schools. Even before becoming a preparent, information will help young people make informed decisions about whether or not to take the step into parenthood at all.

GETTING READY FROM THREE TO FIVE

After three years of age, the best approach to readiness is through preschool programming. A preschool environment, particularly based on one of the current models like High/Scope, is the recommended setting. Not that parents or other primary caregivers skilled in early childhood education could not do the job, but in all likelihood they do not have the time, energy, or materials to do it effectively. In addition, exposure to other children is excellent for children at this age, who are in the process of moving away from the "me" stage and who are also in the process of developing independence.

ASSESSMENT

To provide optimal programming, a developmental review is suggested for every child. The developmental review is a two-part process: (1) an introductory consultation meeting with the parents that includes a developmental assessment to find out where the child is in all five areas of development and (2) a follow-up consultation with the parents that includes a full report with recommendations and a home program based on the assessment. Assessment can now be done without putting the child through any kind of formal testing. A parent questionnaire gives reliable and valid information on developmental areas. If necessary, depending on the particular situation, a teacher questionnaire can be used to get the information entirely or in supplemental form.

THE CHILD DEVELOPMENT INVENTORY

The parent questionnaire for assessment is called the Child Development Inventory. It was designed by Harold Ireton, Ph.D., and published by Behavior Science Systems, Inc. It contains 300 questions and takes about 30 minutes for most parents to complete. The format is a question sheet with a corresponding bubble answer sheet. When scored by a professional, it provides a profile of the child's development in these categories: letters and numbers, social, gross motor, fine motor, language, and self-help. Letters and numbers are related to cognitive skills, and self-help is close to self-esteem.

The manner in which the questions are ordered is a major reason for the reliability and validity of the instrument. In each area, the items are not sequenced in developmental order, but are mixed up. Therefore, the parent who is answering the questions cannot be influenced by the natural tendency to try to make the child look more advanced. Questions about four-year-old development appear side by side with those about two-year-old development and all the other preschool years as well. This format puts the parents at ease. They find themselves in the position to evaluate honestly what their child can do without being influenced by what they think their child *should* be able to do.

If it is too difficult for the parent to answer the questionnaire because of any kind of language problem, the teacher can carry out the assessment with a specially designed teacher questionnaire called the Teacher's Observation Guide. It too was designed by Harold Ireton. This questionnaire can also be used by a teacher to supplement parent information.

FORMAL ASSESSMENT INSTRUMENTS

Most screening instruments for children from birth to five are not highly reliable or valid, primarily because of the nature of the young children who are assessed. Young children do not possess the necessary skills to take a standardized test. They are easily distracted, they are not usually comfortable with strangers, and they can often answer a question or do a task one way and then do it again another way. In addition, they cannot use reading and writing as a means of showing mastery of a skill. They also grow and develop quickly. What they cannot do one day, they may be able to do the next day. Moreover, because children come from such diverse cultural backgrounds, words and specific concepts mean different things to different children. The two most commonly used developmental screening tests with the highest validity and reliability are the Denver Developmental Screening Test (DDST) developed by William K. Frankenburg, M.D., and Josiah B. Dodds, Ph.D., and the Early Screening Inventory developed by S. J. Meisels and M. S. Wiske. Meisels wrote an excellent book on assessments, *Developmental Screening in Early Childhood: A Guide*. His instrument is explained in that book, along with the most up-to-date information about the available assessments and their uses.

Most developmental screening instruments cover the years from birth to age five. Unless there is knowledge or suspicion of delayed development or evidence of a problem, there is no need to give any kind of screening instrument to children under age three. This includes the Child Development Inventory for parents as well. Under normal circumstances it is advisable to do an assessment as part of a developmental review at around age three. It should be repeated at age five if there were any deficit areas identified at age three.

PRESCHOOL PROGRAMMING

Developmentally, the time is right for preschool. If development has moved along an optimum path during the first three years, a developmental review will show that the child has acquired all the foundation skills in all five areas—cognitive, motor, social, language, and self-esteem. If that is the case, the child is ready to reap the rewards of preschool, an opportunity to experience continued growth in all areas under the direction of a trained professional in a stimulating environment. If, for whatever reason, development has not moved along an optimum path during that time, a developmental review will show the area(s) in which foundation skills are lacking. Such a review will reveal a profile in all five areas. The profile will enable the teacher to provide both an appropriate program for the child in the preschool setting and a home program for the parents to follow. Both programs should include remediation in the area(s) of delay and enrichment in the area(s) of strength.

While the process of going from "me" to others and developing independence may be slowed down or be more difficult for a child who is not well developed in one or more areas, the information available about the child will be helpful to a trained teacher working on the goal of complete school readiness for the child by age five.

THE PARENT CONFERENCE

The parent conference process should begin with a developmental review. After that, each conference is for the purpose of updating the child's program both in school and at home. There is a short parent questionnaire that can be given to parents to fill out prior to the conference. It is called the Child Development Review, also developed by Harold Ireton. The teacher can combine that information with other information observed in the classroom to help work effectively with the parent on behalf of the child.

CHECKING READINESS AT FIVE

For the child who has had remediation, readiness should be checked again by developmental review at five years old. By that time, the intervention techniques implemented in the preschool years may have been effective, and in that case the child will be ready to start school. The process of going from "me" to others and of developing independence will continue for the child on the kindergarten level.

If, however, the intervention techniques implemented in the preschool years were not effective and the child is not ready to start school, there are four optimum choices of programming for the child:

1. The child can start school in a regular classroom with an additional support program in that classroom designed to continue to remediate the deficit area(s).
2. The child can start school in a regular classroom with an additional resource support program outside the classroom designed to remediate the deficit area(s).
3. The child can start school in a regular classroom in which a special education teacher is also assigned to help the child accomplish schoolwork that may be too difficult because of the deficit area(s). One special education teacher may be available to help one or more children with deficit area(s). This type of setup is referred to as the *inclusion model.*
4. The child can start school in a special classroom designed to meet the needs of children with special needs.

OPTIMAL PARENTING

A parent who has become comfortable with effective parenting techniques will automatically do optimal parenting, automatically provide an optimal environment for child growth and development. During the first 18 months, a child develops trust. That means a parent should provide a consistent set of parent–child interactions. From 18 months to three years, a child develops autonomy. That means a parent should set up the child's environment so that exploration can take place safely and sufficiently. During the third and fourth years, a child develops initiative. That means a parent should allow the child to make decisions and also let the child make some individual plans. During the fifth year the child develops industry. That means a parent should encourage the child's uniqueness. The child now needs parental encouragement for creativity, the key to life's success from this time forth.

The concept of stages is very important, because there are serious consequences in adult life if any of the stages are not handled properly by the parents. The child may become an adult with impaired ability to trust, or with less autonomy, initiative, and/or industry than is optimal. These deficiencies may be irreparable by that time (Seefeldt, 1993, pp. 228–230).

INDEPENDENCE

The ideal preschool program builds on the readiness established from birth to three. It is a planned educational experience that further develops readiness. It fosters a child's cognitive, motor, social, and language skills, and the child's self-esteem to a level of independence. This is the goal or meaning of readiness.

INTERDEPENDENCE

The ideal preschool program turns out a child who is truly ready for school, truly independent, and truly ready to participate in a kindergarten program. An independent child is ready to be interdependent, to take on first the role of a cooperative kindergarten student and later the many different roles that will emerge in the years ahead. A well-functioning family, along with a high-quality preschool, work together to help a child develop independence. The true goal for the independent person is interdependence. In the school years it will show up as the child's ability to form relationships with peers. Later in life it will take the form of the adult's ability to unite in marriage with an independent partner, to unite in a work environment with one or more independent workers, and to unite in an environment of friendship with a group of friends. In each of these settings, the relationships multiply. For example, at home they go from spouse to parent, to grandparent, and so on. At work there are endless combinations, and so it is with friends.

CHILD-CENTERED PRESCHOOL PROGRAMMING

There are two world-renowned programs for preschool children that excel in getting young children ready for school. Many other preschools have incorporated aspects of these fine programs into the way they handle children.

These programs exemplify a child-centered approach that stimulates critical thinking and problem solving along with creativity. These two programs and others that use some of the same ideas demonstrate techniques that are excellent for developing school readiness. One is the Reggio Emilia approach, and the other is High/Scope.

Reggio Emilia

The preschool in Reggio Emilia in Italy is based on the idea that all children are different. The teachers design a curriculum, and parent volunteers work alongside the teachers. Classwork is organized around themes that allow children to learn a variety of skills and help them understand the world. The program is unusually comprehensive. In class, each child's special qualities are recognized and nurtured. Teachers often leave a tape recorder on an activity table in order to learn how children are reasoning and expressing themselves. There is never a prescribed curriculum; it is always generated from the interests of the children and the resources of the teachers and parents. Children are taught to express themselves in as many different ways as possible. Their expression represents their growth in the world of learning.

Parent Involvement in Reggio Emilia

Parent involvement is a natural and integral part of Reggio Emilia's programming. At the individual classroom level, classroom teachers meet with the parents to discuss the child as part of a particular group. Teachers also meet with the parents in small groups to discuss the more individual needs of each child. Conferences are set up with parents to discuss particular problems if necessary. There are also organized meetings to help parents with parenting skills. These are set up to discuss topics like the role of the father, children's fears, and so on. Some of these meetings have an invited expert to deal with topics like fairytales, children's sexuality, and others. Parents and teachers also come together to improve the school environment. They work on building furnishings and equipment, rearranging the educational space, and more. Parents teach children topics like origami and cooking through a laboratory experience. For holidays and celebrations, the whole community gets involved. Children, parents, grandparents, friends, and other townspeople can be seen together. This program includes a day when parents spend a whole day in their children's classes. Also, small groups of children visit one another's homes or go on outings together—to a gym, a swimming pool, and other locations (Edwards, Gandini, & Forman, 1994, pp. 97–99).

High/Scope

The High/Scope curriculum grew out of a pilot preschool program designed in the 1960s to help disadvantaged preschoolers. Many Head Start programs follow this curriculum. The major tenet of the program is the concept of *plan-do-review.* The children first plan what they will do for an activity session. Then they follow through with their plans, and then they tell about the experiences they had. High/Scope is a child-centered program that gives children choices and the opportunity to create and problem-solve. Although a schedule is followed, the activities are flexible, providing experiences full of variety and novelty. The structure of the program helps to develop independence, autonomy in learning, an internal locus of control, intellectual stimulation, and a sense of responsibility. It has centers or areas where children can discover basic concepts like math, science, reading, writing, or self-awareness, and other centers or areas where they can create using a variety of materials. Group and cooperative activities are also emphasized. This gives the children the opportunity to grow in the area of social problem solving. There is exposure to a teacher who is well trained in bringing out positive behavior in children. Such classrooms usually have few or no discipline problems.

High/Scope Parent Involvement

High/Scope and other exemplary programs based on the High/Scope method have parent involvement programs that are designed to inform parents about what is happening with their children in the school. In addition, there are educational programs for parents. Speakers are invited, and programs are planned to give parents important information about bringing up children in the early years. They are successful in creating support for the school and for enriching the relationship of the parents with their children.

In contrast to the parent involvement in the Reggio Emilia system, the parents are peripheral to the High/Scope program. They are invited guests, brought in whenever possible. They are not an integral part of the educational system in which their child is participating.

THE NEXT STEP IN PARENT INVOLVEMENT

Because our society takes parents away from young children in order to work, we need to be able to accommodate our parents' needs in their actual parental role. If they cannot be learning on site from trained early childhood professionals as they do in Reggio Emilia, they need to be able to learn vital early childhood parenting skills some other way.

There is little built into our best programs in terms of parent training that would be equivalent to teacher training. Yet parents today need the same skills that early childhood professionals need. What has happened is somewhat of a reversal. Before day care and preschools became so prevalent, most child care was done by families at home. Support came from grandparents available to participate in child care and from aunts, uncles, cousins, and even older brothers and sisters. Child care often fell into place naturally. When the family structure started changing, however, child care became more difficult. First the nuclear family lost its support system. Then the nuclear family itself became a threatened unit. Losing the thread of grandparent and extended family knowledge, new parents became a generation not knowledgeable about the skills of child care. In the face of the difficulties faced by the nuclear family, parents struggling to take care of their children turned to the day care and preschool system for help. Because the parent population using that system has limited knowledge of child care, they need child care training. First the early childhood professionals needed this knowledge to be able to do their jobs. Now it is time to turn around and share these newly acquired and vital child care skills with the parents.

Our preschool teachers can help parents learn to bring high quality to a child's educational environment. They can go beyond telling parents what they should do and can show them how to do it. They can teach parents how to listen to children and how to encourage them. They can teach parents organizational skills that will give children structure at home. They can teach parents to display a curiosity that will stimulate children to figure out things for themselves. They can advise parents to share an interest with children through a hobby, art, building, cooking, crafts, drama, music, nature, reading, or sports. They can do all of these things, and they should. The rewards for parents and their children will be worthwhile (Otterbourg, 1994, p. 2).

The program started in Reggio Emilia takes a successful approach to parent training by having the parents volunteer in the classroom and by having them integrated into the school programming. This is reminiscent of the Montessori directress system. Maria Montessori invited the parents to attend the school to see the directress as a model and to be able to treat children at home in the way they were treated at school. The parents in a Reggio Emilia program have the same opportunity.

Parent training in the United States is not as well developed as it is in the Reggio Emilia program. It has to be more direct. There needs to be recognition that there is a way to handle children that helps them to develop to their highest potential in all areas and also leads them toward independence and eventual interdependence. Highly trained early childhood professionals in our exemplary preschool programs have this information and apply it with the children in their classrooms. What is missing now is the follow-through of the parents being able to handle children in the same optimum manner in their homes. Parents need to be taught how to organize for their children home environments that allow choice and a high degree of variety and novelty. They need to know how to set up centers for activities. They need to know how to provide children with materials for creating projects. They need to know how to set up group and cooperative activities with their own children and with their children's friends. They need to know how to have a relationship with their child that gives support, choice, and direction. The High/Scope program and other exemplary programs have a large impact on the functioning level of preschool children, but they would have an even greater impact with parent follow-through commensurate with the school programming.

Throughout the book, the guidelines for spending time with children and doing activities with them have been clearly expressed. They have been designed to be the foundation for a high-quality parent involvement program in any daycare or preschool setting. They are all important, and they all bring with them great rewards in terms of child progress. They should be available to every parent. In addition, the one concept that underlies them all is just *spending time.* What the parent actually does with the child when they are together is sometimes less important than the fact that the parent and child do spend time together. As long as this time is spent pleasantly, lovingly, and with interest, it will have a positive effect on the child's development.

READY FOR SCHOOL

Parents ready to parent will get children ready for school. While children develop at different rates, there are clear markers that signal to onlookers that a child is truly ready for school. These children

- Know their first and last names
- Can tell you their address or phone number
- Know their parents' or guardians' names
- Can catch a large ball most of the time
- Can run and stop on signal
- Can usually hop on one foot and skip
- Can hold a pencil
- Can use scissors
- Like to write and draw (can usually write their name or nickname)
- Can count (often "skip" counting by twos, fives, or tens)
- Like to tell riddles and jokes
- Can copy shapes (circles, squares, triangles, and rectangles)
- Can sort things (beans or pennies) in categories by color, shape, and kind
- Can fill in the missing part (on pictures of people, figures, animals, or a house) (Otterbourg, 1994, pp. 18–19)

It is no accident when you find a child ready for school. An excellent early environment has clearly been a part of that child's life. A broad overall set of experiences is certain to have taken place.

CHAPTER 9

Areas of Development

INDEPENDENCE

Traditionally the areas of development are taught as if they are five parts of the whole child. Figure 9.1 is a closer representation of how this process works. There are specific cognitive, motor, and social skills that develop both independently and in a connected way. Language skills develop that are directly connected to those skills and also as a completely separate process occurring in a language-rich environment. Self-esteem represents the development of the whole child. It grows from accomplishment in all other areas of development and on its own from a feeling of self-worth. The child who achieves self-esteem is the child who has independence and is ready to function independently and effectively in all settings—family, school, and eventually work. Development in each area is critical to independence. If there is a delay or disability in any one area, independence will not be achieved. Areas of delay that are worked with successfully by trained professionals can help a child to achieve a normal level of self-esteem. If a delay is caused by a disability, the area can still be worked with by a trained professional to ameliorate the condition. If it is ameliorated to the child's highest potential, there is also a possibility that the child will achieve a functional level of self-esteem.

INTERDEPENDENCE (COOPERATION)

A child who actively functions positively and cooperatively in a setting is exhibiting interdependence (see Figure 9.2). This is the child who is achieving at relationships, being a brother or sister, son or daughter, nephew or

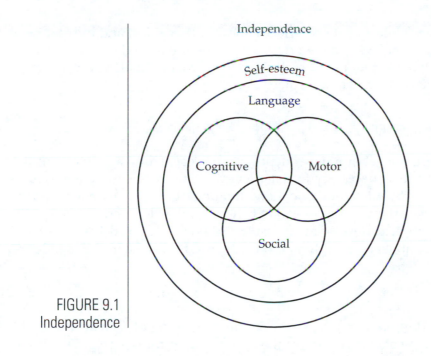

FIGURE 9.1
Independence

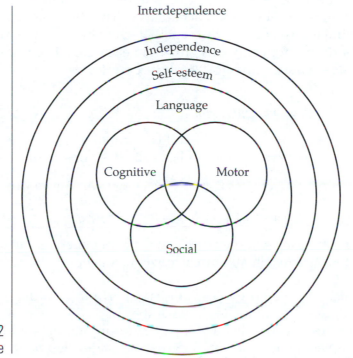

FIGURE 9.2
Interdependence

niece, grandchild, neighbor, friend, and at other roles, and eventually at being a husband, wife, and worker. An independent child will be able to experience the joy not only of high self-achievement but also of working together as a partner or as a member of a group.

INDEPENDENCE AND INTERDEPENDENCE

Only the first level of independence can be reached by age five. This is a foundation level necessary for later levels of independence to emerge. As the child grows into adulthood, new situations, experiences, and responsibilities arise. Many of these require continued development in each of the areas. Continued development results in more advanced levels of independence and consequently in more advanced levels of interdependence.

AREAS OF DEVELOPMENT

It is important for parents to have an understanding of each area of development to be able to maximize the opportunities for their child's growth. Following are brief, concise descriptions of the areas, presented in such a way that parents can use them as guidelines. Just as a child needs a balanced diet of foods from each of the five food groups to have a healthy body, so a child needs a balanced routine that will foster development in all areas. As seen in Figures 9.1 and 9.2, any area that is neglected will affect all the others in some way and ultimately interfere with the goals of independence and interdependence. The following is information about the areas of development presented in a way that parents will be able to use it as important background information for direct parent–child interactions. There is an endless opportunity for children's growth in each area. Each specific accomplishment lays the groundwork for future successes.

Cognitive Development: Learning about the World

This comes about first as the child continually experiences the environment in different ways and then as he or she develops an understanding of those experiences. All learning is accomplished through the five senses.

Motor Development: Movement in a Purposeful Manner

- *Gross motor:* Large muscle movement generated by the child
- *Fine motor:* Small muscle movement generated by the child

While the parent provides various opportunities and exposures for movement, the concept relates to what the child can eventually generate alone. Open areas like big blanket space, child-proof rooms, and playgrounds are examples of environments for gross motor development. The availability of manipulatives provides the milieu for fine motor development.

Social Skills: Relationships

There is an important sequence that encourages strong, healthy social interaction. It goes from relationship to relationship almost like the circles created when a small pebble hits a pond. The first and most important relationship is mother–child. From there the concept expands to parent–child. It then goes on to family–child. These primary relationships create a comfort level with people that allow future healthy relationships to develop with other adults and peers outside the family.

Language: Receptive and Expressive Speech Communication

This expertise arises out of the developmental processes in all the preceding areas. Through parent–child interaction, language is both modeled and reinforced to foster language development. The richer the quality of the language environment provided, the higher the level of language the child will exhibit.

Self-Esteem

Self-Worth

A message should be given to all children that they are important, lovable, capable, and worthy of respect. It includes the concept of individuality, uniqueness, and being special. This is a message of unconditional love, separate from any action the child may do. Additional self-worth is gained through achievement of language skills, cognitive understanding, gross motor and fine motor abilities, and social skills. Self-esteem arises from self-sufficiency, the ability to accept and assume responsibility and to take charge of the process of self-fulfillment. It does not arise from indiscriminate overuse of adult attention and praise.

Dynamic Interaction

To develop the child's self-esteem, it is important to provide rich interaction experiences for the child in all areas of development. The parent plays a major role. The parent has control of the process by designing much of the child's cognitive, motor, social, language, and emotional environment. This design manifests itself in the development of methods of interaction in each of the aforementioned areas. This is a dynamic, never-ending process that undergoes constant revision and progress.

Creativity

Creativity is another aspect of development that is important to a child's self-esteem. While the years from birth to three are critical for facilitating these areas of development, the years from three to five are the time to begin to stimulate creativity. This period follows the foundation years and relies on a basic level of skill development. Creativity "is a special condition, attitude, or state of being that nearly defies definition" (Clark, 1988, p. 46). Although few professionals can agree on a definition, almost everyone has a feeling for what it means. Creativity itself is made up of four parts: rational thinking; emotion and feelings; talent related to mental and physical prowess; and consciousness resulting in imagery, fantasy, and breakthroughs to the preconscious or unconscious states. Everyone has the potential for being creative (Clark, 1988, p. 47).

It is important for parents to have an understanding of creativity and to be able to foster its growth in children. Living in a society that values rational, material gains makes it even more important for parents to create environments for children that value their intuition and feelings. Although it is not something anyone can teach directly, it is something anyone can respect and foster. It requires veering away from the old-fashioned emphasis on right and wrong answers and presenting children more with choices. It involves setting up situations partially and allowing children to complete them. It relies on giving children materials and information and allowing them to put together a product. It stresses the process of an activity over the end result. Parents can become models of creative acts and attitudes.

While creativity used to be almost omitted from the educational setting, it has recently taken on a major role. Learning information used to be the end goal of most teachers in most classrooms. Today, learning to *use* information in a creative way has become a more accepted part of the educational setting.

THE PLAY-AND-LEARN SYSTEM

The way to provide an optimum learning environment for a young child is through applying the play-and-learn system to all areas of child development. The play-and-learn system begins with the four areas of development: cognitive, motor, social, and language. Self-esteem is developed through these areas as well as through discipline and the way children are guided and supported by their parents. Within each area there are many milestones. For each milestone, any number of play activities can be designed, carried out, and then evaluated (Figure 9.3). Evaluation provides two dif-

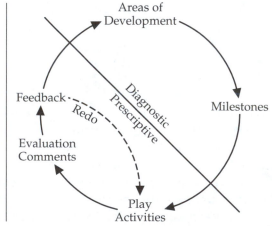

FIGURE 9.3
The Play-and-Learn
System

ferent kinds of feedback. It either gives the go-ahead to work on another milestone with a new play activity, or gives an indication to redo the activity. The same activity can be redone, or a similar one can be set up. Application of this process can and should be made in each area of development. The whole system of leading a child toward independence works by developing the child in each area of development in an interconnected manner.

PARENTS AND THE SYSTEM

Parents enter the system first by drawing on their own background, experience, ideas, intuition, and knowledge. Here are some quotes from leading authorities in the field of education that can help parents become comfortable as facilitators of their child's development:

"Every child has a gift and a talent. We accept the challenge to find and nurture those qualities in each child."—"Tesseract" curriculum, Educational Alternatives, Inc.

"When students are enjoying what they are learning, they stay engaged longer and learn better."—Stuart Schwartz, Ph.D., *Exceptional People*

"Parents know more than they think they do."—Anonymous

"Don't be overawed by what the experts say. Don't be afraid to trust your own common sense."—Benjamin Spock, M.D., and Michael B. Rothberg, M.D., *Dr. Spock's Baby and Child Care*

"Position yourself to occupy the center of the child's universe, not the other way around. As your children grow, those orbits can expand around the stable, secure centerpoint that you as a parent provide."—John Rosemond, *Parent Power*

Ideas like these and others give parents the confidence to develop their own children. From this base of confidence, they will be ready to generate the whole process of providing an optimum learning environment for their child.

APPLYING THE SYSTEM

The play-and-learn system should be used to turn a personalized diagnosis into a personalized prescription for the child. The parent can be taught to use the developmental information in this book to put together this diagnosis and then the prescription. The parent can then be taught to implement the prescription. The process is ongoing and works to create an independent child. The elements of the prescription come from information gained about the child through personalized experience.

The Personalized Diagnosis

First, information comes from going over all of the areas of development. Then analysis is done to see what kinds of things the child can do in each area—milestones. Analysis is also made of milestones that lie just ahead. Part IV contains information about areas of development and milestones. The Diagnostic Record (see Figure 9.4) can be used to make a personalized diagnosis based on that information. For each area of development, the parent can select current milestones or the next milestone ahead for their child.

The Personalized Prescription

On the basis of the child's milestones in each area of development, the parent can be taught to select or design a directed, focused, and appropriate play situation—play activities. These activities can then be evaluated by comments that give parents feedback ("New" or "Redo") about what kinds of play activities to set up next. A personalized prescription should include a play activity for each area of development. New activities can be chosen or designed for each area on the basis of the evaluation and feedback, or the same or similar ones can be used over and over. Part IV contains information about play activities that can be selected or designed by the parent to enrich current milestones and to prepare for upcoming milestones as well. The Prescriptive Record (see Figure 9.5) can be used to make a personalized prescription based on the diagnostic information. For each milestone, the parent can select a *play activity*. Then the parent can carry out the *evaluation comments.* From the evaluation comments, the parent will get *feedback*

Name_____ Age _____ Date _____

Area of Development	Milestone Numbers	Milestones
Cognitive		
Motor		
Social		
Language		

FIGURE 9.4
Diagnostic Record

Name_____   Age _____   Date _____

Area of Development	Milestone Numbers	Play Activity	Evaluation Comments	Feedback	
				New	Redo
Cognitive					
Motor					
Social					
Language					

FIGURE 9.5
Prescriptive Record

("New" or "Redo") and then either select new play activities or continue with the same ones, variations of the same ones, or made-up related ones.

The Diagnostic Record and the Prescriptive Record

Parents can use the Diagnostic Record (see Appendix A) to make an analysis of their child's development. This analysis can be used as preparation for the next step, using the Prescriptive Record (see Appendix B) to make a plan for play activities that will appropriately foster development in all areas. The Diagnostic Record gives a developmental projection of the child, while the Prescriptive Record gives the parent's selection of enjoyable activities to do with the child. While the Diagnostic Record can be used for months at a time, the Prescriptive Record can be changed more often for variety. Because development is rapid in the first two years of life, the Diagnostic Record can be changed more frequently during that time as well. The Diagnostic Record in Appendix A and the Prescriptive Record in Appendix B can be copied for continued use by parents. Teachers who work with children daily can guide parents in making both diagnoses and prescriptions for their children.

Play Activities

Each play activity has been designed with several variables for personalization and to facilitate one or more milestones. Each play activity has been designed to stimulate parents to create other similar activities. Once the parents begin interacting positively and successfully with their child, they should find themselves getting new ideas and being able to create new play activities that will facilitate development, be fun to do, and also be personalized.

The play activities in any one area of development interact with those in other areas. For example, a language activity like describing to a child what you are doing while cooking dinner has benefits in other areas as well:

1. *Cognitive:* The parent is helping the child to learn about the world.
2. *Social:* The parent is engaging the child in the parent's own activities and thereby strengthening the parent–child relationship.
3. *Self-esteem:* By sharing the adult world with a child, the parent is communicating to the child a sense of self-worth.

Any and all play activities chosen to enhance a particular area of development will have positive benefits in at least one other area of development. While the play activity may facilitate more than one area of development, the write-up on the Prescriptive Record should go under the original target area of development.

Each play activity is written in such a way that it can be personalized. A particular object may be mentioned for suggested use, but the parent should feel free to substitute any other object that might be preferable to either the child or the parent.

OVERALL STAGES OF DEVELOPMENT

Besides being able to look at a child's development in terms of milestones within areas of development, it is important for a parent to understand development in terms of overall stages of development. Putting the two together enables parents to have a broader picture of their child. It can be helpful in terms of expectations. The following is a series of general descriptions for a parent to refer to for guidance. While they are presented by stages in terms of months and years, those months and years are only approximations. All children develop at different rates.

Birth to Three Months

This is an exciting time in the lives of parents. Day-by-day development unfolds right before their eyes. Newborns respond to their environment and grow in response to it. They begin to process information through their five senses—sight, sound, taste, touch, and smell. They begin to learn about how they fit themselves into the world. They are making a transition from the womb to life in the outside world.

Three to Six Months

These babies begin to develop muscle control, start to move with purpose, and learn how to sit up. They begin to see themselves as unique. They become familiar with their environment and get to know the people around them. They begin to interact with things in the environment and with other people as well. They are becoming dynamic, contributing members of their family, who affect its lifestyle.

Six to Twelve Months

These more mobile babies understand much more about the environment. They start to remember objects that are out of sight. They can distinguish between family members and strangers. During this period they may make their first utterances, marking the beginnings of vocal communication. Many take their first steps and say their first words around this time. You can see these babies beginning to understand new words. These important skills of awareness indicate a first level of independence.

One to One and a Half Years

Babies now begin both walking and talking. Their walking is toddling, and their talking is mostly with single words; they continue to develop both. They have a quest for independence, and they learn about the world through trial and error and experimentation. This is the time even a casual observer will notice that babies have "a mind of their own."

One and a Half to Two Years

These older toddlers are in perpetual motion. They are always involved in new activities. They experiment by taking things apart and by putting them back together. They use words for self-expression, often two-word combinations. They are possessive about their toys and belongings, a possessiveness that should be respected.

Emerging is a time often referred to as the "terrible twos." This is brought on by a new sense of self-awareness. That too should be respected and channeled in a positive direction whenever possible. Now is the time for parents to work with children and guide them rather than focus on strictly enforcing rules.

Two to Three Years

Two-year-olds are self-centered thinkers. They have developed a degree of independence that makes them difficult to manage. They get attached to stuffed animals or dolls or other objects like blankets. They play, touch, and experience much in their environment. They are expanding their motor skills and their vocabulary. The older twos are increasing their attention span. They show a dramatic increase in motor skills and the ability to communicate. Their play experiences are noticeably richer. Balanced or advanced development in all areas should be emerging, reassuring a parent of the child's future success.

Three to Four Years

Three-year-olds may be well-developed young people, who lead a life full of contrasts—from running fast to sitting quietly, from enjoying the playground to concentrating on a puzzle. Sometimes they express themselves with grown-up words and phrases, using proper grammar and word usage; but they may still exhibit some premature speech. Some will be able to tell stories and play games; others will be limited in this area. They know the difference between good and bad behavior but need firm guidance to be able to control themselves. Since they can learn rules and understand instructions, they can participate in cooperative play. They are rapidly building their vocabularies and can benefit from having things explained to them.

Four to Five Years

Four-year-olds continue to grow in independence. They benefit from nurturing guidance. Their bodies continue to grow, and they can do more and more physical activities. Skipping, jumping, throwing, kicking, and somersaulting are some of the motor skills they have developed. At the same time, they are achieving fine motor skills like being able to cut and draw. They are beginning to understand concepts in greater depth. They can understand directions that have more than one step and stories with details. Some can write their names and recognize letters and words. Some even begin writing. As a group they enjoy having their ideas written down for them by adults. Some can play group games with rules. They have a desire for independence that incorporates a sense of responsibility. They understand gender differences but have no preference for playing with either boys or girls. They have inquiring minds and can solve simple problems. They like sorting and sequencing and have a positive attitude toward cleaning up and doing chores. "Why" and "how" questions are prevalent and provide parents and teachers with many opportunities to teach.*

SUMMARY

Education from birth to age five is the foundation for all future education. As hard as it is to believe that the developmental educational experiences for young children are vital, we know that they are.

From the days of remedial reading to the current days of flourishing tutoring agencies, there have been massive support groups for our children. Today our tutors work day in and day out picking up the pieces of missed educational experiences. Each and every one of them is busy filling in im-

---

*Adapted from the Developmental Chart of the Wings Personal Learning System and from Developmentally Appropriate Practices in Early Childhood Programs Serving Children from Birth through Age 8.

portant educational building blocks. Each and every one of them believes in the education of foundation.

When all parents have the information they need to bring up children in the early years, all children will achieve to their fullest potential and grow up to lead productive lives. No more children will be abused, neglected, or killed. No more children will grow up to abuse, neglect, or kill. Early parenting skills education is the insurance we have for child success, and it is the best crime and violence prevention program available. We cannot afford not to use it.

SUGGESTED READINGS

Carnegie Corporation of New York. (1994). *Starting points.* New York: Carnegie Corporation of New York.

This report is available directly from the Carnegie Foundation in complete form, and it is also available in an abbreviated form. It contains excellent research information about the devastating and lasting effects of a deprived environment on the lives of children ages birth to three.

Collins, S. (1995). *Our children are watching: Ten skills for leading the next generation to success.* Barrytown: Barrytown Ltd.

This book is about leadership in general, both for parents and for managers in the workplace. It teaches about leading an adult life of choice as a model for leading children and workers to success.

Meisels, S. J. (1992). *Developmental screening in early childhood: A guide.* Washington, DC:. National Association for the Education of Young Children.

This book is a thorough overview of screening instruments, with useful information about the instruments and their practical application.

Trelease, J. (1989). *The new read-aloud handbook.* New York: Penguin Books.

While parents are continually told that reading to their child is beneficial, many do not know how to do it. This book tells how and what to read to children.

PART IV

The Child-Centered Activity-Based Program

"The most important aspect of the child's play is not the finished product but the doing."

—Members of the Boston Children's Medical Center and Elizabeth M. Gregg, *What to Do When There's Nothing to Do*

CHAPTER 10

The Play-
and-Learn
System

The areas of development—cognitive, motor, social, language, and self-esteem—are broad categories. Each one encompasses many milestones. They come about by an attempt to describe child development.

Play activities are as numerous and as endless as the parents who are available to play with their children. The play activities that are important to foster child development come about by a two-part process relating to each area of development:

1. What skills are appropriate for a child at each developmental level?
2. What is appropriate for an individual child?

This process is at the heart of developmentally appropriate practices, a concept developed by the National Association for the Education of Young Children (NAEYC).

What follows is an indispensable personalized activity-based system to help every child from birth to age five to reach full potential. It is a program based on areas of development and play activities for parents and their children. It is for administrators to embrace, for teachers to teach to parents, and for parents to have the privilege of carrying out. Some children will benefit from all of the activities; all children will benefit from some of them. All schools should become aware of this approach and try to offer it as a way to implement parent involvement early. This program has lasting effects.

Sample play activities are provided for one or more developmental milestones. Each sample can be used as a model for inventing other personalized activities for a child. Because memory is the most important skill for school success, many of the activities include a memory development component.

To facilitate child learning, actions should first be initiated from left to right. Then, if appropriate, a second round can be carried out from right to left. In addition, motions for a circle or moving in a circle should be first initiated in a clockwise direction. Then, if appropriate, a second round can be carried out in a counterclockwise direction.

Play activities should be matched to developmental milestones that have been reached or to ones that are just ahead. When they are matched to milestones reached, they serve the purposes of reinforcement, enrichment, and expansion. When they are matched to those just ahead, they serve the purposes of working on and preparing for the next milestone. One cannot teach development, but parents have the opportunity to foster development and thereby speed up a process that would take longer if not facilitated.

The next four chapters represent a workable system. First, there is general information about the area of development. Next comes a running description of that area through a series of selected milestones. Milestones are not ends in themselves. They represent a broad range of learning, including activities similar to the selected milestones. For example, if the milestone is that a child can stack three blocks, the true meaning is that the child can do all activities that take the same kind of motor control as is needed for stacking three blocks—pushing a toy car, handling a doll, or rolling clay into a ball. The milestone is a sample of development and is not to be considered a crucial childhood experience.

The milestones of development that follow were compiled from many different sources of early childhood development. A major proportion of the items are the items listed in the NAEYC's Developmentally Appropriate Practices in Early Childhood Programs Serving Children from Birth through Age 8. Others are from the developmental chart in *Quality Child Care* by Ellen S. Cromwell. Another source is the developmental chart produced to go with the Wings Program published by Intelligy. Most charts are different from each other because the entries are all approximations. All children are different from each other because children develop at different rates in different areas depending on both their heredity and on their individual developmental environments. Following each set of milestones are sample play activities matched to the milestones.

The system can be activated by using the sheets in Appendix A and Appendix B—the Diagnostic Record and the Prescriptive Record. The parent can first find the diagnostic level of the child in all four areas of development and then use that diagnosis to design a prescriptive set of play activities. Almost all of the 180 activities can be done with household items or no items at all.

This system, which is set up for maximum efficiency, is based on developmentally appropriate practices and on the principles of education expressed by David Elkind in his landmark book *Miseducation: Preschoolers at*

Risk. These activities are designed to be informal and made up of the kinds of natural parent–child interactions that stimulate young children. The whole range of normal child care activities—cooing, rocking, feeding, and playing—naturally stimulate a baby. Most of the time, doing what comes naturally to a parent is exactly what the baby needs. No authority in child psychology, pediatrics, or child psychiatry advocates the formal instruction of infants and toddlers. What they do advocate is providing young children with a rich and stimulating environment that is warm, loving, and supportive of the child's own learning priorities and pacing. It is in this supportive, nonpressured environment that infants and young children develop security, positive self-esteem, and a deep enthusiasm for learning (Elkind, 1987, pp. 8–9).

The essence of this system is a caution: Don't overdo it. Parents should let their child be the guide. Responding to a child's needs and interests is the goal. As long as the activity remains as play, it is being done correctly. If it becomes boring or repetitious for the child, the parent should be cautioned to stop it.

Along with respect for their child, parents must also be taught to respect themselves. If an activity becomes unpleasant, tedious, boring, or in any other way a problem for the parent, it is time to stop the activity and either do something else or switch to another activity. If the parent is not enjoying the activity, it is not considered effective and should not be continued. The activities require two parts, a parent and a child. For true success, both parts should be functioning optimally.

Children learn most effectively through play. Play is a primary vehicle for and indicator of mental growth. Play enables children to progress along developmental sequences. In addition to its role in cognitive development, play serves important functions in motor, social, language, and self-esteem development. Therefore, child-initiated, child-directed, and parent-supported play is developmentally appropriate and highly effective (Bredekamp, 1986, pp. 1–3).

Parents should facilitate a child's successful completion of tasks by providing support, focused attention, physical proximity, and verbal encouragement. Parents need to be taught to recognize that children learn from trial and error and that children's misconceptions reflect their developing thoughts. Children learn from their own mistakes. Parents need to be given this awareness. Knowledgeable parents will know how to leave a problem with their child and then, if appropriate, encourage the child to find alternatives. Parents can be taught to plan open-ended activities that have more than one right answer and also to value the uniqueness of their own child (Bredekamp, 1986, p. 10).

CHAPTER 11

A Practical Approach to Cognitive Development

Through play, children learn about the world. They experience what is wet, what is dry, what hurts, what can be lifted, what is for pushing, what is for pulling, what makes things stop, what makes things go, what makes some things hold together, and what makes others fall apart. They even find out what they can do alone and when they need help. Children experiment by seeing, feeling, hearing, tasting, and smelling. They drop, kick, throw, and make a mess to experience life and as a result build cognitive skills (Boston Children's Medical Center and Gregg, 1968).

Certain basic experiences have a major impact on cognitive development:

- Tactile and eye–hand coordination
- Listening skills
- Body-in-space awareness
- Auditory and visual tracking, discrimination, and memory

Play activities in these areas also build cognitive skills:

- *Comprehension:* Another word for *comprehension* is *understanding.* Children show that they want to understand because they have a natural curiosity.
- *Memory:* Another word for *memory* is *remembering.* Children who can store and retrieve information can learn successfully.
- *Evaluation:* Other terms for *evaluation* are *planning, coping skills, practical judgment, decision making,* and *leadership.* Experiences in these areas are not easy to provide, but they are valuable.
- *Convergent problem solving:* Another way to say this is *correct answer finding.* Children can be given situations that require skills like thinking, reasoning, sorting, or sequencing to work out the answer.
- *Divergent problem solving:* Other words for this concept are *diversity, fluency, set change, originality,* and *new ways of looking at things.* Children who know more solutions to a problem and more ways to accomplish a task have many more options for success. (Adapted from Meeker, 1988)

Learning about the world is most effectively accomplished by an interactive process, in an environment created for active explorations and interactions with adults, other children, and materials. The process of engaging in such interactions results in learning. Finished products or "correct" solutions that conform to adult standards are not accurate criteria for judging whether learning has occurred. Much of a young child's learning takes place when the activities are self-directed. Successfully navigating an obstacle course or pouring water or beans from pitcher to pitcher makes children feel successful and also teaches a great deal. Such learning situations are devoid of adult judgments.

Play interaction, according to Jean Piaget, enables children to progress through cognitive development in prescribed stages:

- *Sensorimotor intelligence—infancy:* Intellectual growth occurs through the senses and inborn reflexive actions. Gradually, the beginning of symbolic thought develops, as is evidenced by improved memory.
- *Preoperational thought—preschool years:* The ability to use language develops and rapidly advances intellectual growth. The child operates in the world through egocentric perception.
- *Concrete operational thought—primary children:* The child moves on to concept development and the ability to see the point of view of others. Use of classification, seriation, one-to-one correspondence, and causality are tools for more abstract thought and the processing of information.

A child's mental processes for understanding knowledge develop gradually, and cognitive abilities evolve over a long period of time. Piaget attributes cognitive development to maturity, experiences, and social interactions. Knowledge is constructed as the child organizes and structures experiences (Bredekamp, 1986, pp. 3–4; Wilson, 1990, pp. 124–125; Wortham, 1990, p. 100).

Providing opportunities for varied experiences are basic to conceptual development. These include imitation, verbal stimulation, reading, and singing. Every challenging event adds to the child's wonder. Part of the whole process is encouraging curiosity and a desire to learn (Maxim, 1990). The child's experiences form the basis for the development of cognitive abilities.

MILESTONES OF COGNITIVE DEVELOPMENT FROM BIRTH TO FIVE YEARS

Age Range	Milestone	Activity
Birth to 3 months	1. Responds to sound and touch	1, 2, 3, 4, 5
	2. Looks at faces, patterns, objects	1, 2, 3, 4, 5
	3. Follows a moving object with eyes	4, 5
	4. Explores surroundings	3, 4, 5
3 to 6 months	5. Watches own fingers and hands	6, 7, 8, 9, 10
	6. Explores things by putting them in mouth	6, 7
	7. Reaches for a hanging object	8, 10
	8. Is attracted to people more than to objects	9, 10
	9. Responds to a sound that is out of sight	10
	10. Reaches and grasps for an object	6, 7, 8, 10
	11. Uses objects to make noise	6, 8, 10
	12. Searches for a partially hidden object	6, 7
	13. Anticipates reappearance of an object	6, 7, 9, 10
	14. Grasps two objects at the same time	6, 7, 8, 10
	15. Visually follows a fallen object	6, 7, 8, 10
	16. Imitates a vocal sound	9, 10
	17. Imitates and repeats an action	6, 7, 9, 10
6 to 12 months	18. Begins to develop concepts of in and out	11, 15
	19. Begins pointing	12, 15
	20. Performs action in order to get a result	13, 15
	21. Uncovers a hidden object	14, 15
	22. Puts objects into a container	16, 17, 18, 19
	23. Puts down one object to reach for another	16, 17, 18, 19
	24. Explores an object in a number of ways	16, 17, 18, 19
	25. Understands that objects have a front, back, top, and bottom	16, 18, 19
	26. Imitates hitting two objects	18, 19
	27. Imitates scribbling	20
1 to 1½ years	28. Uses trial-and-error approach	21, 22, 23, 24
	29. Uses an object to touch another object	21, 22, 23, 24
	30. Follows an object even when out of sight part of the time	22, 23
	31. Uses an object purposefully	21, 22, 23, 24
	32. Imitates any body gestures	21, 22, 23, 25

Age Range	Milestone	Activity
	33. Imitates new actions	21, 22, 23, 25
	34. Imitates household activities	22, 23
	35. Manipulates small objects	23, 24
1½ to 2 Years	36. Uses an object to affect another object	26, 27, 28
	37. Climbs to get something	29
	38. Moves around an obstacle if necessary	29
	39. Acts and uses toys in a functionally appropriate manner	26, 27, 28, 30
	40. Imitates actions and words from memory	28, 29, 30
2 to 3 years	41. Begins understanding size	31
	42. Begins understanding spatial relations	31
	43. Begins awareness of quantity	32
	44. Begins awareness of similarities	33
	45. Begins to sort	34
	46. Begins understanding part/whole relationships	35
3 to 4 years	47. Understands size	36, 37
	48. Understands spatial relationships	38
	49. Understands quantity	39
	50. Understands similarities	37, 39, 40
	51. Understands sorting	39, 40
	52. Understands part/whole relationships	39
	53. Makes comparisons by differences and similarities	37, 39, 40
4 to 5 years	54. Understands order by size or series	41
	55. Understands the events and the order of events in stories	41, 42
	56. Understands one-to-one correspondence	41, 43
	57. Understands subgroups	44
	58. Understands cause and effect	41
	59. Can count to 50 plus	41
	60. Understands and follows simple directions	41, 42, 44, 45
	61. Pretends and role plays	45

The items are numbered, but within an age range the order is not important. The stages of development are categorized by ages, but the ages are approximate. The order of the stages is the important thing.

ACTIVITIES FOR COGNITIVE DEVELOPMENT FROM BIRTH TO FIVE YEARS

Age Range	*Milestones*
Birth to 3 months	1 through 4

1. Hello and Goodbye—1, 2

ABOUT THE ACTIVITY   The more contact the parent has with the baby, the better. At this point, the best educational toy is the parent.

HOW TO PLAY   Hold the baby on your lap. Look at the baby and say, "Hello." Then say, "Goodbye," and look away. Repeat the words and the actions over and over. Keep creating with the idea. Add a handshake with "Hello" and a wave with "Goodbye." Extend the activity in any way that is comfortable for you and the baby.

2. Sing—Hum—Whistle—1, 2

ABOUT THE ACTIVITY   Music is soothing to a baby. It is also a means of communication. Since the baby will recognize a simple tune repeated over and over, singing, humming, and whistling are all ways to build memory skills.

HOW TO PLAY   Sing, hum, or whistle while you are with the baby. Excellent opportunities are bath, changing, or feeding time.

3. The Rocking Chair—1, 2, 4

ABOUT THE ACTIVITY   A rocking chair is a highly recommended piece of equipment from the time of pregnancy to the end of the developmental years. Movement is both calming and stimulating to the newborn and even to the unborn baby.

HOW TO PLAY   Hold the baby on your shoulder. Let the baby explore your face by touching you. Then hold the baby in your arms or on your lap. Let the baby grasp one of your fingers. Babies can grasp at birth as an inborn reflex, not as a conscious action. Talk to the baby in a natural manner as you interact.

4. The Packsack—1, 2, 3, 4

ABOUT THE ACTIVITY   Closeness and contact with the parent stimulate development. Movement also fosters development.

HOW TO PLAY   Take the baby with you from room to room. Put the baby on your body in a baby packsack, specially made for carrying an infant on your chest. The baby will be facing you. Talk to the baby about what you are doing, about what the baby is seeing, and about any important sounds you hear. Let the baby touch any interesting textures around you.

5. Looking—1, 2, 3, 4

ABOUT THE ACTIVITY   A newborn spends most of the time lying down and looking up and at the sides of the crib. Making the baby's looking experiences as meaningful as possible is beneficial.

HOW TO PLAY   There are several things you can do to the crib to make it more interesting. You can tie a piece of elastic across the crib and have threaded on the elastic four bulldog clips. From these clips you can attach many different items—a colored sock; a colored plastic measuring cup or spoon; a bell; colored paper cut into a shape, a letter, a number, or with a word written on it; a picture of the baby and other pictures of family members; colored cloth, ribbon, or pom poms; or any other interesting pictures or items that are safe and available (Figure 11.1). It is a good idea to change these items often and also to talk about them when you are with the baby. You can move these clips with items on them across the elastic and encourage the baby to follow the objects as you move them. In addition, there are suction cup clips available in most office supply stores that you can attach to the sides of the crib to hang any of these items. The baby will not be able to reach or grasp any of these items until about three months old. At that time you may want to move these items out of reach.

Age Range	*Milestones*
3 to 6 months	5 through 18

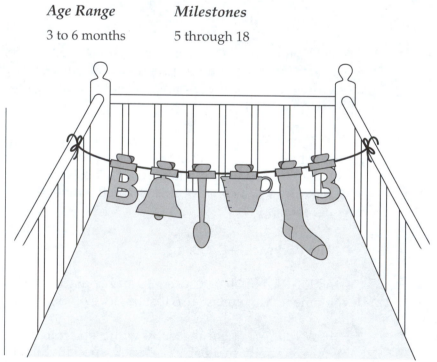

FIGURE 11.1
Looking

6. Chew a Toy—5, 6, 10, 11, 12, 13, 14, 15, 17

ABOUT THE ACTIVITY   The baby at this time is actively learning about the world through the five senses. Objects that are appealing and also safe for the mouth are appropriate.

HOW TO PLAY   Have available a group of objects that stimulate one or more of the five senses and are safe for exploration by mouth. Some suggestions are: a smooth clothespin (the old-fashioned kind, without a spring), a sponge, large empty spools of thread tied together securely by a ribbon, a set of brightly colored scrunchies (cloth-covered elastic hair ties), a smooth plastic bracelet, a rattle, the squeeze toy described above, or another object that is safe, not small enough to be swallowed, and easy to wash. As the baby plays with the object, name it and talk about its color, texture, uses, and other interesting attributes. Whatever you say is information that is being processed and therefore expanding the baby's knowledge. Do some of the same play activities with these objects as you did with the squeeze toy described below. In addition, encourage the baby to bang two of the toys together.

7. Squeeze a Toy—5, 6, 10, 12, 13, 14, 15, 17

ABOUT THE ACTIVITY   The baby at this time is gaining control of the world through hand movements. Things that invite touch will be helpful for encouraging a baby to use those hands.

HOW TO PLAY   Make a squeeze toy that is small and soft for the baby to hold and manipulate. An easy way to do this is to take a knee-high stocking and stuff it with cotton. You can tie it off at the end or tie it in segments. The baby will enjoy playing with the soft squeeze toy in a natural way. In addition, you can hide part of it and see if the baby can still find it. You can hide it behind your back and see if the baby will try to look for it before you bring it back in sight. You can see if the baby can grasp two of these at the same time, or if the baby can grasp two of the segments at the same time. You can drop this soft, quiet toy while you and the baby are on a chair and see if the baby follows it as it falls. You can drop it and retrieve it and then give it to the baby to do the same thing. You can take turns playing with this very soft toy. Try to imitate what the baby does and then see if the baby will try to imitate what you do.

8. Reach, Grasp, and Move—5, 7, 10, 11, 14, 15

ABOUT THE ACTIVITY   The baby will probably be reaching and grasping well by four to five months. At this time you can substitute large binder rings for the bulldog clips. These are also available from an office supply store. You can hang rings from rings or tie ribbons on them. You can also attach to the rings empty spools of thread, plastic measuring cups or spoons, or any other safe and convenient items with holes in them.

HOW TO PLAY   Encourage the baby to reach for the items and to move them. You can also participate in the activity by talking about what you or the baby is doing with the items.

9. Mirror Magic—5, 8, 13, 16, 17

ABOUT THE ACTIVITY   A mirror by itself is a magical toy that never shows the same thing twice. A baby will look and react over and over again. If you interact with the baby with this toy, the baby will get even more out of the experiences.

HOW TO PLAY   Look in the mirror together with the baby. Ask questions like "Who is it?" and "What is that?" The baby will respond with delight. Then do some actions and try to encourage imitation. Nod your head, make a clucking sound, or make some simple movements with your hands, feet, or upper body. You can use a large wall mirror or a small unbreakable play one.

10. Bath Splash—5, 7, 8, 9, 10, 11, 13, 14, 15, 16, 17

ABOUT THE ACTIVITY   Once the baby can sit up, he or she can play well in the bath. Hands will be free to hold things and splash, and feet will be free to kick.

HOW TO PLAY   Place a few bath toys in the water at bath time and let the baby play with them freely. Move the baby's hands to splash, and encourage imitation. Then move the baby's feet to splash, and again encourage imitation. Take one of the toys and use it in different ways: Hold it high and watch the baby reach for it. Drop it in the water and listen together for the splash. Drop it in the water behind the baby and see if the baby turns to the sound. Drop it in the water from up high and see if the baby follows it down. Make some sounds you have heard the baby make and see if the baby will imitate them. Push, pull, or squeeze a toy and see if the baby will imitate what you have done. Imitate any of the baby's movements in the bath. Then see if the baby will imitate them back.

Age Range	*Milestones*
6 to 12 months	18 through 27

11. Container Time—18

ABOUT THE ACTIVITY   Babies at this age love to empty and fill containers. The recycling bin is the place to go to generate this activity. It is good to find containers of various sizes and shapes and smaller items that the babies can put in and empty out. The items chosen should not be small enough to be swallowed. Possibilities include the chew toys from Activity 6, blocks, or smaller containers that can fit into larger ones. The Color Boxes from Chapter 2 can be used with one or two items, and the Shape Boxes from Chapter 2 can be used as described.

HOW TO PLAY   Give the baby a safe container and one or two objects that can be placed inside it. Encourage the baby to empty and fill the container. Be sure to take your turn with this activity and also to describe the activity verbally. Carefully say for the baby "in" when the object is in the container and "out" when the object is out.

12. Pick and Choose—19

ABOUT THE ACTIVITY   At this stage the baby is showing the beginnings of preference. This starts with pointing.

HOW TO PLAY   You can play this anywhere there is room to place two interesting items—on the floor, on the high chair, or on any other kind of flat surface or tray. Place the items in front of the baby but just out of reach, and then ask, "Which one do you want?" After the baby points to one of the items, move the item within range for the baby to take it. Feeding time can be made more fun with this pointing activity. You can have the baby point to a spoon or a cup, then a piece of soft bread or a piece of banana, and then some other food item.

13. Drop and Retrieve—20

ABOUT THE ACTIVITY   Babies in this stage like to drop and throw things. They know how to hold on and let go, and they love to do it over and over. Part of the idea of this activity is to make the parent's retrieval responsibility easier, and the other is for play. In addition, the whole activity teaches cause and effect.

HOW TO PLAY   Tie a foot-long string or ribbon to as many play objects as are available. Then tie these onto the key places where the baby sits and plays—the high chair, a swing or bounce chair, a crib, or a stroller. Let the baby drop and throw objects at any time. Be there to encourage retrieval.

14. Where Is It?—21

ABOUT THE ACTIVITY   Babies at this time have memory of objects that are out of sight. They remember who their parents are, even when the parents are out of sight. That is why they begin to fuss about being with strangers. A game using this memory can be fun.

HOW TO PLAY   Take out a washcloth and a few toys. Take turns hiding a toy under a wash cloth and then lifting up the washcloth to find the hidden item. Help the baby as much or as little as is necessary to both hide and uncover the object.

15. Water or Sand Exploration—18, 19, 20, 21

ABOUT THE ACTIVITY   Water and sand are two types of play environments that are stimulating for many play activities.

HOW TO PLAY   Share water or sand play with the baby. Water toys and sand toys can be emptied and filled many times over. They can also be used for pointing activities. In addition they help a baby work toward a desired result of building, moving, or experiencing. A toy hidden in the sand or under water can be uncovered by memory.

16. Empty and Fill—22, 23, 24, 25

ABOUT THE ACTIVITY   The baby by this time may have quite a lot of mobility. This will keep him able to carry out an activity for a longer time. While the baby could put in and take out one or two items in a container from age six to nine months, the baby can now become immersed in an empty–fill activity.

HOW TO PLAY   Set up the baby with a Color Box from Chapter 2. You can have a good time with it together. Another idea is to set up a big container with discarded mail in it. Take turns taking out a piece of mail. Talk to the baby about the different pieces of mail. Point out alphabet letters, numbers, shapes, and words of interest. Feel free to count the mail pieces; order them by size; or sort them by size, shape, color, or texture.

17. Clothes Pin Drop—22, 23, 24

ABOUT THE ACTIVITY   Old-fashioned clothespins, without a spring, and a metal baking pan are good for this activity.

HOW TO PLAY   Take ten clothespins and place them around the edge of the baking pan. Show the baby how to pull them off and drop them into the pan. Take turns doing this with the baby. Then set up clothespins again and restart the play.

18. Pots and Pans—22, 23, 24, 25, 26

ABOUT THE ACTIVITY   Pots and pans are well known as favorite toys for babies this age. Letting nature be the guide, it is worthwhile to take out the pots and pans.

HOW TO PLAY   Put a plastic cup in a pot and cover the pot with the lid. Watch the baby open the lid and discover the cup. Allow the baby to bang two lids together to the beat of marching music like a set of cymbals. Hide the cup in one of three covered pots. Let the baby find it. Then let the baby hide it for you.

19. Coffee Can Drop—22, 23, 24, 25, 26

ABOUT THE ACTIVITY   Cut a circle the size of a plastic milk carton cap in an empty coffee can lid. Place the lid back on the can. Then collect ten milk carton caps.

HOW TO PLAY   Take turns placing the round caps into the round circle cut into the lid of the can. After the can is filled with the ten caps, show the baby how to take the lid off the can and empty it out. Put the lid back on and play again.

20. Scribble It—27

ABOUT THE ACTIVITY   Since this is the very beginning of the baby's ability to put crayons to paper, it is good to do it in as controlled a way as possible.

HOW TO PLAY   Tape a large sheet of brown paper to the floor. Hand the baby two or three thick crayons and guide the scribbling. Allow as much free scribbling on the paper as possible.

Age Range	Milestones
1 to 1½ years	28 through 35

21. Pull Toy—28, 29, 31, 32, 33

ABOUT THE ACTIVITY   A toddler likes to pull practically anything attached to a string or a rope. There are many pull toys you can buy and an endless variety you can make. The ones you make can involve the added creativity of simulating a train, car, boat, or other form of transportation.

HOW TO PLAY   Make a train, car, or boat for your toddler by putting one or a series of any of these items onto a string: empty spools of thread, pine cones, small boxes, hair rollers, or other small items. Take turns with the toddler pulling the toy. Pretend you are going on all kinds of trips to all kinds of destinations. Take the toy around corners and to different parts of the house. Encourage the toddler to imitate you.

22. Housekeeping—28, 29, 30, 31, 32, 33, 34

ABOUT THE ACTIVITY   Since toddlers can push and pull, they are interested in imitating many housekeeping activities. Sweeping and mopping are very appealing to toddlers.

HOW TO PLAY   Cut the handle of a broom or a mop to the toddler's size. Then get your full-sized broom or mop and start to clean. As you do, talk about how you clean and encourage the toddler to do the same. Any meaningful help the toddler can give will be beneficial to you both.

23. Cooking toys—28, 29, 30, 31, 32, 33, 34, 35

ABOUT THE ACTIVITY   Plastic containers, plastic plates and cutlery, plastic cups, and some old pots and pans are excellent toys for toddlers. They can explore all aspects of these items and also experience the beginnings of pretend play.

HOW TO PLAY   Set aside an empty drawer or cabinet to store special play cooking equipment for the toddler. Let the toddler play freely and also show him or her what you are doing with similar items. Encourage any toddler activities that look similar to real cooking activities.

24. How It Works—28, 29, 31, 35

ABOUT THE ACTIVITY   The toddler's curiosity is growing by leaps and bounds. Any way to stimulate and enrich it is worthwhile.

HOW TO PLAY   Show the toddler how things work. Explain as much as you can of different routine procedures—opening a door with a key, zipping a zipper, pouring water, and more.

25. Follow the Direction—32, 33

ABOUT THE ACTIVITY   The toddler can understand simple directions and also has strong enough body control to go into different places and spots.

HOW TO PLAY   Put each of these direction words on a separate index card: *under, next to, inside, behind,* and so on. Take turns picking a card and then give your child a direction based on the word on the card. Use sentences like these: "Go *under* the table." "Stand *next to* the door." "Sit *inside* the bathtub." "Go *behind* the tree."

Age Range	*Milestones*
1½ to 2 years	36 through 40

26. Blocks or the Bottle Cap Substitute—36, 39

ABOUT THE ACTIVITY   Building skills are becoming more advanced.

HOW TO PLAY   Start with free play and exploring with blocks. You can imitate what your toddler does. You can also make some of your own simple structures and watch for imitation. Large, safe bottle caps can provide another interesting medium for beginning building skills. This concept is explained further in Chapter 2.

27. Puzzled—36, 39

ABOUT THE ACTIVITY   Choose an appropriate puzzle for this developmental stage. Then encourage the toddler through each step of the activity. Homemade as well as purchased puzzles are effective.

HOW TO PLAY   Set out a puzzle before the toddler. A purchased puzzle will have the age range identified. Homemade ones can be made in several different ways. One is to write the child's name on a piece of construction paper and have the toddler scribble crayon decorations on it. Then cut the paper into several puzzle pieces. Another is to write the child's name on a long sheet of construction paper and cut it into a strip. Then cut the strip into rectangles, with one letter per rectangle. Have the child put the pieces together. Then take your turn with the puzzle.

28. Play Ball—36, 39, 40

ABOUT THE ACTIVITY   This is a good time to introduce free play and experimentation with a ball, preferably a large rubber one or a small beach ball. Since the ball never does the same thing twice, use it to stimulate you to think of new and personalized ideas that will be effective for you and your toddler.

HOW TO PLAY   Sit opposite the toddler and roll the ball back and forth. Then think of other rolling games. One idea is something like bowling. Set up a small configuration of blocks or bottle caps. Then take turns rolling the ball to knock over the configuration. You can each set up a configuration for the other to knock down. Think up as many ball games as are fun and appropriate for you and your toddler to play.

29. Animals and Their Sounds—37, 38, 40

ABOUT THE ACTIVITY   Young children identify closely with the world of animals. They find animals cute and fun to imitate. They will enjoy pretending to be like animals and also saying their sounds.

HOW TO PLAY   List on index cards many different animals to which the child has been exposed. Take turns picking a card and then acting out the animal, including the sound it makes—for example, dog with a woof, cat with a meow, lion with a roar, duck with a quack. Have fun with this game by climbing up on chairs and moving around objects.

30. Body Identification—39, 40

ABOUT THE ACTIVITY   Older toddlers have a lot of memory about different body actions. This is an excellent age to introduce body part identification along with simple body actions.

HOW TO PLAY   Put as many body part words as you wish on separate index cards. Examples are: *hand, mouth, eyes,* and *toes.* Take turns picking a card and then giving the child a direction based on the word on the card. Use sentences like these: "Wave hi with your *hand.*" "Smile with your *mouth.*" "Close your *eyes.*" "Wiggle your *toes.*"

Age Range	*Milestones*
2 to 3 years	41 through 46

31. Cars on the Road—41, 42

ABOUT THE ACTIVITY   Play experiences can become more representational at this age. They can have more meaning and be more personalized and directed.

HOW TO PLAY   Set up a road system on a carpet or floor. Get out all the toy cars, trucks, and trains available and start to play. There are different ways to make the roads. You can use two ribbon strips to outline a road wide enough for the chosen cars. You can use masking tape to do the same thing. You can use material or wrapping paper that can be cut into long strips. You can even use a wide sheet of brown paper on which you can draw a road and any other landscape you wish. Use all kinds of language and enjoy your road adventure together.

32. Rice Is Nice—43

ABOUT THE ACTIVITY   At this time the child is gaining an understanding of quantity.

HOW TO PLAY   Put dry, uncooked rice in a small juice cup, about half full. Then get out a large cup. Have the child pour the rice from the small cup into the large cup. It will look like less in the large cup, but point out to the child that the amount of rice remains the same. Have the child pour the rice from the large cup into the small cup. It will look like more in the small cup. Again point out to the child that the amount remains the same. Together enjoy sharing this pouring activity. After each time the rice is poured, say, "The same." Encourage the child to say it as well.

33. Match Maker—44

ABOUT THE ACTIVITY   Visual discrimination is quite well developed, and this opens up the door to a wide range of matching activities. A technique for providing an endless number of play opportunities is to use a set of 3″ × 5″ index cards and your choice of children's stickers.

HOW TO PLAY   Make two sets of identical cards with matching sets of stickers on them. Start by laying out five sticker cards. Then take turns with the child picking from the match pile and making a match. If the child is ready to choose matches from a larger number of choices, set up the next round with more choices. Choose appropriate stickers—ones with fine differences in discrimination or ones with greater differences—depending on the child's ability and preference. A wide range of stickers is usually available in variety stores.

34. Sorting It Out—45

ABOUT THE ACTIVITY   A set of any kind of blocks is good for this activity. The first part of this activity is excellent for sorting, and the second part develops visual discrimination on the first level and memory on the highest level.

HOW TO PLAY   Choose a category to sort by. Color is good for a start. Find a good-sized container from the recycling bin. If that doesn't work, find another plastic container, preferably the size of a fruit bowl or a large mixing bowl. Take turns with the child putting all blocks of a selected color inside the container. When that task is accomplished, take out a set of three that are different shapes. Then, as the child watches, take one shape away and ask, "What shape is missing?" When the child says the correct shape, say something like, "I can't fool you." If the child does not say the correct shape or does not say anything at all, you say, "The _____ is missing." Try the activity again, sorting by shapes. Take turns with the child putting all blocks of a selected shape inside the container. When the task is accomplished, take out a set of three that are different colors. Then, as the child watches, take one color away and ask, "What color is missing?" When the child says the correct color, again say something like, "I can't fool you." If the child does not say the correct color or does not say anything at all, you say, "The _____ is missing." Try this activity by sorting other colors, other shapes, or by size. When you get up to selecting the missing one of three, you can also ask the child to have closed eyes when you take one of the blocks away. After the guess is made, whether it is right or wrong, show the child the actual block that was removed.

35. Piece of the Pie—46

ABOUT THE ACTIVITY   Around this time the child is starting to understand the concepts of part and whole. This makes paper plates an excellent play material because you can cut them into four, five, or six pie-shaped pieces.

HOW TO PLAY   First take away one piece and ask the child to replace it accurately. Then take away two, then three, and ask the child after each one to replace them. Have the child do the same activity with you. You can both color designs on the plates before you cut them.

Age Range	*Milestones*
3 to 4 years	47 through 53

36. Size It Up—47

ABOUT THE ACTIVITY   Since the concept of size has become more fixed, use different objects in the house to seek and find.

HOW TO PLAY   Take turns finding a big object and then ask the child to find a little example of the same object. Then take turns finding a little object and asking the child to find a big one. For example, you can find a big pencil and ask for a little one, a big sock and ask for a little one, a little shirt and ask for a big one. It will be fun hunting up items that will have size matches.

37. Stringing Pasta—47, 50, 53

ABOUT THE ACTIVITY   There are different sizes of pasta that you can use for stringing. Stringing can be the end goal of the activity, or the child can make a necklace to wear. Plain pasta can be used with yarn, or the child can paint the pasta with food coloring.

HOW TO PLAY   Rigatoni is the largest size, for the children with the least motor control. Macaroni, shells, and other sizes are for fingers with more control. A child has the option of using pasta pieces that are exactly the same or ones that are different. Different ones lend themselves to patterns. Take turns with the child telling which piece of pasta should go on next. Describe the pieces by color, size, or shape. For additional memory development, you can give two or three directions, like "first a big one and then a small one" or "first a red one, then a yellow, and then a blue."

38. I See—48

ABOUT THE ACTIVITY   The child is learning more and more about the environment every day. This activity provides a good way to both acknowledge and stimulate the child's new interest in detail.

HOW TO PLAY   Sit together on a couch or on two comfortable chairs. Face the same wall of the room. The more detail there is on the wall, the better it is for this activity. Take turns with the child asking, "What do you see?" and "Where is it?" Then take turns answering something like, "I see a picture" and "It is over the sofa."

39. Terrific Ten—49, 50, 51, 52, 53

ABOUT THE ACTIVITY   Exposure to the quantity of 10 in a play way provides a foundation for the many mathematical activities that will soon be ahead for the child.

HOW TO PLAY   Collect simple household objects that can be found in units of 10. Some examples are: clothespins (the kind without springs), buttons (not small enough to swallow), large paper clips, bottle caps, rubber bands, pencils, crayons, markers, and so on. Start using them in the group of 10. Take turns with the child saying, "Give me some." Wait until you get some. Then say, "Give me all of them." After you get some, count them. Then after you get all of them, count them again. Then select five different items. Ask the child to close his or her eyes. Then take away one item. When the eyes are opened, ask the child which item has been taken away. Take turns with this game and increase the number of items if appropriate.

40. Sort It Out—50, 51, 53

ABOUT THE ACTIVITY   Use catalogs or magazines for cutting out pictures. Cutting can be an activity that you do together. Give as little or as much help to the child as needed in the actual cutting. The focus of this activity is on finding the pictures to cut out.

HOW TO PLAY   Think of different categories to sort by. Some examples are: things that happen during the day and things that happen at night, food and drinks, men and women, boys and girls, indoor scenes and outdoor scenes. Choose a category and begin finding the pictures. After you have a nice collection, begin sorting the pictures into two piles. Counting the pictures in each pile adds to the fun.

Age Range	*Milestones*
4 to 5 years	54 through 60

41. A Picture Is Worth a Thousand Words—54, 55, 56, 58, 59, 60

ABOUT THE ACTIVITY   You need a catalogue or magazine with colorful pictures in it. Categorization is the focus as with the last activity, but the concepts are deeper and more refined.

HOW TO PLAY   Look at the pictures together. As you look, use any of the following questions that relate to a particular page and take turns answering them. Continue as you both like with more pages and more questions.

1. What can walk, talk, eat, sleep, breathe, fly, sit, stand, hear, think, drive?
2. Which one is the biggest, smallest, softest, hardest, cutest, happiest, funniest?
3. Which have you never seen, seen often, always wanted to see, never wanted to see?

4. Name what you see on the page in order of size from smallest to biggest and then from biggest to smallest?
5. What is the same about _____ and _____? What is different about _____ and _____?
6. Find all the squares, circles, triangles, and any other noticeable shapes.
7. Why is the person happy, sad, tired, angry, or scared?
8. What do you think happened before this picture took place? What is happening now? What do you think will happen next?
9. Count by pointing with your finger the number of people, animals, cars, trees, food items, or other appropriate pictures.
10. Whom do you like in the picture? Why? Is there anyone you do not like? Why?

42. Hear It, Picture It, Draw It—55, 60

ABOUT THE ACTIVITY   Being able to understand the spoken word is important for reading comprehension. Reading aloud to children helps them with their reading comprehension.

HOW TO PLAY   Choose a children's book together with the child. Read aloud a vivid paragraph to the child. Then ask your child to draw the picture it brings to mind. Next, if age- and ability-appropriate, ask the child to read a paragraph to you for you to draw. Continue reading aloud vivid paragraphs and taking turns drawing the pictures as long as there is interest.

43. Talk about a Picture—56

ABOUT THE ACTIVITY   Talking about a picture enables you to see it in greater detail, to get more out of it.

HOW TO PLAY   Choose a picture from a book, a painting, a photograph, a drawing, or even a view from a window. Then take turns telling what you see. What each of you says enables the other one to see more detail and meaning than either of you was able to see before.

44. Field Trips in and Around the House—57, 60

ABOUT THE ACTIVITY   Each room in the house and the outdoors holds a wealth of information that can be uncovered through play.

HOW TO PLAY

- **IN THE KITCHEN,** look for a category of items, such as utensils. Take turns finding spatulas, egg beaters, can openers, scoops, salad servers, and more. Each time you find one, describe its use. If the child does not know a name or use, fill in the information. Other categories include food, dishes, and pots and pans. Sample subcategories include foods that are vegetables, dishes that are plastic, and pots and pans that have lids.

- **IN THE BEDROOM,** look for a category of items, such as jewelry. Take turns finding earrings, necklaces, bracelets, charms, rings, and more. Each time you find one, describe it, tell why you like it, when it is worn, whether it reminds you of something. Use the jewelry to create, role-play, enjoy. Help the child out naturally and as needed. Other categories include clothing, toys, and furniture. Sample subcategories include shirts, toys with parts, furniture with drawers, and many other variations.

- **OUTDOORS,** look for a category of items, such as things that are hard. Take turns finding stones, branches, and any other creations of nature. Each time you find one, describe its size, its color, and why you like it. Maybe you will think of a way to use it. Collect nature's treasures in a brown bag, small bucket, or other easy-to-carry container. Back at the house, if time, energy, and interest permit, make a nature collage. Other categories include things that are green, soft, wet, and so on. Sample subcategories include green things that are big, soft things that move, and wet things that will soon dry.

45. Do What It Says—60, 61

ABOUT THE ACTIVITY   Participation and action add to the effectiveness of activities. Being able to act out a word or words makes learning to read them easier and more fun.

HOW TO PLAY   Write directions on index cards, one direction per card, and place the pack of cards face down in front of you and the child. Take turns picking a card and following the direction on it. You can start this game on the simplest level with one-word directions, and then gradually increase to two, three, and four words. If age- and ability-appropriate, you can play this game with sentences and then short paragraphs. The following are examples of directions in ascending order:

Hop   Jump   Kick   Clap   Walk   Skip   Hide   Sing   Talk
Stand up. Sit down. Clap hands. Bend down. Bump elbows.
Tie the shoe. Touch your toes. Write your name. Open the door.
Sit in the chair. Turn on the light. Pick up the paper. (See Figure 2.3 in
    Chapter 2.)

CHAPTER 12

A Practical Approach to Motor Development

Children have an inborn drive to move. Motor development in children from birth to age five varies. Children start to walk earlier or later, and it does not mean they are more or less intelligent. Physical stimulation by adults does, however, help the child develop motor coordination earlier. Early mobility fosters confidence and also enhances visual, spatial, and tactile facility. In addition, mobility helps the child to satisfy natural curiosity by broadening the child's opportunities for exploration.

Thus, providing an environment that promotes physical development is both desirable and possible. It arises naturally out of normal baby and child care situations. Every contact that includes moving, touching, and holding the child can be performed in a way that enhances development. These contacts include carrying the child, changing, washing, feeding, and playing.

These practices have positive results with all children. They are especially helpful to children with delayed development because of the way they help the child structure his or her body. Certain activities can help prevent deformities, correct bad posture, improve balance, and speed up development.

Motor activities contribute directly to the development of the brain and to the organization of the nervous system. From birth to three months, relaxation techniques represent the majority of the movements. From three to six months, exercises are for preparation of the sitting position. From six to twelve months, mastering the sitting position and preparing for the standing position become the focus. From nine months on, interactions are for developing play, mastering the standing position, and preparing for movement independence.

No area of development functions in a vacuum. All activities designed for physical development should be accompanied by talk, song, rhythm, and music. A calm atmosphere should be provided as much as is possible. It is easy to see how parent–child physical interaction will promote bonding, the foundation for social and cognitive development.

Major strides in muscle development take place from birth to fifteen months, the months that take the child from no motor skills at all through to being a very accomplished toddler. Any positions or activities that cause the child to use muscles will be effective. In addition, any environments that stimulate movement are appropriate.

Play activities are a major part of child development because it is play situations that encourage movement. Babies move to get a toy or object of interest. They also strive for new positions to be able to do, see, or experience pleasure (Levy, 1973).

The general area of motor development is made up of two parts—gross motor, which has to do with large body movement, and fine motor, which has to do with hand and finger control. These two parts are mixed in the chart that follows.

Motor development is a transformation of a young child's muscles and general body build, a changing of body proportions and physical skills. The baby shows rapid growth during the first year, with major changes in ability developing quickly. The toddler's round, babylike shape grows slimmer and increases in size, with a consequent increase in motor abilities. During the preschool years, the muscle and skeletal systems continue to develop, and the head and brain reach almost their adult size, again with new skill capability as a result. All physical growth throughout the developmental years from birth to age five brings with it new opportunities for both gross and fine motor development (Spodek & Saracho, 1994, p. 82).

MILESTONES OF MOTOR DEVELOPMENT FROM BIRTH TO FIVE YEARS

Age Range	Milestone	Activity
Birth to 3 months	1. Keeps arms and legs bent and fists clenched	1, 2
	2. Follows object with eyes	3
	3. Lifts head and chest while lying on stomach	4
	4. Holds head steady while upright	5
3 to 6 months	5. Looks, reaches, and grasps at the same time	6, 7, 10
	6. Sits supported	6, 7, 8, 10
	7. Rolls from back to stomach	9, 10
6 to 12 months	8. Transfers object from one hand to the other	11, 15
	9. Creeps forward or backward	12
	10. Pulls to standing	13, 14
	11. Sits unsupported and reaches	15
	12. Puts objects into a container	15
	13. Brings hands together to body midline	15, 16
	14. Uses pincer grasp (thumb and forefinger)	15, 17
	15. Hands object to another person	15
	16. Crawls	18, 19
	17. Crawls upstairs	18, 19
	18. Rolls or pushes an object	20
	19. Walks holding onto furniture	20
	20. Walks	20
1 to 1½ years	21. Stacks about two blocks or similar objects	21, 22
	22. Begins to scribble	23
	23. Starts to throw objects	24
	24. Crawls downstairs	25
1½ to 2 years	25. Turns a knob	26
	26. Stacks about six blocks	26
	27. Uses a push or pull toy	27
	28. Kicks a ball	28
	29. Begins to run	27
	30. Walks up and down stairs	29
	31. Jumps	30

Age Range	Milestone	Activity
2 to 3 years	32. Begins to show hand dominance	31
	33. Stacks about eight blocks	31
	34. Throws a ball overhead	32
	35. Climbs in and out of an adult chair	33
	36. Climbs on a gym set	33, 34
	37. Rides a tricycle	35
	38. Walks upstairs with alternating feet	34
	39. Coordinates a two-handed activity	31
	40. Walks downstairs alternating feet	34
3 to 4 years	41. Cuts and pastes	36
	42. Ties a knot	37
	43. Strings large beads	38
	44. Scribbles or draws	39
	45. Begins to hop	40
4 to 5 years	46. Cuts on a line with scissors	41
	47. Prints most upper-case and some lower-case letters	41
	48. Writes numbers up to 10	41
	49. Prints name	42
	50. Fastens, buckles, or ties	43
	51. Catches a ball	43, 44
	52. Colors within lines and does puzzles	42
	53. Walk upstairs without holding a rail	45
	54. Skips	43
	55. Learns to ride a two-wheeled bike, to roller skate, and to do somersaults	43

The items are numbered, but within an age range the order is not important. The stages of development are categorized by ages, but the ages are approximate. The order of the stages is the important thing.

PLAY ACTIVITIES FOR MOTOR DEVELOPMENT FROM BIRTH TO FIVE YEARS

Age Range	*Milestones*
Birth to 3 months	1 through 4

1. Relax the Baby—1

ABOUT THE ACTIVITY   The newborn's body is tense. The effects of having been in the fetal position can still be seen.

HOW TO PLAY   Lay the baby on a soft surface like a bed. Pat the baby slowly, regularly, and softly on the arms, legs, and tummy. Gradually you will feel the body relax. Then slowly open and close the arms across the baby's chest. Slowly, holding the baby under the knees, push the legs up and down to extend and stretch out the muscles.

2. Opening the Hand—1

ABOUT THE ACTIVITY   The newborn has a reflex grasp, left over from the fetal position. It is helpful to loosen it up.

HOW TO PLAY   Lay the baby on a soft surface like a bed. Begin the loosening at the shoulder by making regular pats along the arm to the hand. As the arm relaxes and the hand opens, raise the baby's arm. When the hand opens, take the baby's hand and stroke the baby's face and body, then your own face and body, and then your hand.

3. Look at It—2

ABOUT THE ACTIVITY   Sight is developing as soon as the baby is born. Providing opportunities for focusing and following an object help the baby adjust to the new outside world.

HOW TO PLAY   Lay the baby on a soft surface like a bed. This can also be done in a crib or stroller. Cross the baby's arms across the chest. Then open them up. Cross and open a few times in a row. After this movement, the hands will probably lie somewhat open at the baby's sides. Hold out a soft small toy or object for the baby to touch. A small puff ball, a small stuffed animal, a rattle, or another soft object can be used. After the baby has experienced touching the toy or object, hold it out so that the baby can see it. Then move it slowly from left to right across the baby's view. Move it in such a way that you are aware of the baby tracking it.

4. Baby Up—3

ABOUT THE ACTIVITY   Positioning the baby on the tummy opens up a new view and develops new body awareness.

HOW TO PLAY   On the bed or other soft surface, place the baby on the tummy. Place a small soft pillow, if available, under the tummy. The baby should lean on the hands or forearms and be encouraged to push up with the arms. Stroke the length of the back to encourage raising the head and back.

5. Head Up—4

ABOUT THE ACTIVITY   This is an activity to do while holding the baby. It is for strengthening the neck and back muscles.

HOW TO PLAY   Hold the baby with the baby's back against you. Support the baby with one hand on the baby's chest and one hand on the baby's knees. With the baby facing away from you, bring the baby over to a mirror. Let the baby lean over as far as desired toward the mirror. Interest in the baby's image in the mirror will encourage the baby to straighten from the back and neck.

Age Range	Milestones
3 to 6 months	5 through 7

6. Look, Reach, and Grasp—5, 6

ABOUT THE ACTIVITY   Muscle development is the key for this age range. This activity strengthens the gross motor neck and stomach muscles as well as the fine motor reach and grasp techniques.

HOW TO PLAY   Lay the baby on a soft surface like a bed. Have the baby grasp your thumbs and encourage a pull-up. Next, while you hold down the baby's legs, move and support the baby's head to encourage the baby to rise up toward you. Show a small toy or appealing object to encourage the baby to rise and move toward you. Then encourage the baby to reach for and grasp the toy or object.

7. Look, Reach, and Grasp Again—5, 6

ABOUT THE ACTIVITY   Whereas Activity 6 was designed to strengthen the neck and stomach muscles, this activity is designed to strengthen the neck and back muscles. Neck, stomach, and back muscle development are precursors to the sitting position.

HOW TO PLAY   Hold the baby face down with one hand on the knees and the other under the chest. Place the baby in a position with his or her hands bouncing on a table or on the floor. Place a toy or interesting object just in front of the baby. You will start to feel the back and neck being held up. At some point you will see full support of the baby on outstretched arms. In this position, allow the baby to reach for and grasp the toy or object.

8. Pull to Sitting—6

ABOUT THE ACTIVITY   This is direct preparation for sitting.

HOW TO PLAY   Place the baby on its back on a bed or on a soft surface. Hold the baby's head and right shoulder up. Raise the baby slightly, turning the chest over to the left so that the baby rests on the left shoulder, then on the left elbow, then on the left hand, and then eventually ends up in the sitting position. Repeat the activity from the other side.

9. Rolling Over—7

ABOUT THE ACTIVITY   The beginning roll is from back to stomach.

HOW TO PLAY   Place the baby on its back on a bed or soft surface. Holding the legs, flex the right leg. From the hip, naturally guide the baby from left to right as you face the baby, gently turning the baby from back to tummy. You can repeat this activity several times.

10. Pedaling—5, 6, 7

ABOUT THE ACTIVITY   This position is good for developing control with feet and back muscle development for both sitting and turning over.

HOW TO PLAY   Place the baby on its back in a crib where something is hanging down above the baby's tummy. (Refer to Cognitive Development Activities numbers 5 and 8 and to Figure 11.1.) Hold the baby gently by the hands with outstretched arms. Draw attention to the hanging toy and encourage the baby to reach for it with the feet. Move the baby a little further away from the toy to increase difficulty.

Age Range	*Milestones*
6 to 12 months	8 through 20

11. Shape Up—8

ABOUT THE ACTIVITY   Supported or unsupported sitting will work for this activity. The Shape Boxes described in Chapter 2 are recommended for this activity.

HOW TO PLAY   Place the baby in a sitting position. Sit across from the baby. Take a Shape Box and give one to the baby. Take out your shape. Move it back and forth from hand to hand and then place it in the correct hole of the shape box. Encourage the baby to go through the same motions, first moving the shape from the Shape Box back and forth from hand to hand and then placing the shape in the correct hole in the Shape Box. Use all three Shape Boxes, taking a turn with each one. If you have the large container that has a lid with three shapes in it as shown in Chapter 2, use that one as well in this activity. Help the baby as much or as little as is necessary in fitting the correct shape into the correctly shaped hole.

12. You Can Get It—9

ABOUT THE ACTIVITY   The Name Toy described in Chapter 2 is recommended for this activity. The one to use is the one that stands up.

HOW TO PLAY   Place the Name Toy on the floor a good distance away from the baby. Then kneel behind the toy in a crawling position. Let the picture side of the toy show to the baby. Then tell the baby to come to you and to (*Baby's Name*). Point to the baby's picture as you say (*Baby's Name*). After the baby gets there, let the baby play with the card. Then repeat the activity with the name side of the card showing to the baby.

13. Hoop It Up—10

ABOUT THE ACTIVITY   The crib is the standard place for a baby to learn to pull up to a standing position. A coffee table is also a good height. Of course, it should be cleared of breakable items. A hula hoop placed around your waist can be held out securely in front of you for a baby to use as a support for pulling up. The hoop gives the baby an appropriate-sized handle.

HOW TO PLAY   Hold a hula hoop around you securely. Then position yourself near the baby. Tell the baby to grab on to it and to pull up. With your body you will be able to control the pull-up activity well.

14. Who Is That?—10

ABOUT THE ACTIVITY   This is an effective position for holding the baby at almost any time. It will allow the baby maximum view and also maximum muscle development leading to the standing position.

HOW TO PLAY   Hold the baby against you facing away from you. Put one hand under the baby's knees and the other under the chest. Give less support under the chest by gradually lowering your hand. Bring the baby over to a mirror in this position. Encourage the baby to lean toward the baby image in the mirror, as will be natural. Say something like, "Who is that?" over and over. Expect a big smile with some appropriate vocalizations. After the response, say something like, "Yes, you are right. That is (*Baby's Name*).

15. Sitting on a Stool—8, 11, 12, 13, 14, 15

ABOUT THE ACTIVITY   Sitting the baby on a stool strengthens the back muscles and frees the arms for play.

HOW TO PLAY   Seat the child on the stool with feet on the ground, ankles at right angles to the feet, knees at right angles to the thighs, and hips at right angles to the trunk. Sit behind the baby, holding the baby by one thigh alone and avoiding support for the back. Give the baby time to find and gain balance. A baby close to unsupported sitting may accomplish this milestone by straightening the back, turning from side to side, and feeling support from having the feet on the ground. Remove support from the baby's thigh if you see and feel that the baby has attained sitting balance.

Independent sitting, or even minimally supported sitting, opens up avenues for different kinds of play. Give the baby a small toy or interesting object and take turns with the baby transferring it from one hand to the other. Then take turns passing it back and forth to each other. With a container, take turns putting the object in and taking it out. Take turns clapping your hands—first you, then the baby, and so on. Fill a container with raisins or Cheerios. Take turns with the baby picking up one piece at a time with the forefinger and thumb and eating it.

16. Clap Hands—13

ABOUT THE ACTIVITY   Nothing brings a baby's hands together at the midline better than a clapping-hands activity. Either supported or unsupported sitting is appropriate for the baby.

HOW TO PLAY   Place the baby in a sitting position across from you. Tell the baby to watch you play with a ball and then clap hands for you. Then give the ball to the baby to do something with it. Then clap for the baby. Take turns playing with the ball and clapping for each other.

17. Paper Clip It—14

ABOUT THE ACTIVITY   Paper clips are light and safe. They are also easily accessible. Be careful when you use them that you watch the baby to make sure that they cannot be swallowed. Either supported or unsupported sitting is appropriate for the baby.

HOW TO PLAY   Place the baby in a sitting position across from you with two bowls in front of you both. Fill one bowl with paper clips. Take turns using the pincer grasp to take one paper clip out at a time and transfer it to the other bowl. Help the baby as much or as little as is necessary. Try to empty the filled bowl one by one until all the paper clips have been transferred to the other bowl.

18. Creeping on the Tummy or Crawling on All Fours—9, 16, 17

ABOUT THE ACTIVITY   Creeping and crawling develop over time from exposure to opportunity. This mobility helps the baby get things and go places.

HOW TO PLAY   Place the baby down in a creeping or crawling position in a large, safe, open area. Get down with the baby and imitate the baby's movements. If you do what the baby does, the baby will feel in charge and happy and will tend to do more of these movements. Imitate the new movements as well. If the baby totally stops the movements, you can intercede with yours, and the baby will probably imitate you.

19. Hand Walking—9, 16, 17

ABOUT THE ACTIVITY   The baby will enjoy this activity. At the same time, it is excellent preparation for creeping and crawling.

HOW TO PLAY   Put the baby down on a table or on the floor by the hands. Hold the baby by the thighs. Walk the baby like a wheelbarrow. When the baby does well, change the area of support to the knees. Then change it to the ankles.

20. Ready, Set, Walk—18, 19, 20

ABOUT THE ACTIVITY   Independent walking will arrive one day all on its own. There is a lot of fun to be had just before that day arrives. A hoop and a roll or push toy can provide many happy hours of fun.

HOW TO PLAY   Get a hula hoop. Stand opposite the baby, each of you holding onto it. Take some steps together. Holding onto the hoop, you can move forward, backwards, and sideways. Then begin sidestepping, first clockwise and then counterclockwise. Sidestepping to music is even better. A toy shopping cart or baby carriage is excellent for pushing. These toys are good because they can be weighted by blocks or other heavy things to support the baby. As the baby pushes the toy, generate some pretend play. Talk about a shopping trip or an imaginative experience with doll play.

Age Range	*Milestones*
1 to 1½ years	21 through 24

21. Stacking Two—21

ABOUT THE ACTIVITY   Look around the house for different things a toddler can stack. Toddlers who have just learned to walk love to experience new things.

HOW TO PLAY   Collect your stacking equipment. These are some suggestions, but you might come up with other items: cans of soup, mini-cereal boxes, plastic measuring cups, bars of soap, and so on.

22. **Where Is the Nut?—21**

ABOUT THE ACTIVITY   The measuring cups are used for a stacking or nesting activity. The nut is to make the activity more interesting. Other objects can be substituted for the nut, like a large bottle cap or a block that fits into the cups.

HOW TO PLAY   Present the toddler with the two cups and the nut or its substitute. Separate the two cups and hide the nut under one of them. Tell the toddler to guess under which cup it is. When the toddler finds it, say something like, "You guessed it!" Whichever it is in, the toddler should pour it into the other one. The last step is first to stack and then nest the cups. Take your turn and repeat the activity over and over.

23. **Paper Plate Scribbles—22**

ABOUT THE ACTIVITY   This is a good time to introduce paper plates as a medium of art. Older children can use them in many different ways.

HOW TO PLAY   Give the toddler a paper plate. Demonstrate with sturdy crayons how to crayon on the plain surface and how to do it on the ribbed part of the plate.

24. **Bean Bag Toss—23**

ABOUT THE ACTIVITY   Since the toddler has just learned to throw, bean bags are a soft and appealing item for channeling this energy. Homemade bean bags can be made from socks stuffed with dry beans and tied at the ends.

HOW TO PLAY   Get a plastic tub, wash basin size, a large shoebox, a clean waste paper basket, or some other container of choice. Also get a supply of a dozen or more small bean bags. Put the container in the middle. Stand on opposite sides of the container, not too far away, each of you with a good supply of bean bags in front of you on the floor. Take turns throwing a bean bag into the container. When all bean bags have been thrown, whether or not they are all in the container, take a new supply, rotate your positions a quarter turn clockwise, and begin again.

25. **Crawling Up and Down—24**

ABOUT THE ACTIVITY   A small step is needed for this activity. A good way to get one is by setting up a board. One suggestion is a large wooden kitchen cutting board placed on two sets of double phone books (see Figure 12.1).

HOW TO PLAY   Tell the toddler to climb up on the board. Then guide the toddler slowly down.

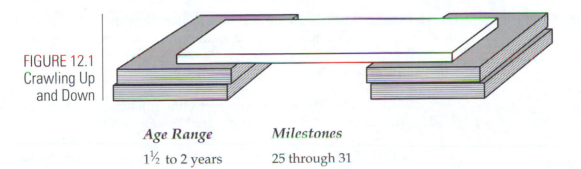

FIGURE 12.1
Crawling Up
and Down

Age Range	*Milestones*
1½ to 2 years	25 through 31

26. Roll Out the Blocks—25, 26

ABOUT THE ACTIVITY   A 16-ounce plastic jar is perfect for this activity. Also have on hand as many blocks as it can hold, preferably at least six.

HOW TO PLAY   Take turns opening the lid by unscrewing it and rolling out the blocks. Then take turns stacking the blocks. Bottle caps can be used as well. Select ones that can be stacked because of gradations in size.

27. Push or Pull—27, 29

ABOUT THE ACTIVITY   Push toys and pull toys are both recommended for toddlers. Push toys have a firm handle and a unit at the bottom to push. Pull toys have a string handle and a unit with wheels on it at the bottom to pull.

HOW TO PLAY   All you have to do is take out the push and/or pull toys. For young toddlers, these toys are a great success all on their own. You may even notice your child begin to run.

28. Kick the Ball—28

ABOUT THE ACTIVITY   It is easy to overlook the coordination needed for kicking a ball. A good size to use is an 8" to 10" round ball. A good place is outside in a yard.

HOW TO PLAY   Place a rope across a field to divide it into two territories, the child's and yours. Take turns kicking across the rope into the other person's territory. Take as many kicks as is necessary to get the ball across to the other side of the rope.

29. Walking Up and Down—30

ABOUT THE ACTIVITY   A small step is needed for this activity. You can make one as described in Activity 25. See Figure 12.1 for an illustration.

HOW TO PLAY   Hold the toddler by the hand and tell him or her to walk up on the board. Keep holding one hand and tell the toddler to walk down.

Then take your turn to walk up and then down. Tell the toddler to hold your hand. You can repeat the activity as many times as there is interest.

30. Jumping Jack—31

ABOUT THE ACTIVITY   Acting out a rhyme enhances its meaning for a child. In this case, part of the benefit is a physical exercise.

HOW TO PLAY   Place a candle or an unbreakable candlestick on the floor. If you do not have either of these, place another object on the floor—a crayon, pencil, block, book, or other unbreakable item. Tell the toddler to stand behind the object and get ready to jump over it when you say the words "Jack jumped over." Begin saying the rhyme "Jack Be Nimble, Jack Be Quick."

Jack be nimble.
Jack be quick.
Jack jumped over the candlestick.

Repeat the rhyme and take your turn to jump. Do the activity as many times as both of you want.

Age Range	*Milestones*
2 to 3 years	32 through 40

31. Red and Blue Blocks—32, 33, 39

ABOUT THE ACTIVITY   The block activity is now expanded to include eight blocks, four red and four blue. Crossing the midline of the body with the hands helps to develop hand dominance. Stacking blocks builds fine motor control.

HOW TO PLAY   Sit across from each other at a table or on the floor. Set the eight blocks in a pile in front of you both. First, pick up one block at a time, hold it directly in front of the child, and tell the child to take it. Notice with which hand the child takes it. Because hand dominance is developing, the child may take all the blocks with the same hand, right or left. If the child uses a mixture of some rights and some lefts, you will see that hand dominance is not developed.

Next, tell the child to sort the blocks, putting all the red blocks on the right side and all the blue ones on the left. You can talk about the concept of 4 and 4 and how together they make 8. Tell the child that you are going to pick up blocks randomly. If you pick up a red one, the child is to take it with the left hand. If you pick up a blue one, the child is to take it with the right hand. Each of those movements requires the child to cross the midline of the body with the hands. After the child has all the blocks, tell him or her to set them up for you to play, with the red ones on your right and blue ones on your left. Let the child pick blocks for you. Then you pick them up, also by crossing the midline.

The third part of the activity is to stack the blocks. Take turns with this activity as well. Each time one of you takes a turn, stack them in a different sequence. Tell what your sequence is going to be before you stack—for example, every other one a red and a blue, two reds and then two blues, four reds and then four blues.

32. Basket Ball—34

ABOUT THE ACTIVITY   Any opportunity to channel the newly formed throwing ability is a good one. All athletes who have excelled in a sport had early experiences with that sport.

HOW TO PLAY   Use a laundry basket and a play ball for this activity. Stand on opposite sides of the basket. First throw the ball back and forth to each other over the basket. Next take turns throwing the ball into the basket. Start with a distance close enough to provide 100 percent success. Little by little, back away from the basket to make the activity more challenging.

33. Pop Goes the Weasel—35, 36

ABOUT THE ACTIVITY   This is a variation of a traditional circle game. All circle games should proceed first in a clockwise direction and then in a counterclockwise direction.

HOW TO PLAY   Put an adult chair in the middle of the circle. Tell the child you will both walk around the chair to the tune of "Pop Goes the Weasel." Tell the child that when you get to the words "Pop goes the weasel," the child should bend down and then pop up and climb into the chair. Lend as much or as little assistance as is needed for the child to get into the chair. Begin to walk around the chair singing these words:

> *All around the cobbler's bench*
> *The monkey chased the weasel.*
> *The monkey thought it was all in fun.*
> *Pop Goes the Weasel.*

Repeat the activity.

34. Stepping Up and Stepping Down—36, 38, 40

ABOUT THE ACTIVITY   A kitchen stepladder is excellent for this activity if a safe staircase is not available.

HOW TO PLAY   Fold out the stepladder so that three steps are available. Hold the child's hand as the child tries to step up to the top of the ladder using alternating feet. Never let go of the child's hand. Tell the child there is a rhyme that goes with the three steps up and the three steps down. Tell the child to say the rhyme while going up and down the stepladder. These are the words:

> *One, two, three.*
> *Look at me.*
> *Three, two, one.*
> *That was fun.*

Each number is to be said as each step is made. For "Look at me," tell the child to do a motion with the right hand while you continue to hold the left.

35. The Bicycle Song—37

ABOUT THE ACTIVITY   Riding a tricycle requires a solid cross-patterning movement with the legs.

HOW TO PLAY   Tell the child to lie down in front of you, legs out front. Hold each of the child's legs under the knees as you would hold handlebars on a bicycle. Then, to the words of "Daisy, Daisy," move the child's legs up and down in a bicycle-pedaling movement. You can take turns having the child pedal your legs as well. These are the words:

> *Daisy, Daisy,*
> *Give me your answer, do.*
> *I'm half crazy*
> *All for the love of you.*
> *It won't be a stylish marriage*
> *I can't afford a carriage.*
> *But you'll look sweet upon the seat*
> *Of a bicycle built for two.*

Age Range	*Milestones*
3 to 4 years	41 through 45

36. Collages—41

ABOUT THE ACTIVITY   There are as many varieties to this activity as there are people who make the collages. Cutting out the items is one way to set up the materials. Another way is by tearing the items, which is very good preparation for fine motor development and refined use of scissors.

As with any of the other play activities, playing along is always better than just giving directions for the child to play.

HOW TO PLAY   Put out any kind of construction paper you have available for the background. Then round up the supplies for making a collage.

Since there are so many choices, try a different one each time you play. Some ready-to-paste materials are: crackers, raisins, dry puffed cereals, colored paper scraps, cotton balls, and scraps of colored cloth. Some materials for tearing are: old magazines and newspapers, old sheets or other scrap material not needed for something else, different textures of paper—smooth, bumpy, heavy, thin, tissue, and different colors of paper—both construction and copy machine weight.

Then demonstrate, using the pincer grasp (thumb and forefinger), how to tear different shapes—tiny, big, thin, wide, and more. Tell the child to tear what is desired to make a collage. Color, shape, and texture designs can be considered.

Then explain the pasting. Get out child-safe white paste. Tell the child to use the applicator or a plastic spoon to scoop out a reasonable amount of paste from the container and put it on the background paper. Then tell the child to spread the paste on the background paper with the forefinger and middle finger. Once the paste is spread, the child is ready to paste the chosen torn pieces onto the paper. The result will be a personal design that will give the child pride. In this activity, the process is more important than the product.

37. All Tied Up in Knots—42

ABOUT THE ACTIVITY   Being able to tie a knot is the first step in being able to tie a bow.

HOW TO PLAY   Tie a long ribbon onto a door knob. Each end should hang down at least 18 inches. Show the child how to tie a knot with the ribbon using the two ends that are hanging down. Tell the child to tie a knot. Then you tie one. Take turns tying as many knots as possible with the hanging ribbon.

38. Stringing Large Beads—43

ABOUT THE ACTIVITY   Large beads can be used for this activity, but the variety of pasta called rigatoni is even better. Yarn of any size can be cut, but 18" to 24" is suggested for use as a necklace.

HOW TO PLAY   Cut two pieces of yarn to a desired length, one for the child and one for you. Tie one bead or one piece of rigatoni to the end of each piece of yarn. Put Scotch tape on the other ends of each piece to make firm tips for threading beads. Demonstrate how to thread the beads or the rigatoni. Then begin the beading fun together. If desired, tie each beaded yarn into a necklace when you are finished.

A variation is to give each other beading directions. This will work especially well with the colored beads—for example, "(*Child's Name*), string the red, then the blue, then the yellow." It could also work with the rigatoni if you paint them first with a mixture of food coloring and water.

39. Draw It Out—44

ABOUT THE ACTIVITY   Thick crayons can be a valuable tool for children of this age. They are made to be manipulated by small hands. Scribbles, some simple shapes, and the beginnings of representational art will show up.

HOW TO PLAY   Set up the child with paper and thick crayons. Even paper bags can be cut open for a good coloring surface. This activity has no rules. Just encourage whatever you see and watch the techniques grow. Of course, you are welcome to draw as well.

40. Walk, Hop, Stop—45

ABOUT THE ACTIVITY   Singing and movement go hand and hand.

HOW TO PLAY   There is a movement song to the tune of "Frère Jacques" that makes moving fun. Join hands with the child and move in a circle to the following words:

Walking, walking, walking, walking,
Hop, hop, hop.
Hop, hop, hop.
Running, running, running.
Running, running, running.
Now let's stop.
Now let's stop.

Age Range	*Milestones*
4 to 5 years	46 through 55

41. Make a Set of Flash Cards—46, 47, 48

ABOUT THE ACTIVITY   As children get better at using scissors, opportunities to cut will be welcomed. As they get better at drawing and writing, opportunities to practice those skills will be welcomed as well.

HOW TO PLAY   Get a supply of plain white copy paper, about 25 sheets. Show the child how to fold the sheets in half and then in half again two at a time. Then show the child how to cut the sheets on the folded lines. Once the sheets are cut, there will be paper for 100 flash cards.

Take 26 of the flash cards and tell the child to write on them the 26 capital letters. Take 26 more flash cards and tell the child to write on them the 26 lower-case letters. Take 10 cards and tell the child to write on them the numbers from 1 to 10, and 10 more for the child to write the number words from *one* to *ten.* Let the child write as many of the letters and numbers as is possible. For any that the child cannot write, write it in pencil so that the child can trace it. Work on the project with the child, watching true independent work and assisting where necessary.

There are many possibilities for playing with the flash cards. They can be used in the traditional way. They can be used for simple matching games—capital to lower case and numerals to number words. They can also be used for the game of concentration, using the letter and number matches. Concentration can be played with five pairs to start and then with additional pairs as the child gains expertise with the matches.

For ordinary flash cards, you can add interest by making the child's response a game of speed. The object is to try to say the letter or number quickly, before the caller puts it out of sight. The focus of the activity is changed from whether or not the child knows the answer to how quickly the child can say the answer.

42. Color by Letter—49, 52

ABOUT THE ACTIVITY   Many commercial color-by-number sets are too complicated for children this age. It can be more appropriate and even more fun to make your own, as shown in Figure 12.2.

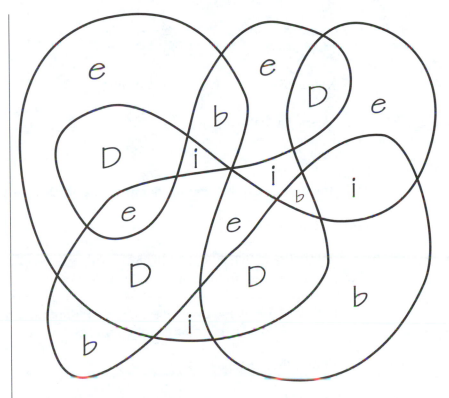

FIGURE 12.2
Color by Letter

HOW TO PLAY   Draw a free-form shape that contains various segments. Tell your child to print his or her name under the free-form shape. Then tell the child to trace over each letter using a different color crayon. If there is more than one of a particular letter in the name, tell the child to color all examples of that letter the same color. Then put a different letter from the child's name in each of the segments in the free-form shape. The colors of the letters in the child's name now represent the key for coloring the free-form shape. The child is now ready to proceed to color by letter. Participate as much or as little as is necessary to make the coloring activity a success.

43. Picture It; Do It—50, 51, 54, 55

ABOUT THE ACTIVITY   Representational pictures are becoming clearer now.

HOW TO PLAY   As in Activity 41, guide the child in making the flash cards. This time the child should make eight. Write a sentence on each flashcard and tell the child to illustrate the sentence on the back. Then put the flash cards in a pile. Take turns picking the flash cards and acting out the sentence or the picture. Some suggested sentences are:

> *Buckle the shoe.*
> *Tie the shoe.*
> *Throw the ball.*
> *Catch the ball.*
>
> *Ride a bike.*
> *Roller-skate.*
> *Do a somersault.*
> *Hop.*
> *Skip.*

Help the child with the activity as much or as little as is necessary.

44. Catch It—51

ABOUT THE ACTIVITY   Ball skills are important to development and can reward a child with many happy hours of play.

HOW TO PLAY   Stand opposite each other. Play catch with a ball 8" to 10" in diameter. Move farther and farther apart as you both gain expertise.

45. Phone Book Steps—53

ABOUT THE ACTIVITY   Use three phone books to create a two-step set of stairs. You can also use thick books to make the stairs.

HOW TO PLAY   Put two thick telephone books side by side and a third one on top of one of them. On the ground, put a masking tape path leading up to the telephone books. It can be straight or curved. Tell the child to follow the path leading to the steps and then to climb up the steps without holding on to you while climbing. Then take your turn.

CHAPTER 13

A Practical Approach to Social Development

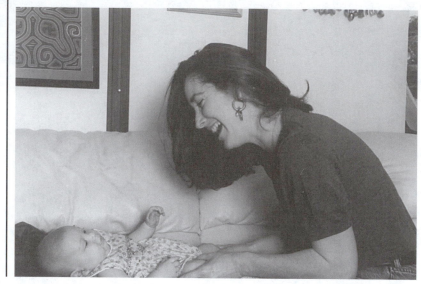

Relationships are what social development is all about. The early relationships that adults form with a baby have a significant impact on the baby for years to come. Though it sounds simple to bring up a child, actually it is deceptively difficult.

Providing an optimum environment for social interaction is not easy from the beginning. Some new parents think the newborn will be helpless and ready to be controlled, directed, and molded into whatever form they wish. However, it turns out that each baby is a unique person right from the start, with individual wants, needs, and feelings. The new baby has a complex genetic potential that plays an important role in how social interactions and social development will progress. Trying to control a child who is trying to become independent makes social development a process that is a challenge to the most educated and best prepared of parents.

Control over the baby starts out at 100 percent. During fetal development, the parents can completely control the environment of the unborn baby. It is advisable that they both do so by reducing stress for each other. The mother can take complete control over the food she eats for nourishing the baby; by physically exercising her body in such a way as to provide healthy, physical movement for the growing fetus; and by choosing to play soft music, to read aloud as she reads, and to talk in a way that will expose the unborn baby to the highest quality information and language. While newborns still need to be almost completely controlled, day by day they learn to take more control of their environment.

During the first eight months, babies remain quite dependent. Then, with the onset of mobility, children's independence increases rapidly. The parents' task—trying to fill the dependent needs of the baby while at the same time trying to help the baby become independent—is a complicated balancing act.

In the preschool years, social relationships become significant. Adult–child relationships continue to affect children, and child–child relationships also influence children's social skills. These relationships affect feelings of security, attitudes toward others, and future social patterns. Children who have well-developed social skills when they start regular school will most likely adjust well to school and not have behavior problems.

Social skills directly affect academic achievement. From the work of Piaget, we know that such skills improve cognitive development by giving children alternative perspectives and access to new information. Social relationships with more competent peers have the most positive impact on the academic functioning level of young children (Spodek & Saracho, 1994, p. 172).

Throughout the first five years, the child will achieve many social milestones. Specific parent–child activities will be beneficial in helping the child reach these milestones, and others will be appropriate once a child is functioning at a particular level. All should be done in a way that offers love, security, and respect to the child. Young children need to feel protected and cared for in order to be able eventually to protect and care for both themselves and others. The early childhood parent–child social activities in the years from birth to five lay the foundation for the child to be able to have functional social skills after that.

MILESTONES OF SOCIAL DEVELOPMENT FROM BIRTH TO FIVE YEARS

Age Range	Milestone	Activity
Birth to 3 months	1. Cuddles when held	1, 2, 3, 4
	2. Responds to human voices	1, 2, 3, 4, 5
	3. Smiles socially	1, 2, 3, 4, 5
3 to 6 months	4. Shows pleasure	6, 7, 8, 9, 10
	5. Initiates social interactions	7, 8, 9
	6. Uses gestures to show likes and dislikes	8, 9, 10
6 to 12 months	7. Reacts appropriately to strangers	11, 12
	8. Responds playfully to a mirror	13, 14
	9. Plays "Peek-a-boo"	15
	10. Shows preference for people, objects, places	16, 17, 18
	11. Drinks from a cup	19
	12. Responds to praise	19, 20
1 to 1½ years	13. Likes routines and rituals	21, 23, 25
	14. Follows simple directions	22
	15. Enjoys stories	23
	16. Helps with household tasks	24
	17. Enjoys sharing rhymes and songs	25
	18. Initiates household activity	24
	19. Can undress self	22
1½ to 2 years	20. Imitates others	26
	21. Solitary play—coloring, building, books	27
	22. Plays simple games	28
	23. Attempts to put on clothes	29
	24. Plays parallel with other children	30
2 to 3 years	25. Is possessive of objects and loved ones	31
	26. Resists change, likes routines	32, 33
	27. Takes pride in achievements, resists help	34
	28. Puts on clothes with supervision	35
3 to 4 years	29. Plays in groups	36, 37, 38
	30. Dresses without supervision	39
	31. Bathes with supervision	40
4 to 5 years	32. Does dramatic and creative play	41, 42, 43, 44, 45
	33. Plays cooperatively with other children	42, 43, 44, 45

The items are numbered, but within an age range the order is not important. The stages of development are categorized by ages, but the ages are approximate. The order of the stages is important.

PLAY ACTIVITIES FOR SOCIAL DEVELOPMENT FROM BIRTH TO FIVE YEARS

Age Range	*Milestones*
Birth to 3 months	1 through 3

1. Rock-a-Bye-Baby—1, 2, 3

ABOUT THE ACTIVITY   The baby needs to be rocked as much as possible. The body contact is important. A bouncer chair or any other kind of rocker should not be used if the parent is available to hold the baby.

HOW TO PLAY   Hold the baby in your arms in the most comfortable way possible. Then rock the baby to the tune of "Rock-a-Bye-Baby." Establish eye contact with the baby as you rock and sing. The words are:

Rock-a-bye baby
In the treetop.
When the wind blows,
The cradle will rock.
When the bough breaks,
The cradle will fall.
Down will come baby,
Cradle and all.

2. Where Is (Baby's Name)?—1, 2, 3

ABOUT THE ACTIVITY   The baby needs to be touched as much as possible. It is also good for the baby to feel movement as much as possible. Putting the baby's name in a song makes it personal and of high interest.

HOW TO PLAY   Sit the baby in your lap. Put the baby in a position in which you can clap the baby's hands to the beat of the song. Clap together as you sing the song. These are the words:

Where is (Baby's Name)?
Where is (Baby's Name)?
Here I am.
Here I am.
How are you today, (Sir or Ms.)?
Very well I thank you.
Raise your right hand.
Raise your left hand.

3. The Grand Old Duke of York—1, 2, 3

ABOUT THE ACTIVITY   This song includes bouncing and a ride in the air upwards. The bouncing movement is calming to the baby, and the upward movement is stimulating. When the baby is moved up, the baby will learn by experience the meaning of *up.* When moved down, the baby will learn about *down,* and when moved halfway up, the baby will learn about that, too.

HOW TO PLAY   Sit the baby on your knee facing you. Support the baby around the chest under the arms. Then bounce and sing together. These are the words:

The Grand Old Duke of York (Bounce)
He had ten thousand men. (Bounce)
He marched them up the hill, (Baby up)
And he marched them down again. (Baby down)
When they're up, they're up, (Baby up)
And when they're down, they're down, (Baby down)
And when they're only halfway up, (Baby halfway up)
They're neither up nor down. (Baby up, then down)

4. If You're Happy and You Know It—1, 2, 3

ABOUT THE ACTIVITY   The baby can be propped up across from you for this song. Eye contact is very important. This is a happy song that makes everyone smile.

HOW TO PLAY   Sit the baby comfortably across from you. Rock together as you sing, and do the motions to the words with the baby's hands, head, and feet.
These are the words:

If you're happy and you know it, clap your hands. (Clap hands)
If you're happy and you know it, clap your hands. (Clap hands)
If you're happy and you know it, your face will surely show it.
If you're happy and you know it, clap your hands. (Clap hands)

If you're happy and you know it, pat your head. (Pat head)
If you're happy and you know it, pat your head. (Pat head)
If you're happy and you know it, your face will surely show it.
If you're happy and you know it, pat your head. (Pat head)

If you're happy and you know it, stamp your feet (Stamp feet)
If you're happy and you know it, stamp your feet (Stamp feet)
If you're happy and you know it, your face will surely show it.
If you're happy and you know it, stamp your feet (Stamp feet)

5. Pat-a-Cake—2, 3

ABOUT THE ACTIVITY   Babies enjoy the rhyming words and the actions that go with it.

HOW TO PLAY   Sit the baby comfortably across from you, propped up and secure. Say the rhyme to the baby and do the motions with the baby's hands. These are the words:

> *Pat-a-cake, pat-a-cake, baker's man. (Clap hands)*
> *Bake me a cake as fast as you can. (Clap hands)*
> *Roll it and stir it (Roll then stir baby's hands)*
> *And mark it with a* (Baby's first initial). *(Make initial on baby's palm)*
> *Put it in the oven (Move hands forward)*
> *For* (Baby's Name) *and me. (Point to baby and then to you)*

Age Range	Milestones
3 to 6 months	4 through 6

6. See It, Hear It, Feel It—4

ABOUT THE ACTIVITY   Exploring through sight, sound, taste, touch, and smell is at the heart of baby's functioning.

HOW TO PLAY   Collect some interesting items from around the house and give them to the baby for exploration. Here are some ideas: Small boxes with and without lids, foam rubber or sponges, a strainer, an egg carton or muffin tin, a loaf of bread (in the bag), and a variety of cushions. Name them, talk about them, and play along as much as you like.

7. I Can Do It—4, 5

ABOUT THE ACTIVITY   Imitation is the first level of activity. It prepares a child for the next level, initiating the activity. Talking to and playing with a baby come naturally. Whatever gestures or sounds you use for imitation should be ones that come naturally.

HOW TO PLAY   Sit on the floor or in another comfortable spot with the baby. Place yourselves where you have eye contact. Then begin making gestures or sounds for the baby to imitate. Some favorite gestures and sounds are: Wave hi; wave bye bye; make peek-a-boo; and make any gurgling, cooing, or babbling sounds. Any that are initiated by the baby are for you to imitate.

8. Ready, Set, Play—4, 5, 6

ABOUT THE ACTIVITY   This is related to Activity 10. The face is interesting, and so is the rest of the body.

HOW TO PLAY   As you lie on a bed, place the baby in different positions, each one more fun than the last. One will be more fun than the next. First jiggle the baby above your head. Then swing the baby from the chest to between the knees. Then bounce the baby on your knees. Try other actions that are safe, enjoyable, and comfortable for you both. Let the baby communicate to you through gesture preferences for different types of movements.

9. Give and Take—4, 5, 6

ABOUT THE ACTIVITY   This is a popular game with babies.

HOW TO PLAY   Set up about six safe, easy-to-handle, interesting objects. Give the baby one of them. As you do, say, "I give it to you." Look at the baby and say, "Now, you give it to me." When you get it back, give it back to the baby and say, "I give it to you." Look again at the baby and say, "You give it to me." Keep up the give and take for a while and then switch toys. See if the baby, through gesture, will show you which toy should be used next.

10. Face It—4, 6

ABOUT THE ACTIVITY   This activity reminds us that "the best educational toy is a parent." It is related to Activity 8.

HOW TO PLAY   Hold the baby in a comfortable position. Balance the baby well so that the hands are free to explore your face. The baby will probably naturally grab your nose or an ear, or even reach out toward your eyes. Caution the baby with the word "easy" about touching your face. Encourage the baby to touch your features, and then name each one as it is touched.

Age Range	*Milestones*
6 to 12 months	7 through 12

11. Getting Around—7

ABOUT THE ACTIVITY   The baby's world can start to include other people and other places.

HOW TO PLAY   When you are out with the baby at the mall, in a store, or on the street, talk to the baby about what you see. When you are with other adults, include the baby in the conversation from time to time. The car is another environment to explore and get to know. Point out the tires, the roof, the mirror, and more.

12. Introductions—7

ABOUT THE ACTIVITY   Because the baby is now getting an awareness of strangers, this is a good time to enjoy baby-centered activities that include other people. Play this activity when anyone is in the room who is not part of the immediate family.

HOW TO PLAY   Go through a formal introduction with the baby and all the other people in the room. Use this format: "(*Baby's Name*), this is (*Other Person's Name*). (*Other Person's Name*), this is (*Baby's Name*). Then guide the baby to shake hands with the other person. Continue using this format with each person in the room who is not part of the immediate family.

13. Mirror Movement—8

ABOUT THE ACTIVITY   Mirrors make simple activities more fun.

HOW TO PLAY   Stand in front of a full-length mirror with the baby. Turn on some music that is pleasant for both of you for dancing. Dance together. Emphasize keeping the rhythm as you both enjoy music, loving, and caring. Don't forget to make silly faces in the mirror.

14. The Play Mirror—8

ABOUT THE ACTIVITY   Unbreakable play mirrors are hard to come by, but if you can find one, it will be helpful. There is more information about mirror play in Chapter 2. Supported or unsupported sitting is appropriate for the baby.

HOW TO PLAY   Place the baby in a sitting position, and sit across from the baby. Pass a play mirror back and forth to each other. When you get it, say, "One two three, look at me." Then make a silly face in the mirror. When the baby gets the mirror, say the same rhyme and tell the baby to make a silly face in the mirror. Repeat the activity as long as you and the baby are both enjoying it.

15. Peek-a-Boo—9

ABOUT THE ACTIVITY   Nature somehow makes sure that most babies are exposed to this game in one way or another. This is an appropriate time to introduce this kind of play.

HOW TO PLAY   Hide your face behind your hands or behind a blanket. Suddenly show your face and say, "Peek-a-boo. I see you!" Repeat the activity as long as it holds the interest of both you and the baby.

16. I Found You—10

ABOUT THE ACTIVITY   Once babies can get around, they will.

HOW TO PLAY   Set the baby up to move around in a safe enclosed area. Then turn your back to the baby for a few minutes. Next turn around and say, "I found you!" Let the baby go free again. Then turn around and show surprise about where the baby is. Once again say, "I found you!" Repeat the activity as often as you like.

17. What You See Is What You Get—10

ABOUT THE ACTIVITY   A coffee table cleared of all breakables is a good place for this activity. If the baby has standing balance, the height of the table will be just right. If not, a standard-sized stool will make a good chair for the baby. Stand behind the baby to give standing or sitting support when and if it is needed.

HOW TO PLAY   Place all the play objects in the center of the table, out of the baby's reach. Then ask the baby, "What do you want?" After you see a point or hear a sound or maybe a word, give the baby what was selected Any safe and interesting items or playthings can go on the table—a doll, a toy, a toy car or boat, yarn, a mitten, a hat, and more.

18. Off to See the World—10

ABOUT THE ACTIVITY   This activity is highly unstructured.

HOW TO PLAY   Place the baby on the floor. Allow the baby to move to any location in the room or even to another part of the house. Be sure to keep an eye on the baby at all times to ensure safety. Wherever the baby goes, say, "I like that place." If it is a dangerous location, remove the baby immediately and say, "I do not like that place. Dangerous place."

19. Juice Comes in a Cup—11, 12

ABOUT THE ACTIVITY   Drinking is a social activity, and juice is the baby's social drink. It should be given only in a cup.

HOW TO PLAY   Set up a social drink and snack time for you and the baby. Set up a safe, comfortable table situation in which you both have the same drink and snack from the same plastic cups and dishes. Juice is a suggested drink, and soft crackers or banana pieces are suggested food items. Give the baby as much or as little help in drinking from the cup as is necessary, and be sure to describe to the baby all efforts at cup-drinking success.

20. Book Etiquette—12

ABOUT THE ACTIVITY   Emergent reading and reading awareness should take place gradually from birth on.

HOW TO PLAY   Sit on the floor comfortably with the baby. Have handy a group of books with thick cardboard pages. These are books, but because of their durability they are also toys. Hand each book to the baby one at a time.

If the baby holds it right side up, say, "You're holding the book right side up." If the baby holds the book upside down, change the position to right side up and say, "You're holding the book right side up." Phrase repetition gives the activity an element of fun.

Continue this activity with page turning. Give the baby the book right side up. Then say, "Turn the page." If the baby does it correctly, say, "Turn another one." Keep giving the page-turn direction until the whole book has been finished. No reading is necessary for this activity. Give as much or as little help as is necessary for turning the pages.

Age Range	*Milestones*
1 to 1½ years	13 through 19

21. Singing Time—13

ABOUT THE ACTIVITY   Because toddlers enjoy routines and rituals, it is a good idea to set up a special singing time.

HOW TO PLAY   Start off with a name song. An excellent one is "Where Is (*Baby's Name*)?" in Activity 2. Another one is "Mommy's Dress." Sing this first using the word "Mommy," and the color the toddler is actually wearing. Then substitute the baby's name for "Mommy." Keep the color consistent throughout the song. Each time you sing it, choose another color. Red, yellow, blue, and green are good beginning colors. These are the words:

> *Mommy is wearing a red dress, red dress, red dress.*
> *Mommy is wearing a red dress all day long.*
> (Baby's Name) *is wearing a red* (article of clothing),
> *red* (article of clothing), *red* (article of clothing).
> (Baby's Name) *is wearing a red* (article of clothing)
> *all day long.*

After the name song, sing the alphabet song. Point to the letters of the alphabet as you say each one. (See Appendix C.) After the alphabet song, sing the number song. A traditional number song in our culture is "Ten Little Fingers." Show each finger on the toddler's hands as you sing the numbers in the song. Show the toddler how to use each finger as a finger stretch. It is sung to the tune of the old-fashioned "Ten Little Indians" song. The last line is "Ten little fingers on your hands."

After the number song, introduce a new song. One suggestion is "Open Shut Them." These are the words:

> *Open shut them (Hands open, hands closed)*
> *Open shut them (Hands open, hands closed)*
> *Give a little clap, clap, clap. (Clap hands)*
> *Open shut them (Hands open, hands closed)*
> *Open shut them (Hands open, hands closed)*

Put them in your lap, lap, lap. (Hands in lap)
Creep them, creep them, slowly creep them (Hands creep up)
Right up to your chin, chin, chin. (Hands to chin)
Open up your little mouth, (Open mouth)
But do not let them in. (Hands away)

Other favorites can be sung as well. A good way to end the routine is with a circle song. An excellent one is "Walk, Hop, Stop" in Activity 40 in Motor Development. Another suggestion is "Ring Around a Rosie."

To establish a routine, the Singing Time activity should start with a name song, go on to the Alphabet Song, then to the number song, then another favorite song, and finally a circle song.

22. Where Is It?—14, 19

ABOUT THE ACTIVITY   The toddler can follow simple directions and also find objects that are out of sight.

HOW TO PLAY   Send the toddler on errands and see what you get. Make up your own directions—for example, "Bring me the ball." "Sit on the chair." "Put this brush on the table." "Change your clothes." "Take off the hat."

23. Story Time—13, 15

ABOUT THE ACTIVITY   Because toddlers enjoy routines and rituals, it is a good idea to set up a regular story time.

HOW TO PLAY   Start off with a picture book. Read the story and have the toddler participate as much as possible. Talk together about the pictures and about the story content.

Next read a book that has large print so that you can point to the words as you read them. Have the toddler read as many words from recognition as possible. Recognition will come from repetition.

Last, let the toddler choose a storybook. If it is long, read only part of it and continue with it the next time. End the routine by reading word cards and acting out the words as explained in Activity 45 in Cognitive Development. Use only one-word directions. Start the game off with three cards—Hop, Jump, and Clap. Add additional cards after the toddler has mastered these.

24. Imitate Me—16, 18

ABOUT THE ACTIVITY   Toddlers enjoy imitating adults.

HOW TO PLAY   Sit on the floor or in some other comfortable place with the toddler. Start with some warm-up imitations like these: "I touch my head. Now you do it." "I clap my hands. Now you do it." "I stand up. Now you do it." Continue with some real household tasks: "I vacuum the floor.

Now you do it." "I dust the furniture. Now you do it." "I wash the dishes. Now you do it."

25. Partners in Rhyme—13, 17

ABOUT THE ACTIVITY   Because toddlers enjoy routines and rituals, it is a good idea to set up a sequence of "Partners in Rhyme" activities.

HOW TO PLAY   Sit opposite the toddler on the floor. Start with the song "Row, Row, Row Your Boat." Hold each other's hands in a parallel way. Let the toddler's feet stretch out to meet the inside of your thighs. Then pull each other back and forth to the song of "Row, Row, Row Your Boat." Ease up as you pull so that the toddler can get the exercise of using arm muscles to pull you.

Next enjoy the song "The Wheels on the Bus" together. Do all the motions opposite each other. Do these motions with enthusiasm. They all serve as good exercise. Third, take the toddler's legs under the knees and push the legs back and forth to the tune of "Daisy, Daisy." The words are in Activity 25 in Motor Development. Finish up with a horsey ride to the tune of "Ride a Cock Horse." These are the words:

> *Ride a cock horse*
> *To Banbury Cross*
> *To see a fine lady*
> *Upon a white horse.*
> *With rings on her fingers*
> *And bells on her toes,*
> *She shall have music*
> *Wherever she goes.*

Age Range	*Milestones*
1½ to 2 years	20 through 24

26. Tap a Pattern—20

ABOUT THE ACTIVITY   The senses of sight, sound, and touch can be heightened with this tapping activity.

HOW TO PLAY   Sit across from each other at a table. Tap on the table once and have the toddler tap once after you. Then tap twice and have the toddler tap twice. Then tap three times and have the toddler repeat that. If three times is the hardest the toddler can do, stop with that and practice it several times. If three taps go well, try three in a pattern like *long, short, short* or *short, short, long.* Continue with expanded patterns that are appropriate for the toddler. You can do some with syllables like *ap-ple tree* for *long, short, short,* or use the child's name. Tell the toddler to tap for you. Then try to imitate that as well.

27. The Special Bag—21

ABOUT THE ACTIVITY   An old tote bag, a plastic beach bag with handles, or even a medium-sized paper shopping bag is good for this activity. Fill it with items of special play interest to the toddler. Besides a sketch pad, thick crayons, and a few sheets of stickers, nothing should go in the bag that is consumable. Change some or all of the items each time you set it out for play. Suggested items for this bag are: sketch pad and thick crayons, blocks, books that encourage reading (those with simple pictures and clear large print words), playing cards, bean bags, an old pocketbook with old keys and an old wallet, costume jewelry, handkerchiefs, small dolls or stuffed animals, a sheet or two of stickers to be used with the sketch pad, raisins or Cheerios in a small plastic container, toy cars, or any other items of interest to the toddler that are also safe to use independently.

HOW TO PLAY   Take out this bag for play when it is a good time for both you and for the toddler to be playing alone. Set up a special spot in the house for playing alone. Put the special bag there. Then turn on a timer for ten minutes. Tell the toddler to play with the special bag in the special spot until the timer rings. When the ten minutes are up, decide together whether to set up this play alone time for another ten minutes or to end the activity.

28. Seek and You Shall Find—22

ABOUT THE ACTIVITY   Toddlers enjoy finding things, but they will need audible or visible clues.

HOW TO PLAY   Set a cooking timer for one minute. Listen together to the ticking sound. Tell the toddler you are going to hide the timer in another room. Hide it, come back to the room, and tell the toddler to look for the timer and bring it to you. Remind the toddler to listen for the ticking sound and to move closer to it as it gets louder.

Prepare seven index cards, each with a different number on it from 1 to 7. Show the toddler the cards with the numbers on them, and say that you are going to hide them in another room. Hide the cards so that a small piece of each card shows as a clue. Come back into the room and tell the toddler to look for all seven cards and bring them to you. Remind the toddler to look for the little pieces of the cards that will be showing. When the toddler comes back with the cards, count them together. Tell the toddler to put them in order from 1 to 7. Give as much or as little help as is necessary.

Remember, you are still the best educational toy! Tell the toddler you are going to hide yourself in another room. Hide so that you are still a little visible. Call to the child to come and look for you. Your voice and the visible part of your body will serve as clues.

Tell the toddler to hide in another room. After a short time, go in the other room and look for the toddler. Find the toddler. Hug and laugh together to end the activity.

29. Dressing—23

ABOUT THE ACTIVITY   Use a parent's clothes for this activity. If a toddler can handle the parent's clothes in a play situation, there will be carryover to the child's own dressing capability.

HOW TO PLAY   Lay out several articles of clothing that you do not mind the toddler wearing. Then give short directives: "Put on the shirt." "Put on the shorts." "Put a sock on the left foot." "Put on the belt." Help the child as much or as little as necessary.

30. Theme Play—24

ABOUT THE ACTIVITY   Setting up a theme situation can facilitate parallel play with two or more toddlers. Successful and easy-to-set-up themes include: the store, cooking, and dress-up.

HOW TO PLAY   Set up a theme area for play. If it is the store, take out some cans, cartons, boxes, shopping bags, plastic food, a play telephone, coupons, and so on. Let the toddlers stack, line up, pretend, or create. For a cooking theme, provide some plastic dishes, cups, cutlery, pots, pans, a play stove or one drawn on a carton, and whatever else is available. Let the toddlers pour, mix, serve, and create. Whatever the theme, set up what you have and watch the toddlers play. Guide as much or as little as is necessary.

Age Range	*Milestones*
2 to 3 years	25 through 28

31. My Family—25

ABOUT THE ACTIVITY   Talking about the family promotes the bonding process.

HOW TO PLAY   Take out some family pictures. Look through a family photo album or use the "My Family" book explained in Chapter 2. Take turns pointing to people in the pictures. When you point, tell the child to say who is in the picture. When the child points, you say who it is. Try to identify the people by name and also by relationship—mother, father, sister, brother, aunt, uncle, cousin.

32. Stations—26

ABOUT THE ACTIVITY   Since children at this time begin to resist changes, this changing activity can be beneficial. It makes a game out of moving on to another activity.

HOW TO PLAY   Set up four stations on a big play area. Here are some examples: (1) a large piece of paper and thick crayons for a free-form coloring activity, (2) a set of blocks or a big basket of bottle caps, (3) a group of children's picture books, and (4) a group of age-appropriate puzzles. Get some soft music ready. Tell the child to start playing at one station when you start the music and to go to another station when you stop the music. Give the child a chance to play at all four stations and even to repeat stations if desired.

33. Stop the Music—26

ABOUT THE ACTIVITY   This is another way to make a game out of changing activities.

HOW TO PLAY   Spread out four different pieces of colored paper on the floor. Get some playful music ready. Tell the child to play freely while you play the music and to move to a colored square once the music stops. You can play and stop the music four times so that the child can move to the four different designated spots.

34. Describe the Object—27

ABOUT THE ACTIVITY   The child will be successful every time because whatever the child brings can be right.

HOW TO PLAY   Describe an object in a particular room and ask the child to bring it to you. Give as much or as little description as you think is necessary to get the object of your choice. If the child does not bring what you had in mind, try again with more explicit descriptions. After the child has brought you all the requested objects, describe them one by one and ask the child to put them back where they were.

35. Dress the Parent—28

ABOUT THE ACTIVITY   Being able to put clothes on a parent will enhance the child's skill at dressing.

HOW TO PLAY   Take out some clothes large enough for you to wear over your own clothes—for example, a jacket, a sweater, a big shirt, socks, shoes, or a belt. Tell the child to pick one item and to put it on you. Give as much or as little assistance as is necessary.

Age Range	*Milestones*
3 to 4 years	29 through 31

36. Marching Band—29

ABOUT THE ACTIVITY   Marching to music is a successful group activity. Homemade instruments are easy to make and much more fun than purchased instruments, which also can be used. Select music with a clear beat.

HOW TO PLAY   Make some homemade instruments. Two pot lids make cymbals. Small plastic containers filled with uncooked rice or paper clips make nice maracas. A closed plastic container with a spoon makes a good drum. Give each child an instrument. Take one yourself and lead the children as you all march to music and keep rhythm with the instruments.

37. Hokey Pokey—29

ABOUT THE ACTIVITY   The Hokey Pokey is a popular group game. It is excellent for following directions, learning body parts, using creativity, and enjoying a group.

HOW TO PLAY   Tell everyone to stand in a circle. Then begin the song. Everyone should both sing and do the actions. These are the words:

> *You put your right hand in. (Put right hand in toward the circle)*
> *You put your right hand out. (Take right hand out away from the circle)*
> *You do the hokey pokey, and you turn yourself about. (Wiggle your body*
> *   and turn around)*

Repeat the stanzas with these body parts: left hand, right foot, left foot, whole self, and any other part—shoulder, elbow, knee, and so on.

38. The Mulberry Bush—29

ABOUT THE ACTIVITY   "Here We Go Round the Mulberry Bush" is a popular circle game that is excellent for creative thinking and creative expression. For this and any other circle games, move around the circle in a clockwise direction. If you repeat the activity to give everyone a second turn, move around the circle in a counterclockwise direction.

HOW TO PLAY   Everyone walks around in a circle clockwise to the tune of "Here We Go Round the Mulberry Bush." Each person gets a chance to make up an original stanza starting with the words, "This is the way we . . ." That person acts out the motions as well. These are the words:

> *Here we go round the mulberry bush, the mulberry bush, the mulberry bush.*
> *Here we go round the mulberry bush so early in the morning.*
> *This is the way we (pretend action), (pretend action), (pretend action),*
> *This is the way we (pretend action) so early in the morning.*

39. The Dressing Game—30

ABOUT THE ACTIVITY   Once children can dress without supervision, they enjoy changing clothes.

HOW TO PLAY   Ask the child to go to another room and change one item of clothing or to change the way of wearing a particular item. When the child returns, try to guess what has been changed. Then take your turn. Go to another room and change something about what you are wearing.

40. Bath Directions—31

ABOUT THE ACTIVITY   The bath can provide an opportunity for following directions. Following one direction is easy, following two is fun, and following three is a challenge.

HOW TO PLAY   Give three bath directions. Tell the child not to follow any of them until all three are remembered. These are some examples: "Wet the wash cloth, put soap on it, and wash your arms." "Soap your legs, and then your tummy, and then your neck." "Rinse your legs, then your tummy, then your neck."

Age Range	*Milestones*
4 to 5 Years	32 to 33

41. Art—32

ABOUT THE ACTIVITY   Through art children should be allowed to explore, be original, and experiment, free of adult standards. They should understand that art is a process and not a product for pleasing someone else. Self-expression and creativity are the goals.

HOW TO PLAY   Set up a table and chair area specifically for child art. Put out the materials selected and let the child create. Some suggested materials are: crayons, paper, paintbrushes, poster paint, tempera paint, chalk with black or dark blue paper, modeling materials like clay or Play-Doh, yarn, thick pencils, glue, scissors, paint containers, sponges, paper plates, scraps of material, wrapping paper, and wallpaper.

42. Puppet Play—32, 33

ABOUT THE ACTIVITY   Puppets can be made from the simplest materials: wooden spoons, spatulas, dish mops, strainers, hairbrushes, and more. The handle is for holding the puppet, and the flat, wide part is for making the face. Decorate the face part with wiggle eyes, yarn, felt, ribbon, sequins, buttons, and more. A sock can be turned into a puppet with a moving mouth.

It can be further designed with felt, yarn, or buttons. Popsicle sticks or tongue depressors with construction paper heads are also easy to make. In addition, lunch bags with faces on them are popular puppets and are usually played with well.

HOW TO PLAY   Children will know exactly what to do with puppets. You will see natural puppet conversations going back and forth. Participate with a puppet of your own as much or as little as you wish.

43. Water and Sand Play—32, 33

ABOUT THE ACTIVITY   The most formed toys provide the least value for children, and the least formed toys provide the most value. Water and sand play provides relaxation, manipulation, experimentation, and conversation.

HOW TO PLAY   Set up water play in a wading pool or bathtub. Have soap available to make bubbles. Put out play equipment: funnels, sponges, corks, play boats, egg cartons, cups, and more. Children will use these to design boats and rafts and to create all kinds of water sprays, falls, and splashes.

Set up sand play in a sandbox. Put out mold equipment: cans, buckets, milk cartons, funnels, cookie cutters, paper cups, plastic containers, and more. Children will use these to make houses, automobiles, space ships, skyscrapers, and other objects.

44. My Day—32, 33

ABOUT THE ACTIVITY   Dramatic play is successful at this age. It is personal play, a chance for self-expression. It is creative expression, one of the most effective forms of children's communication. Children love to pretend.

HOW TO PLAY   Set up a pretend restaurant for children's play. A table and chairs are a good start. Then set up the rest as much as possible. Some helpful items are: apron, menus, a restaurant sign, eating utensils, a tablecloth, placemats, napkins, a play telephone, and any play kitchen equipment. Play with the children as much or as little as you wish. Other possible themes are school, business office, and theater.

Set up a pretend doctor's office for children's play. A bed or cot is a good start. Then set up the rest as much as possible. Some helpful items are: a white shirt, gauze, cotton, Band-Aids, a play telephone, and a play doctor's bag with equipment. Play with the children as much or as little as you wish.

Set up a pretend beauty parlor for children's play. A big easy chair is a good start. Then set up the rest as much as possible. Here are some helpful items: curlers, wash basin, comb, brush, blunt scissors, apron, towels, empty plastic shampoo containers, magazines, and mirror. Play with the children as much or as little as you wish.

45. Row, Row, Row Your Boat—32, 33

ABOUT THE ACTIVITY   This is a creative cooperative activity. It also provides a strong gross motor exercise.

HOW TO PLAY   Two children should sit opposite each other with their hands pulling each other's and their feet apart touching each other's. They should pull each other back and forth as they sing "Row, Row, Row Your Boat." After singing and pretend rowing through the song, they should repeat the activity, but faster. Then they should repeat it all again, but this time calling it fastest.

CHAPTER 14

A Practical Approach to Language Development

Children are born with the potential to speak any language known to human beings. That means that they can make all the sounds used in all languages. Because as a rule they are exposed to only one, the sounds of that language are reinforced, and little by little the sounds of the other languages are extinguished. If there is exposure to two or three languages, all of those sounds will be saved. The reason a child learns to speak a particular language is only because that is the language the child has heard. It follows, therefore, that the richer and higher the quality of that particular language exposure, the richer and higher the quality of the language the child will have.

Language development is critical. It is the key to academic success. Advanced language development in the early years is correlated with later school success.

If parent–child language influences child language development, and if child language development influences child achievement, then it is important that parents learn how to create a language-rich environment. Many techniques of positive language have been identified and can be taught to parents.

Opportunities for child language development grow and develop as the child grows and develops. The play activities that follow make use of the principles of language development. They provide a language environment that establishes the opportunity for language interactions between the child and the parent. These include parent observation of the child, giving the parent information about the child's world of language. They also include listening to children and hearing conversational cues that help a parent not only communicate with children but also be able to stimulate child language appropriately.

The following are a few of the basics of language stimulation that are appropriate throughout the developmental years from birth to five:

Self-talk: Talk to the child about what you are doing. Describe each activity as you are doing it. For example, "I am cracking an egg, putting it in a bowl, stirring it."

Labeling: Talk to the child about what the child is doing. Describe each activity as the child is doing it. For example, "You are pouring the paints, dipping the brush, painting blue, straight lines."

Repeating: Repeat back to the child exactly what the child has said. If any parts of the child's speech are unclear, be sure to emphasize your clarity on those parts.

Expansion: Repeat back to the child exactly what the child has said, expanding the concept with appropriate meaning. For example, if the child says "Ba," say something like, "Oh you want the bottle," or if the child says "Ball," say, "Oh you want the red ball."

Expatiation: Repeat back to the child exactly what the child has said, expanding the concept with new meaning. For example, if the child says, "It is cold," say something like, "It is cold in winter."

Open-ended questions: Ask questions that do not have one right answer but can be answered in many ways. The following are excellent question formats:

What do you think would happen if . . . ?
How did you do that?
Can you think of another way?
Where could we do that?
What can you tell me about . . . ?

The basic acquisition of grammatical speech is accomplished by age three and a half. By the time a child turns six, there is a speaking vocabulary of about 2,500 words. Such development takes place naturally within the framework of a rich language environment, but it will not take place in a deprived environment (Spodek & Saracho, 1994, pp. 291–204).

MILESTONES OF LANGUAGE DEVELOPMENT FROM BIRTH TO FIVE YEARS

Age Range	Milestone	Activity
Birth to 3 months	1. Responds to pleasure with vocalizations	1, 2, 3, 4, 5
	2. Responds to sounds with vocalizations	2, 3, 4, 5
	3. Smiles	1, 2, 3, 4, 5
	4. Responds to pleasure with gurgles	1, 2, 3, 4, 5
	5. Produces random vowel-like sounds	1, 2, 3, 5
	6. Responds to loud sounds with vocalizations	4
	7. Responds to human voices with vocalizations	1, 3, 5
3 to 6 months	8. Responds to changes in speech with vocalizations	6, 7
	9. Responds to facial expressions with vocalizations	6, 7
	10. Recognizes familiar objects by name	7, 8, 9
	11. Recognizes people by name	7
	12. Babbles vowel and consonant sounds	7, 10
	13. Imitates sounds	8, 9, 10
	14. Vocalizes to toys and mirror image	10
6 to 12 months	15. Responds to rhythm with vocalizations	11, 12, 13, 14
	16. Makes word-like sounds	12, 13, 14, 15
	17. Says "Da-da" and "Ma-ma" as sounds	12, 13, 15, 16
	18. Vocalizes playfully when left alone	17, 18
	19. Enjoys simple songs and rhymes	19, 20
	20. May understand and respond to one or two words other than name: "No," "Sit down"	17
1 to 1½ years	21. Uses single words, about a ten-word vocabulary	21, 22, 23
	22. Imitates words	21, 22, 24, 25
	23. Uses inflections	21, 23
	24. Makes one-word requests	21, 22, 25
	25. Identifies one facial part and some body parts	21, 22, 24
	26. Follows simple directions	21, 22, 24, 25
	27. Puts two words together	21, 22, 23, 24
1½ to 2 years	28. Imitates phrases	26, 27
	29. Gives own name and refers to self as "I" and "me"	28, 29, 30
	30. Has a 50- to 300-word vocabulary	27, 29
	31. Identifies parts of face	28, 29

Age Range	*Milestone*	*Activity*
	32. Identifies articles of clothing	27, 28, 29, 30
	33. Follows more complicated directions	28, 30
2 to 3 years	34. Makes words plural by adding an *s*	31
	35. Requests help: "I want juice"	31, 32
	36. Identifies object by description of what it does	31
	37. Understands categories like size, shape, and color	31, 33, 34
	38. Names objects in a picture	35
	39. Follows complex directions	33
	40. Asks *what, where,* and *when* questions	31, 35
	41. Uses three- to four-word sentences	31, 35
3 to 4 years	42. Says first and last name	36
	43. Recites nursery rhymes and songs	37
	44. Uses comparison words like *empty* and *full*	38
	45. Talks in simple sentences	36, 37, 39, 40
	46. Understands basic information	36, 37, 39, 40
4 to 5 years	47. Asks *why* and *how* questions	41
	48. Likes to talk about daily experiences	42, 45
	49. Names almost all body parts	43
	50. Sequences a picture story	44
	51. Uses pronouns like *his, hers,* and *ours*	41, 42
	52. Understands basic verbal information	41, 45
	53. Has some beginning reading skills	43
	54. Has advancing comprehension skills	41, 42, 43, 44, 45

The items are numbered, but within an age range the order is not important. The stages of development are categorized by ages, but the ages are approximate. It is the order of the stages that is important.

PLAY ACTIVITIES FOR LANGUAGE DEVELOPMENT FROM BIRTH TO FIVE YEARS

Age Range	*Milestones*
Birth to 3 months	1 through 7

1. Coo, Babble, Gurgle—1, 3, 4, 5, 7

ABOUT THE ACTIVITY   Responding with the same sounds to a baby's vocalizations encourages the baby to vocalize more.

HOW TO PLAY   Lay the baby down on a bed or flat surface. Lean over the baby so that you make eye contact. Listen for sounds. Whenever you hear one, say it back. You will see smiles, and you will naturally smile back.

2. Sounds Great—1, 2, 3, 4, 5

ABOUT THE ACTIVITY   Soothing sounds like music or a bell encourage the baby to vocalize.

HOW TO PLAY   Lay the baby down on a bed or flat surface. Bring over an interesting supply of things that make soothing sounds. Suggested items are a nice-sounding bell, a glass with a spoon, a music box, two blocks, a popsicle stick and a paper plate, a rattle, a lidded plastic container with paper clips, another one with uncooked rice in it, a bottle cap that clicks when pushed in, and so on. Show the baby each item separately and then make the sound. Respond with a smile to the baby's smile, a coo to a coo, or a gurgle to a gurgle.

3. Doing What Comes Naturally—1, 2, 3, 4, 5, 7

ABOUT THE ACTIVITY   Babies enjoy hearing the rhythm, the beat, and the softness of nursery rhymes and songs.

HOW TO PLAY   Sit with the baby in your lap. Say or sing any rhymes or songs that come to mind. Some old favorites are "This Little Piggy Went to Market," "Where Is Thumbkin?," and "Hickory, Dickory, Dock." Do any hand motions that you know for those rhymes. When the baby babbles, stop and listen and then continue with the rhyme or song.

4. Sound Patterns—1, 2, 3, 4, 6

ABOUT THE ACTIVITY   Hearing just loud and soft sounds and their patterns is stimulating to verbalizations.

HOW TO PLAY   Sit the baby in your lap in a position in which you can clap the baby's hands. Balance the baby well so that you can also clap your own hands. Clap short patterns using loud and soft claps, first with the baby's hands and then with yours. Listen for the baby's vocalization responses. Then continue with another pattern. You can do the same activity with tapping the baby's and your feet, tapping on a table, and tapping together two items like blocks.

5. Babies and Books—1, 2, 3, 4, 5, 7

ABOUT THE ACTIVITY   Reading to a baby as soon as the baby is born is associated with helping the child eventually learn to read. Hearing the rhythm of the words and feeling the warm, physical encounter help a baby associate pleasure with reading.

HOW TO PLAY   Hold the baby comfortably in your lap. Choose a book with large, simple pictures and preferably large, clear words. Point to the different pictures and name them. Talk about the pictures if appropriate. Point to the words as you read.

Age Range	*Milestones*
3 to 6 months	8–14

6. Dance Little Baby—8, 9

ABOUT THE ACTIVITY   Babies love being sung to, especially if the songs involve activity. If you move the baby to a direction word in a song, the baby will learn by experience the meaning of the direction word.

HOW TO PLAY   Stand the baby up on your lap facing you. Establish a pleasant facial expression with the baby. Hold the baby under the arms so that you can bounce the baby easily to the rhythm of the song. Sing and move the baby to the action words of the following song, "Dance Little Baby":

Dance little baby. (Bounce baby)
Dance up high. (Move baby up)
Never mind baby. (Bounce baby)
Mother is nigh. (Hug baby)
Up to the ceiling, (Move baby up)
Down to the ground, (Move baby down)
Backwards and forwards, (Move baby backwards and forwards)
Round and round. (Move baby around clockwise)

7. Spiders Unite—8, 9, 10, 11, 12

ABOUT THE ACTIVITY   Two nursery rhymes about spiders can give a lot of information and also stimulate vocalizations. They are "The Eensy Weensy Spider" and "Little Miss Muffet."

HOW TO PLAY   Sit the baby propped up across from you. Get a small piece of yarn or yarn puff to represent an "eensy weensy" spider and a large piece of yarn or yarn puff to represent a large spider. Take out the tiny piece of yarn or puff and start with the first rhyme, "The Eensy Weensy Spider." Do all the hand motions as demonstration for the baby. Watch for the smiles and babbles, almost as if the baby were watching a show. Repeat the rhyme, involving the baby in the motions as much as possible. Then take out the large piece of yarn or puff and a doll and set the doll up on a pillow. Say and act out the motions to "Little Miss Muffet." Then repeat the second rhyme, involving the baby in the action of the story as much as possible. The words to the rhymes are:

> *The eensy weensy spider went up the water spout. (Twist fingers upwards)*
> *Down came the rain and washed the spider out. (Wiggle fingers downward*
> *   and then open hands outward)*
> *Out came the sun and dried up all the rain, (Palms up)*
> *And the eensy weensy spider went up the spout again. (Twist fingers upwards)*

and

> *Little Miss Muffet sat on a tuffet (Doll on pillow)*
> *Eating her curds and whey. (Doll eating)*
> *Along came a spider (Move spider)*
> *And sat down beside her (Place spider down)*
> *And frightened Miss Muffet away.(Have doll run away)*

8. Sounds Like Bath Time—10, 13

ABOUT THE ACTIVITY   Bath time is a natural time for naming body parts. Splashing also stimulates smiles and sounds.

HOW TO PLAY   Place the baby in the bath in a supported position. Then, in an orderly fashion, wash each part of the body. Use self-talk to describe what you are doing—"I am washing your legs. I am washing your tummy. I am washing your arms," and so on.

9. Sounds Like Feeding Time—10, 13

ABOUT THE ACTIVITY   Feeding time is a natural occasion for naming foods and utensils. The act of eating itself also stimulates the beginnings of conversation, sounds, and facial expressions at this point.

HOW TO PLAY   Place the baby supported in a high chair. Then set up the baby's food. Use labeling to describe what the baby is doing. For example, "(*Baby's Name*) is eating applesauce. Now you are eating green beans. Now you are drinking milk." You can add conversation like, "(*Baby's Name*) is eating from a spoon. You are drinking from a bottle."

10. Jack in the Box—12, 13, 14

ABOUT THE ACTIVITY   Action rhymes are both stimulating and enjoyable for babies. The winding motion and the opening motion in this rhyme allow the baby to cross the midline of the body. This crossing is excellent preparation for eventual reading and writing. To learn to read, you have to be able to cross the midline of the body with the eyes; to learn to write, you have to be able to cross the midline of the body with the hands.

HOW TO PLAY   Sit with the baby in front of a mirror. The baby will probably start babbling just from seeing the image of you and the baby together. Imitate whatever babbling you hear to encourage more sounds. After freely enjoying the mirror images and the sounds, begin the "Jack-in-the-Box" rhyme. Use the baby's right hand to wind clockwise the pretend handle of the pretend jack-in-the-box. Use the right hand also to open the pretend lid from left to right. Repeat the activity with the left hand going counterclockwise and from right to left. These are the words to the rhyme, "Jack-in-the Box":

> *Jack in the box. (Wind baby's right hand)*
> *Jack in the box. (Wind baby's right hand)*
> *Open the lid. (Move baby's right hand from left to right)*
> *And up s/he pops. (Move baby up)*

Age Range	*Milestones*
6 to 12 months	15–20

11. Three Little Monkeys—15

ABOUT THE ACTIVITY   This is a popular song with babies this age. It has a catchy rhythm and interesting hand movements. Either supported or unsupported sitting is appropriate for the baby.

HOW TO PLAY   Sit the baby across from you or next to you on a couch. Sing to the baby the words to this song and direct the baby to do the actions as indicated. These are the words:

> *Three little monkeys jumping on the bed (Move three fingers in a bouncing position on baby's other hand)*
> *One fell down and bumped his head. (Turn one finger away and then bump fist to head)*
> *Mama called the doctor and the doctor said, (Pretend dial a telephone)*
> *Keep those monkeys off of that bed. (Use pointing finger for scolding)*
> *Two little monkeys jumping on the bed (Move two fingers in a bouncing position on baby's other hand)*
> *One fell down and bumped his head. (Turn one finger away and then bump fist to head)*

Mama called the doctor and the doctor said, (Pretend dial a telephone)
Keep those monkeys off of that bed. (Use pointing finger for scolding)
One little monkey jumping on the bed. (Move one finger in a bouncing
       position on baby's other hand)
One fell down and bumped his head. (Turn one finger away and then bump
       fist to head)
Mama called the doctor and the doctor said, (Pretend dial a telephone)
No more monkeys jumping on the bed. (Use pointing finger for scolding)

12. Did You Hear That?—15, 16, 17

ABOUT THE ACTIVITY   Sounds stimulate the baby to make more sounds, and they will stimulate you to talk about them. Listening for sounds also develops auditory discrimination skills.

HOW TO PLAY   Hold the baby and take a "sounds walk" either inside the house or outside. Find things that make a sound. For each one, listen to the sound and then talk about it to the baby. Describe it as loud, soft, ticking, and so on, and tell what makes the sound. Some examples of sounds you might hear are: alarm clocks, dogs barking, thunder, ambulance sirens, airplanes, dishwashers, washing machines, and timers.

13. Radio Rhythm—15, 16, 17

ABOUT THE ACTIVITY   By introducing the baby to the radio, you are introducing the concept of changes. Once you put a cassette or a CD on to play, that is what plays. But you can easily change what you hear on the radio. Those contrasts provide stimulation for the baby.

HOW TO PLAY   Show the baby the radio. Turn it on. Then listen together. Talk to the baby about what you hear. If appropriate, show the baby how to help you change the station. Then listen again. The baby will respond, and so will you. Dance together as is natural.

14. Sounds Great—15, 16

ABOUT THE ACTIVITY   A rocking chair is the place of choice for this activity. The movement in itself is stimulation to baby sounds.

HOW TO PLAY   Sit with the baby on your lap on a rocking chair. Rock with a comfortable rhythm. Look at the baby often and smile. You will probably hear the baby say many different sounds. Listen to each one carefully. Then repeat it back as if it were a real word or words. If you hear something like "ah-da—dit," you could say something back like, "'I like that.' You said 'I like that'" Listen carefully. Have fun. Create.

15. Did You Feel That?—16, 17

ABOUT THE ACTIVITY   Feeling stimulates the baby to make sounds, and interesting things to touch will stimulate you to talk about them. The more talking you do and the higher quality that talk is, the richer the baby's language environment will be.

HOW TO PLAY   Hold the baby and take a "touch walk" either inside the house or outside. Find interesting things to touch. Touch each thing together, and then talk about each one to the baby. Describe them as hard, soft, rough, smooth, and so on. Then, when appropriate, tell how they are used. Some examples are tree bark, towels, cotton, flour, shaving cream or whipped cream, snow, flowers, grass, stones, twigs, carpet, floor, curtains, tablecloth, and napkins.

16. Ma-ma and Da-da—17

ABOUT THE ACTIVITY   Babies start to say these sounds without connecting them to either Mommy or Daddy. *Ma-ma* is often a sound used by the baby to indicate comfort, and *da-da* is often a sound used by the baby to indicate play. Both Mommy and Daddy are needed for this activity.

HOW TO PLAY   Sit the baby between Mommy and Daddy. Hug and talk and play together with the baby. Listen for the key words *ma-ma* and *da-da*. If the Mommy hears the word *ma-ma*, she takes the baby and puts the baby on her lap. She hugs the baby and says something like, "Oh, you said *Mommy*." If the Daddy hears the word *da-da*, he takes the baby and puts the baby on his lap. He hugs the baby and say something like, "Oh, you said *Daddy*." Play, listen carefully, hug, and have fun.

17. Alone and Better for It—18, 20

ABOUT THE ACTIVITY   Playing alone can stimulate vocalizations. It also provides an opportunity to interject from time to time with basic directions.

HOW TO PLAY   Set up a "furniture playpen"—an enclosed, safe play area delineated by easy-to-move furniture like a sofa, chairs, and a suitcase or two. Give the baby a few safe things to play with. Some examples are: wooden spoons, plastic containers, empty boxes, and any other favorite playthings. Listen for vocalizations as an expression of both contentment and exploration. From time to time join the baby to show a new way to use some of the items. Use simple phrases like: "Sit down. Show me the cup. Give me the spoon." You may have to demonstrate new play ideas from time to time. These new ideas will renew the baby's interest in playing alone.

18. High Chair Fun—18

ABOUT THE ACTIVITY   The high chair is a safe place for setting up the baby to watch you work in the kitchen.

HOW TO PLAY   Take out the Alphabet Cards described in Chapter 2. Start with the *B* card. Since the *buh* sound is one of the first sounds a baby learns to say, the letter *B* is one of the first letters a baby can learn to recognize. After the baby becomes familiar with the *B*, give the baby the *D*. The *duh* sound is one of the next sounds a baby learns to say. When you hear the *duh* sound, give the baby the *D* card. Introduce the rest of the alphabet in order from *A* to *Z*. Do not introduce a new letter until you can tell there is recognition of the previous letter. These letters can hang on the high chair for convenience and can be good play toys to accompany a meal.

19. Pat-a-Cake—19

ABOUT THE ACTIVITY   This is the same rhyme used in Activity 5 in Social Skills Development. At this age the rhyme will encourage more vocal participation. There may not be words, but there will be sounds that will be closer to words. The hand movement can also become more sophisticated. The cross-patterning of the hands to the words *pat-a-cake* will be crossing the midline of the body with both hands and eyes, movements that are excellent preparation for the reading process.

HOW TO PLAY   Sit with the baby across from you at a table, on the floor, or in some other comfortable place. Say the rhyme to the baby and do the motions together. See the words and motions in Activity 5. While you did the motions for the baby in the previous activity, this time do the motions opposite the baby. Show the baby how to cross-pattern the hands after each clap.

20. 1, 2, 3, Rhyme with Me—19

ABOUT THE ACTIVITY   These are simple beginning rhymes. Introducing the number concepts of 1, 2, and 3 gives interest and meaning to the rhyme routine. Start with "Hickory Dickory Dock" to emphasize the number 1. Then do "Two Little Apples" to emphasize the number 2. End with the "Three Little Monkeys" in Activity 11 for the number 3.

HOW TO PLAY   Sit with the baby on your lap so that you are both comfortable. Say these simple rhymes to the baby and move the baby with the suggested motions. These are the words:

Hickory dickory dock (Bounce baby)
The mouse ran up the clock. (Move baby up)
The clock struck one. (Show baby's one finger)
The mouse ran down. (Move baby up then down)
Hickory dickory dock. (Bounce baby)

Two little apples (Show baby's two fingers)
Up in a tree (Move baby up)
Smiled at me.(Point with baby's two forefingers to the corners of the mouth)
So I shook the tree (Put baby's two hands together to shake a tree)
As hard as I could, (Shake harder)
And down came the apples, (Move baby's fingers down)
Mm they were good. (Rub baby's palm clockwise around baby's tummy)

Go on to "The Three Little Monkeys." Then say a review sentence like "The clock struck one" (show one finger), "two little apples" (show two fingers), and "three little monkeys " (show three fingers).

Age Range	*Milestones*
1 to 1½ years	21–27

21. Puppets Make Other Puppets Talk—21, 22, 23, 24, 25, 26, 27

ABOUT THE ACTIVITY   Puppets encourage toddlers to talk. Straight conversation may fall flat, but puppet conversations can go on and on.

HOW TO PLAY   Take out two wooden spoons. Draw a happy face on one and a sad face on the other. You can make these faces with a felt tip marker, pieces of yarn, ribbons, or other scraps of material. Sit with the toddler across from you at a table, on the floor, or in some other comfortable place. Hold up the two puppets. Say something happy with the happy face puppet, like, "I love my doll." Then say something sad with the sad face puppet, like, "I lost my shoe." Then offer the puppets to the toddler. Tell the toddler to take a happy spoon or a sad spoon and to say something in a happy voice or in a sad voice. Respond by repeating what was said or by expanding it with a completed sound or an additional word or words and then by making an appropriate puppet response. Take turns with the puppets. Let the conversation grow. You can each take a puppet for talk, or you can make the two puppets have a conversation with each other. One puppet can ask the other puppet to show different facial features like the nose, eyes, or ears. Help the toddler as much or as little as is necessary.

22. Body Apart—21, 22, 24, 25, 26, 27

ABOUT THE ACTIVITY   Language is always stimulated by high-interest topics. The body, which is personal, has high interest.

HOW TO PLAY   Stand up with the toddler opposite you. Tell the toddler you are going to point to body parts on your body and say that you want the toddler to point to the same body part on the toddler's body and say the name of it. If the easy parts are going smoothly, use parts that are less frequently heard—elbows, chin, ankles, heel, wrist, waist, and others. Tell the toddler to take a turn pointing to parts for you to touch and name.

23. Private House—21, 23, 27

ABOUT THE ACTIVITY   Pretend play stimulates language. Toddlers love to hide and get away to a private enclosed spot.

HOW TO PLAY   Make a pretend house for the toddler by draping a sheet or blanket over a card table or over the backs of two or more chairs moved close together. First let the toddler enjoy free, creative play with the new playhouse. Then tell the toddler that you will change the house into different kinds of places. Put in a few props if desired or just let the creativity and language flow from the toddler. The following are examples of changes: tent, cave, airplane, train, spaceship, restaurant, school, and store.

24. Do as I Do and Do as I Say—22, 25, 26, 27

ABOUT THE ACTIVITY   The mirror is an effective stimulant for both movement and language. It encourages vocalizations. Repeating and expanding on vocalizations helps children grow faster in their language development.

HOW TO PLAY   Sit or stand in front of a mirror with the toddler. Start with actions and then switch to words. Make different animated faces. After each face, watch the toddler imitate you. Then move different body parts. After each imitation movement, say, "I see (*Toddler's Name*) move the (*body part*)." Watch for the body movement and listen for the body part name. If you hear only a sound, repeat it back as the appropriate word. For example, if you hear *ah,* repeat it back as *arm.* If you hear *arm,* repeat it back as *arm* or expand it to *right arm* or *left arm.* If you hear *arm up,* repeat it back as "Your arm is up."

25. Build It from Memory—22, 24, 26

ABOUT THE ACTIVITY   Any interactions that build memory are powerful language builders. A set of blocks or bottle caps will be good for this activity.

HOW TO PLAY   Sit with the toddler across from you at a table, on the floor, or in some other comfortable place. Have an ample supply of blocks or bottle caps. Take turns giving each other directions for building a tower of three—for example, "Take the red, then the blue, and then the green. Next take the blue, then the green, and then the red." Or, "Take the blue, then the green, and then another blue." You give the directions first.

Age Range   *Milestones*

1½ to 2 years   28 through 33

26. Match Me—28

ABOUT THE ACTIVITY   Participating in a challenging activity stimulates language.

HOW TO PLAY   Take out several cookie cutters and a pile of index cards. Trace one cookie cutter with a marker on an index card. Then give the toddler the cookie cutter to match it to the shape. Say a sample phrase about the shape like "Matched a star," and tell the toddler to repeat the phrase. Trace as many cookie cutters as you have, one on each index card. Then choose a card from a pile of cards with shapes on them and put out two cookie cutters for choices, one with the correct matching shape on it. Tell the toddler to place the correct cookie cutter on the matching shape. Once the match is made, tell the toddler to say "Matched a (*cookie cutter shape*)." Play all cards through, first matching one to one, then by choosing a match from two, and then by choosing a match from three. Go to four or five choices if appropriate. If the toddler is able to set up matches for you, take your turn as well.

27. Categories Book—28, 30, 32

ABOUT THE ACTIVITY   Since learning about the world for a toddler becomes more complicated every day, any strategy that introduces categories will simplify the learning process by making it more organized.

HOW TO PLAY   Cut out pictures from magazines of things that fit into categories with which toddlers are familiar. Some examples are: flowers, animals, people, toys, and food. If you can find pictures of real items that the toddler has, it will make the book more personal and more interesting. If you still have the box a toy or other item came in, and there is a picture of the toy or item on the box, cut out that picture for the categories book. If there is a food item from a box that the toddler likes, you can cut out the picture from the package and use that for the categories book (see Figure 14.1).

Put a book together that has a series of pages for each of the categories and a title page for the category with the category word on it. Then make a set of index cards to match all the category title pages. Tell the toddler to pick a category card and match it to the title page with that category on it. Then tell the toddler to choose a picture in that category and to talk about it. Take your turn with the next index card, category title, and picture explanation. Keep playing until you have gone through all the categories.

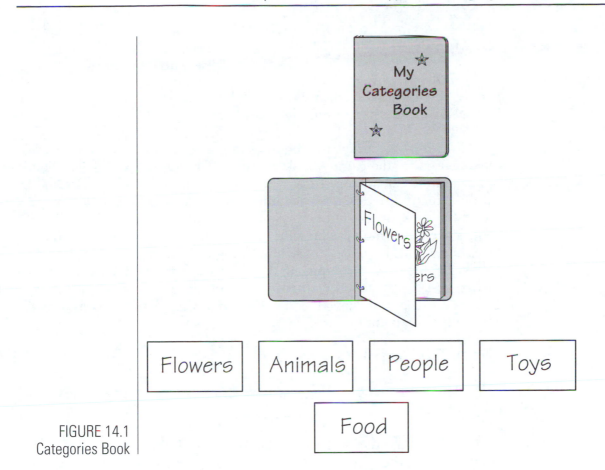

FIGURE 14.1
Categories Book

28. "Simple" Simon Says—29, 31, 32, 33

ABOUT THE ACTIVITY   The word *simple* in this activity means simplifying the traditional "Simon Says" game by leaving out the rule that says not to do the action if you don't hear the words "Simon Says." In this activity, always give the game directions with the words "Simon Says."

HOW TO PLAY   Stand with the toddler facing you. Tell the toddler you are going to give a series of Simon Says directions and that as soon as you have given a direction, you want the toddler to follow it. Follow the directions as you say them to show the toddler exactly what to do. These are examples of directions: "Simon says wave hi." "Simon says wiggle your fingers." "Simon says touch your shirt." "Simon says sit down." When the toddler gets used to basic directions, switch to more abstract ones, like household jobs: "Simon says dust the furniture." "Simon says sweep the floor." "Simon says set the table." If the toddler is able, give the child a turn to give the "Simon says" directions for you to follow.

29. My Story—29, 30, 31, 32

ABOUT THE ACTIVITY   This picture storybook is a follow-up to the "My Family" book introduced in Chapter 2. Use whatever photographs you have available to make this toddler play book.

HOW TO PLAY   Put the photographs in a small picture album similar to the one used for the Family Book. Put the photographs on the right-hand pages and the explanatory story words on the left-hand pages. Use short, simple sentences to describe each photograph. When referring to the toddler in the book, use the toddler's name, the word *I*, and the word *me*. Write about the child as much as possible, mentioning facial expressions and articles of clothing as well as any action taking place in the pictures.

When the book is completed, read it to and with the toddler. Point to each word as you read, and talk together about the pictures. As the toddler gets used to the book, have the toddler read as many of the words as possible when you point to them.

30. Pick-up and Delivery—29, 32, 33

ABOUT THE ACTIVITY   Tying in action with words helps to expand a toddler's vocabulary.

HOW TO PLAY   Take out a large shopping bag. Tell the toddler you need eight items for the bag and that after you get them all, you want to have them all put back. Ask for one item at a time. When the toddler brings you the item, tell the toddler to say, "I got it." When the toddler puts the item in the bag, always say, "Thank you." Select items that the toddler can reach and bring independently and can put away when the game is over. Samples of possible items are: a cup, a spoon, a pillow, a towel, a toothbrush, a stuffed animal, a ball, and an article of clothing. Tell the toddler to take the bag around from room to room and return all the items. Play again if you both wish.

Age Range	*Milestones*
2 to 3 years	34 through 41

31. A What, Where, When Walk—34, 35, 36, 37, 40, 41

ABOUT THE ACTIVITY   Talking about what you see increases attention to detail and stimulates language development.

HOW TO PLAY   Take a walk in or outside the house and stop at an interesting sight. Some examples are: a flower, a bird, a twig, or a sculpture. Ask the following questions:

1. What are more than one called?
2. Do you want it?
3. What does it do?
4. What color is it?
5. Where is it?
6. When did it get here?

Tell the child to ask you any of the above questions about the next item on the walk.

32. If You Want It, Ask for It—35

ABOUT THE ACTIVITY   Mealtime is excellent for using this technique.

HOW TO PLAY   Set out three items and tell the child to ask for one of them. These are sample sentences: "I want the juice." "I want the doll." "I want the car." After the child has said as clear a sentence as possible, repeat the sentence, substituting the word *you* for *I*, and give the child the item.

33. Fun with Big and Small—37, 39

ABOUT THE ACTIVITY   Learning about size by manipulation is stimulating to language development.

HOW TO PLAY   Find as many objects as you can that can be in pairs of big and small—for example, shoes, spoons, bowls, cups, boxes, and pencils. Play together with the objects. You can do many different things:

1. Sort by size.
2. Put the small ones in an order and put the big ones in the same order.
3. Ask for two items by size—the big spoon and the small cup, or the small bowl and the big shoe.

34. Sort It Out—37

ABOUT THE ACTIVITY   Sorting by size, shape, and color stimulates language.

HOW TO PLAY   Tell the child to bring out a group of items—books, toys, or something similar. Tell the child to sequence the group by size. Try to sort it by shape. Try again by color. Play together freely with the items.

35. Reading—38, 40, 41

ABOUT THE ACTIVITY   Reading to a child at this age includes as much child participation as possible.

HOW TO PLAY   Tell the child to sit next to you on a comfortable sofa or chair.

Choose two kinds of books. Start with one that has simple pictures and simple sentences to go with them. As you read, point to the words. After repeating the book several times, let the child fill in the last word. Then, after reading the book, go back and ask the child to name objects on each of the pages.

Now read the second book. This one should have more complicated pictures and more complicated sentences to go with them. This book should give the child information on a topic or be an in-depth story. As you read, point to the words. After reading each page, go back and ask the child what is happening either in the story or in the picture. Ask questions that do not have a right or wrong answer: "How do you think the child feels?" Do not wait long for answers, and give your own answers as well. Feel free to ask *what, where,* and *when* questions. If the child asks you a *what, where,* or *when* question, ask the question back to the child to get the child thinking. Usually, children come up with answers to their own questions. If not, you can go ahead and give your answers as well.

Age Range	*Milestones*
3 to 4 years	42 through 46

36. Story of the Day—42, 45, 46

ABOUT THE ACTIVITY   Listening to a story builds receptive vocabulary. That vocabulary becomes the reservoir from which expressive vocabulary develops. The most interesting stories children can hear are stories about themselves. Such stories also invite participation and are especially suitable for bedtime.

HOW TO PLAY   Start the story with a routine opening. Hearing the same opening each day will help the child learn through repetition. Some good information for the opening is: "This is the story of the day of (*First Name, Middle Name, Last Name*) who was born on (*birthdate*). (*Child's Name*) lives at (*address*). (*Child's Name*) got up in the morning, got dressed, and . . ." From there, both you and the child can tell the daily story. (See Chapter 5 for further information.)

37. Perform-a-Rhyme—43, 45, 46

ABOUT THE ACTIVITY   If you read to the child regularly from a nursery rhyme, song, or Mother Goose book, the child will show an interest in learning some rhymes and songs by heart.

HOW TO PLAY   Choose a familiar rhyme or song. Say it line by line to the child, but leave out the last word in each line—for example, "Twinkle, twinkle, little _____." If that goes well, say the rhyme again, line by line, but leave out the last two words—for example, "Twinkle, twinkle _____." Keep going, leaving out three words, then four, all the way to letting the child sing the whole song.

38. Opposites—44

ABOUT THE ACTIVITY   Seeing a word often makes learning the concept easier. Children also like using cards.

HOW TO PLAY   Make a set of index cards, each with a word on the front and its opposite on the back—for example, *up/down, in/out, open/shut, empty/full, hot/cold, here/there*. Take turns picking a card from the pile. Say the word on the top of the card. Have the child try to guess the opposite word on the back of the card. Then turn the card over to check it. Help the child as much or as little as necessary with reading the words.

39. The Directions Game—45, 46

ABOUT THE ACTIVITY   Listening to several directions lays the ground-work for giving several directions. This activity develops memory directly. Start with two directions and then go on to three or maybe even four.

HOW TO PLAY   Give the child three directions to follow. They should all be directions for enjoyable actions. Tell the child to listen to all of the directions before following all of them—for example, "Touch the chair, then the sofa, and then the carpet." "Pat your head, clap your hands, and then jump." "Touch the floor, cover your eyes, and walk to the wall."

40. What Was That?—45, 46

ABOUT THE ACTIVITY   Listening for information and being able to recall are important skills for language development.

HOW TO PLAY   Tell the child to call the local phone number for the time, find out the time, and tell it to you. If this is easy, tell the child to call back and tell you both the time and the temperature. (Temperature is usually included on the time message.) If that is still easy, tell your child to call back and tell you the time, temperature, and some other information that was included on the message.

Age Range	*Milestones*
4 to 5 years	46 through 51

41. I Remember—47, 51, 52, 54

ABOUT THE ACTIVITY   Understanding and remembering the spoken word is the precursor of self-expression.

HOW TO PLAY   Describe a simple scene and then ask the child to draw it. Tell the child to listen to all of the information, remember it, and then draw it on a sheet of white paper. The following is an example of a scene: "There is a vase with four flowers in it, a red one for Grandma, a yellow one for Grandpa, and two orange ones for us."

Ask questions about the picture when it is done—for example, "Why did you make the vase that shape? How did you make the petals? For Grandpa, which flower is his? For Grandma, which flowers are hers? For us, which flowers are ours?"

42. Picking Pictures—48, 51, 54

ABOUT THE ACTIVITY   Children at this age enjoy cutting out interesting pictures, and they enjoy talking about what they have chosen.

HOW TO PLAY   Tell the child to cut out any interesting pictures from colorful magazines. Then tell the child to sort the pictures into categories: animals, plants, cars, places, things to do, and so on. Label the categories with index cards. Go through the categories one by one and ask these questions:

1. Do you do that?
2. Have you seen that?
3. Do you know about that?
4. If so, where, when, or how?

43. Words, Words, and More Words—49, 53, 54

ABOUT THE ACTIVITY   Vocabulary building is enjoyable in a game format.

HOW TO PLAY   Choose an item that can be called by a lot of different names—for example, *pants.* Then take turns naming as many words as possible for *pants* —*trousers, jeans, shorts, leggings,* and so on. Another example is *cup.* Other words for *cup* are *glass, mug, goblet, tankard,* and so on. A variation is to take turns saying all the words you can think of that belong to a category, such as fruit, flowers, trees, or parts of the body. Some children may enjoy seeing the word written as well.

44. What Happens Next?—50, 54

ABOUT THE ACTIVITY   Children of this age enjoy either drawing or telling the ending as a simple story.

HOW TO PLAY   Tell a short sequential story to the child. Leave off the ending. Tell the child to draw a picture of what happens next or say what happens. Some story examples follow:

1. The seed was put in the ground. The child watered it. The sun shined on it. What happened next?
2. The child woke up. The child got dressed. The child ate breakfast. What happened next?
3. The sun went down. The clouds got gray. The wind started to blow. What happened next?

45. Talk—48, 52, 54

ABOUT THE ACTIVITY   Think about talking. However you can include the child in your world of talk, do so.

HOW TO PLAY   Talk. Talk as much as possible in a positive way to the child. Talk about your work, your day, your activities. Do this at any time, in any place, and as often as you can. Then listen. Listen to your child at any time, in any place, and as often as you can. When your child talks, talk on a similar level. Make your responses equal in length and complexity to what the child is saying. Feel free to repeat and expand. Most of all, feel free to enjoy!

CHAPTER 15

Child-Centered Programming

ADDITIONAL ACTIVITIES

Some activities are excellent for children of any age. For the youngest children, the adult will play a larger role; for older children, the adult will play less of a role. The focus of all the activities that follow is fun and creativity. In addition, the following selected activities help a child develop directly in five areas—cognitive, motor, social, language, and self-esteem.

1. Building with Cards

ABOUT THE ACTIVITY   Use 3" × 5" index cards, an incomplete set of old playing cards, or a used set of children's playing cards. If you use 3" × 5" cards, use colored ones if possible and cut them in half so they are 3" × 2½" in size. Then cut four one-inch slits in each card, one on each of the four sides.

HOW TO PLAY   With the cards, build together with your child. Using the slits to attach the cards to one another, make as simple or as elaborate a structure as you wish.

2. Make a Family House

ABOUT THE ACTIVITY   This is a simple construction-paper house with a door and two windows that open. Behind each opening is a picture. The child's is behind the door, and pictures of two different family members are behind each of the two windows.

HOW TO PLAY   Use two pieces of 9" × 12" construction paper to make the house. Fold one in half so that it is 6" × 12" with the opening on the bottom. Then cut a door and two windows in the half that is showing. Make them so that they can open and close and easily reveal a picture behind them. Put a picture of the child behind the door and a picture of two different family members behind each of the two windows. Fold the other piece of paper in half diagonally so that a duplicate triangle can be cut out and attached to the house as a roof and so that the remaining rectangle can be folded in half and attached to the roof as a chimney. Use glue, staples, or tape to make the attachments, whatever is handy and most appropriate to the age of the child. Make the house as simple or as elaborate as you wish. Have fun with your easy-to-make peek-a-boo house. Play, talk, and create as you open and close the door and windows together.

3. Make Rock Pets

ABOUT THE ACTIVITY   Creating rock pets is easy to do and leads to fun and creative play.

HOW TO PLAY   Go outside and collect interesting-looking rocks. Bring them inside and select any that look like animals. Then use nontoxic tempera paint to make them look even more like animals. Paint pens or durable markers can also be used. Those with fine points can be for facial features. Play, talk, and create with these rock animals. These can also be combined with the activities connected with the Family House.

4. Make Your Own Bean Bags

ABOUT THE ACTIVITY   Play activities with bean bags are especially appealing to children. Bean bags are enjoyable to touch and fun to throw.

HOW TO PLAY   Fill old socks with dried beans or rice. Then tie them to close them up. Use large plastic containers or large plastic cups for games.

Place them in different patterns and take turns throwing bean bags into the containers and cups. Make the games as elaborate or as simple as is appropriate to the age of the child.

5. Make a Collage Box or Can

ABOUT THE ACTIVITY   Making a collage on a box or can turns a collage activity into the production of a functional item. It can also be used as an excellent gift.

HOW TO PLAY   Use magazines that have colorful pictures as a source of cutouts for the collage. Design the collage as you would any other collage, by color or theme, and cut out enough pictures to cover your selected box or can. Cover the box or can with white glue. Then stick on the selected cutouts.

OVERVIEW

Go back and look at the milestones in any area of development. Compare a milestone from birth to three months with a milestone from one and a half to two years. Now compare one from one and a half to two years with one from four to five years. What a comparison!

Notice what the world is like for a baby, toddler, and preschool child. For the newborn, anything pleasant that the baby can see, feel, touch, taste, or smell provides a positive learning experience. Any natural exposure in a pleasant surrounding is what is needed.

From one and a half to two years, the experiences of sight, sound, touch, taste, and smell are much more specific. Parents need to help toddlers to understand what they see and hear, and to be able to effectively manipulate and organize what they touch. Even taste and smell are now part of purposeful activities.

From four to five, the picture changes again. Children are applying well-developed senses to a community environment. They use their senses to see and enjoy total activities. They can go to a puppet show or play, help a parent prepare a meal, visit zoos and museums, listen to music and even distinguish pianos, flutes, drums, trumpets, and more. They can count objects; play school, store, or restaurant; and participate in all kinds of creative role play. They even have begun to read and write. All human growth centers around learning about the world through the five senses, and parents have the opportunity to provide an environment for young children that stimulates that growth and development.

While newborns are busy lifting their heads and developing senses, children from four to five are asking questions that stump adults, questions that need to be answered by an up-to-date encyclopedia. It is a complicated process for a child to develop from newborn to age five. It is one that takes place under the direct guidance of parents. It can proceed smoothly and efficiently from newborn eye tracking to preschool questions about space travel. However, it does not proceed smoothly by chance. It takes well-prepared, knowledgeable, and loving parents.

It is clear that preparing parents is not just a good idea. It is essential. The learning that takes place before children start school is the foundation for everything they will learn in school and, of course, in life. Parents are truly their children's first and most important teachers.

A HIGH TECH VIEW OF GROWING UP

Video Principles of Parenting

PLAY with your child as often as you can.
RECORD your laughter and your smiles.
REWIND and replay all of your child's accomplishments.
FAST FORWARD past the mistakes.
STOP focusing on what your child cannot do.
EJECT your life filled with satisfaction.

Video Principles of Teaching

PLAY as you teach, learn, and love.
RECORD your children's successes.
REWIND and replay all of your fond memories.
FAST FORWARD past the mishaps.
STOP looking at norms.
EJECT lives full of major accomplishments.

Video Principles of Childhood

PLAY long and hard and fair.
RECORD your adventures.
REWIND all of your fond memories.
FAST FORWARD past the mix-ups.
STOP delaying.
EJECT your life full of challenges met and dreams come true.

SUMMARY

The parents of the 1990s find themselves walking on a tightrope. Rich or poor, advantaged or disadvantaged, families with children need help. Earning a living requires a major expenditure of time and effort, and so does taking care of children. However parents work it out, child rearing is inherently stressful. Sometimes job responsibilities will spill over into child care time, and vice versa.

Given this situation, it is essential to build parenting skills programming into parents' lives. It can no longer be left to the occasional optional class at a church or synagogue or to the publication of a new book on child care. Today's lifestyle is not geared toward extras. Classes will be missed, books will go unread, and children will go without care. The end result will be children not ready for school, children not achieving to full potential, and a country without the resources it desperately needs. We did not prepare our parents in 1975 when Burton White suggested it. We did not do it in the 1980s with adequate funding for the New Parents as Teachers (NPAT) program. We did not do it in 1994 after the Carnegie Commission Report came out. We must do it now. It is the best crime and violence prevention program our country could possibly have.

SUGGESTED READINGS

Leach, P. (1978). *Your baby & child from birth to age five.* New York: Knopf.

> *This is the landmark book that followed Dr. Spock as a reliable reference for parents. It contains important basic medical advice for the first five years of life as well as many creative ideas for helping children develop to their full potential.*

Maxim, G. W. (1990). *The sourcebook: Activities for infants and young children.* Columbus: Merrill.

> *This book is an excellent reference for activities for children from birth to age five. For birth to age three it emphasizes home activities, and for ages three to five, it provides many classroom activities and projects.*

Morrow, L. M. (1991). *Literacy development in the early years: Helping children read and write.* Boston: Allyn and Bacon.

> *This book covers much of the research available on the new concept of emergent literacy. It has a lot of information about the effect of parents on their children's learning in the early years.*

Silberg, J. (1993). *Games to play with toddlers.* Mt. Rainier: Gryphon House.

> *This book is specialized for babies from one to two years. The layout and design makes the book easy-to-follow for today's busy parents.*

REVIEW QUESTIONS

Part I

1. Trace the history of early childhood parent education and involvement.
2. What happened in the 1970s to interfere with adequate parent involvement?
3. What must happen in the 1990s to raise the academic achievement level of students?
4. Describe the new model of early childhood parent involvement.

5. What are the optimum characteristics of parent involvement as they exist in the schools today?
6. What are the basics of early learning from birth to eight months?
7. What are the basics of early learning from eight months on?
8. Choose five exemplary toys and tell about them.
9. Discuss toys, games, and play.
10. Describe emergent reading and emergent writing. Compare them to emergent walking and emergent talking.

Part II

11. Why is the word *efforts* a major theme of the book?
12. How can a parent influence a child's self-esteem?
13. What is the meaning of the word *discipline?*
14. Describe and discuss five of the pillars of parenting.
15. Bedtime has its problems. Describe what they are and devise several solutions.
16. Choose an exceptionality and discuss it in terms of both regular and special parenting considerations.

Part III

17. What is Goals 2000? What is goal number 1? What does Goal Number 1 mean to you?
18. Readiness from birth to age three is different from readiness from ages three to five. What are the major differences?
19. Define the areas of development, how they interact, and the meanings of both *independence* and *interdependence.*

Part IV

20. Choose a play activity from any of the areas of development. Try it out with a child of the appropriate age. Write up your experience.
21. Fill out a diagnostic record and a prescriptive record for a child.
22. Design three activities based on three of those already designed in the program.

APPENDIX A

Diagnostic Record

Name _____ Age _____ Date _____

Area of Development	Milestone Numbers	Milestones
Cognitive		
Motor		
Social		
Language		

APPENDIX B

Prescriptive Record

Name _____ Age _____ Date _____

Area of Development	Milestone Numbers	Play Activity	Evaluation Comments	Feedback	
				New	Redo
Cognitive					
Motor					
Social					
Language					

This sheet may be copied for parent use.
Copyright © 1997 by Allyn and Bacon.

APPENDIX C

The Alphabet Song

ABCD

EFG

HIJK

LMNOP

QRS

TUV

WX

Y and Z

Now I know my ABC's.

Next time won't you sing with me?

References and Bibliography

Berger, E. H. (1991). *Parents as partners in education: The school and home working together*. New York: Macmillan Publishing Company.

Bloom, B. (1964). *Stability and change in human characteristics*. New York: Wiley.

Boston Children's Medical Center & Gregg, E. M. *What to do when there's nothing to do*. New York: Dell, 1968.

Bredekamp, S. (Ed.). (1986). *Developmentally appropriate practices in early childhood programs serving children from birth through age 8*. Washington, DC: National Association for the Education of Young Children.

Carnegie Corporation of New York. (1994). *Starting points*. Author.

Clark, B. (1988). *Growing up gifted*. Columbus: Merrill.

Collins, S. (1995). *Our children are watching: Ten skills for leading the next generation to success*. Barrytown, NY: Barrytown Ltd.

Covey, S. R. (1989). *The seven habits of highly effective people*. New York: Simon & Schuster.

Cromwell, E. S. (1994). *Quality child care*. Boston: Allyn and Bacon.

Des Dixon, R. G. (1994). Future schools—and how to get there from here. *Phi Delta Kappan, 75*(5), 360–365.

Edwards, C., Gandini, L., & Forman, G. (1994). *The hundred languages of children: The Reggio Emilia approach to early childhood education*. Norwood, NJ: Ablex.

Elkind, D. (1987). *Miseducation: Preschoolers at risk*. New York: Knopf.

Freed, A., & Freed, M. (1983). *TA for KIDS: Powerful techniques for developing self-esteem*. Rolling Hills Estates, CA: Jalmar Press.

Gartrell, D. A. (1994). *Guidance approach to discipline*. Albany: Delmar Publishers.

Ginott, H. (1965). *Between parent and child*. New York: Avon Books.

Goldberg, S. R. (1981). *Teaching with toys: Making your own educational toys*. Ann Arbor: University of Michigan Press.

Goldberg, S. R. (1986). *Growing with games: Making your own educational games.* Ann Arbor: University of Michigan Press.

Goldberg, S. R. (1990). *The pattern of caregiver-to-child verbalizations in relation to academic achievement for environmentally at-risk preschoolers.* Doctoral dissertation, University of Miami.

Gordon, L. (1994). *52 rainy day activities.* Vancouver: Raincoast Books.

Gordon, T. (1975). *Parent effectiveness training.* New York: Penguin Books USA.

Greene, E. (1991). *Books, babies and libraries.* Chicago: American Library Association.

Harris, T. A. (1973). *I'm O.K.—You're O.K.* New York: Harper & Row.

Henderson, A. T., Marburger, C. L., & Ooms, T. (1992). *Beyond the bake sale: An education guide to working with parents.* Washington, DC: National Committee for Citizens in Education.

Ireton, H. R. (1992). *Child development inventory.* Minneapolis: Behavior Science Systems.

Jones, L. T. (1991). *Strategies for involving parents in their children's education.* Bloomington, IN: Phi Delta Kappa Educational Foundation.

Katz, L. G. (1994). The challenge ahead. *Young Children, 49*(6), 2.

Kunin, M. M. (1995). Family involvement partnership for learning. *Community Update, 24*;3.

Leach, P. (1978). *Your baby & child from birth to age five.* New York: Knopf.

Levy, J. (1973). *The baby exercise book.* New York: Random House.

March of Dimes. (1994). *Men have babies too: A guide for fathers-to-be.* New York: Author.

March of Dimes. (1994). *Be good to your baby before it is born: Preventing birth defects.* New York: Author.

Marshall, R. (1991). The best schools in the world. *Newsweek,* December, pp. 50–58.

Maxim, G. W. (1990). *The sourcebook: Activities for infants and young children.* Columbus: Merrill.

Meeker, M. (1988). *The creative learning workbook.* Vida, CA: SOI Systems.

Meisels, S. J. (1992). *Developmental screening in early childhood: A guide.* Washington, DC: National Association for the Education of Young Children.

Morrow, L. M. (1991). *Literacy development in the early years: Helping children read and write.* Boston: Allyn and Bacon.

National Association of Elementary School Principals and Worldbook Educational Products. (1992). *Little beginnings: Starting your child on a lifetime of learning.* Chicago: World Book, Inc.

Nucci, L. P. (Ed.). (1989). *Moral development and character education: A dialog.* Berkeley: McCutchan.

O'Connel, M., & Bloom, D. E. (1987). *Juggling jobs and babies: America's child care challenge, #12.* Washington, DC: Population Reference Bureau.

Ollila, L. O., & Mayfield, M. I. (1991). *Emerging literacy: Preschool, kindergarten, and primary grades.* Boston: Allyn and Bacon.

Otterbourg, S. D. (1994). *Parent involvement handbook.* Boston: Education Today.

Pennsylvania Department of Public Instruction. (1935). *Parent education bulletin 86.* Harrisburg: Pennsylvania Department of Public Instruction.

Pestalozzi, F. J. (1913).*How Gertrude teaches her children.* London: Allen & Unwin.

Pestalozzi, F. J. (1951). *The education man.* New York: Philosophical Library.

Peterson, N. L. (1987). *Early intervention for handicapped and at-risk children.* Denver: Love.

Riley, R. W. (1994). *Strong families, strong schools: Building community partnerships for learning.* Washington, DC: U.S. Department of Education.

Rogers, F. M. (1994). That which is essential is invisible to the eye. *Young Children, 49*(5) 33.

Rosemond, J. (1992). *Parent power: A common sense approach to parenting.* Kansas City: Andrews/McMeel.

Schlossman, S. L. (1976). Before home start: Notes toward a history of parent education in America, 1897–1929. *Harvard Educational Review, 46,* 436–467.

Schwartz, S. E. (1991). *Exceptional people.* New York: McGraw-Hill.

Silberg, J. (1993). *Games to play with toddlers.* Mt. Rainier: Gryphon House.

Spock, B. (1975). *Baby and child care.* New York: Simon & Schuster.

Spock, B., & Rothberg, M. (1992). *Dr. Spock's baby and child care.* New York: Pocket Books.

Spodek, B., & Saracho, O. N. (1994). *Right from the start: Teaching children ages three to eight.* Boston: Allyn and Bacon.

Sunley, R. (1955). Early nineteenth century American literature on child rearing. In M. Mead & M. Wolfenstein (Eds.), *Childhood in contemporary cultures* (p. 160). Chicago: University of Chicago Press.

Trelease, J. (1989). *The new read aloud handbook.* New York: Penguin Books.

Tuttle, C., & Paquette, P. (1991). *Thinking games to play with your child.* Los Angeles: Lowell House.

United States Department of Education. (1991). *America 2000: An education strategy.* Washington, DC: Author.

United States Department of Education. (1992). *What other countries are doing, National Goal #1.* Washington, DC: Author.

White, B. L. *The first three years of life.* New York: Fireside, 1993.

White, M. R. (1991). *Accreditation criteria and procedures of the National Academy of Early Childhood Programs.* Washington, DC: National Association for the Education of Young Children.

Wilson, L. C. (1990). *Infants and toddlers.* Auburn: Delmar.

Wings Personal Learning System. (1990). *Developmental chart.* Memphis, TN: Intelligy.

Wortham, S. C. (1990). *Test and measurement in early childhood education.* Columbus: Merrill.

INDEX